MIMESIS
INTERNATIONAL

PHILOSOPHY
n. 56

T0258049

MARCO STANGO

THE IDEAL AND THE REAL

Studies in Pragmatism

MIMESIS
INTERNATIONAL

This volume is published with the support of the University of Molise, as part of the project "MyExperience Molise".

© 2022—MIMESIS INTERNATIONAL
www.mimesisinternational.com
e-mail: info@mimesisinternational.com

Isbn: 9788869774126
Book series: *Philosophy,* n. 56

© MIM Edizioni Srl
P.I. C.F. 02419370305

CONTENTS

PREFACE   7

INTRODUCTION   15

1. THE PRAGMATIC MAXIM AND THE NORMATIVE SCIENCES:
PEIRCE'S PROBLEMATICAL "FOURTH" GRADE OF CLARITY   25

2. I WHO? A NEW LOOK AT PEIRCE'S THEORY OF INDEXICAL
SELF-REFERENCE   55

3. A DEWEYAN ASSESSMENT OF THREE MAJOR TENDENCIES
IN PHILOSOPHY OF CONSCIOUSNESS   87

4. DEWEY, SEMIOTICS, AND SUBSTANCES   119

5. CAN THOMISM AND PRAGMATISM COOPERATE?   149

BIBLIOGRAPHY

GIOVANNI MADDALENA

PREFACE

In the one hundred and fifty years of its life, pragmatism has continued to demonstrate its vitality. Vague but powerful since Charles S. Peirce first formulated it in discussion with his pals at Harvard University, pragmatism has been variously interpreted and misinterpreted, to the point that the existence of evident characteristics and structure ascribable to pragmatism has been often doubted.[1] Even today, after many interpretative adventures, pragmatism provokes disparate readings and new paths of inquiry. Marco Stango's book reveals one of these paths, tying the American-born philosophy to classical ancient and medieval philosophy in a way that is truly original. My final remarks will further explain this point of view; however, for the moment, I would like to begin this preface with a brief discussion of Stango's treatment of Peirce and Dewey's works. Doing so will lead us to Stango's overall thesis and to understanding its place within pragmatist scholarship.

In his introduction, Stango raises the oft-discussed question of the continuity or discontinuity among classical pragmatists. Stango

---

1   On the story of the Metaphysical Club, see Louis Menand, *The Metaphysical Club: A Story of Ideas in America* (New York: Ferrar, Straus and Giroux, 2001). Some interesting reconstructions of pragmatism are in Colin Koopman, *Pragmatism as Transition: Historicity and Hope in James, Dewey, and Rorty* (New York: Columbia University Press, 2009), Robert Brandom, *Perspectives on Pragmatism: Classical, Recent, and Contemporary* (Cambridge, MA: Harvard University Press, 2011), Cheryl Misak, *The American Pragmatists* (Oxford: Oxford University Press, 2013), Trevor Pearce, *Pragmatism's Evolution: Organism and Environment in American Philosophy* (Chicago: University of Chicago Press, 2020), and Mathias Girel, *L'esprit en acte. Psychologie, mythologies et pratique chez les pragmatistes* (Paris: Vrin, 2021).

looks to the *Wirkungsgeschichte* of classical pragmatism, which casts some doubt about the unity of the pragmatist project or idea. As a keen scholar, Stango knows that the idea of two pragmatisms – the scientific and realist proposed by Peirce and the subjectivist, nominalist held by other classical pragmatists and re-proposed by Richard Rorty in the second half of the nineteenth century – is untenable on philological grounds. There are too many proofs for the opposite view. Stango himself, in the third chapter, shows how the idea of a purely nominalist approach in Dewey's work does not make sense if one takes his semiotics seriously. Indeed, many years of scholarship support this interpretation, as a variety of authors have shown. For example, the concept of continuity, in different shapes, is the common way through which pragmatists talked about reality. Peirce himself explains to James the strong reliance of his philosophy on this mathematical concept.[2] Numerous scholars have also noticed the dense texture of the relationships among ideas, proposals, inspirations and problems among the classical pragmatists and Stango is no exception.[3] Still, Stango is right in saying that all this work does not change the history of the effects of pragmatism in the nineteenth century, especially when understood as a subversion against classical philosophy in the abandonment of metaphysics. Stango's own ambivalence with respect to this question amounts to an enigma which requires further consideration on the part of the reader. For my part I propose a double solution to the history of the effects of pragmatism: one which takes a philological route and the other a philosophical route.

---

2   See Rosa Maria Calcaterra, "Varieties of Synechism: Peirce and James on Mind-World Continuity", *Journal of Speculative Philosophy* 25 (4) (2011), 412-424, Giovanni Maddalena, *The Philosophy of Gesture: Completing Pragmatists' Incomplete Revolution* (Montreal: McGill-Queen's University Press, 2015), Michela Bella, *Ontology after Philosophical Psychology: The Continuity of Consciousness in William James's Philosophy of Mind* (Lanham: Lexington Books, 2019).

3   See, among others, the publication in Italian of the correspondence between Peirce and James, *Alle origini del pragmatism: corrispondenza tra C. Peirce e W. James*, ed. by Marco Annoni e Giovanni Maddalena (Torino: Aragno, 2011).

The philological solution is that the unity of classic pragmatism, even in its neo-pragmatist contemporary transformation, was not understandable until the relevance of anti-Kantianism was introduced as a proper characteristic of the whole movement. This feature was not completely understood until a thorough study of Peirce's works was completed. Only when one reads the entire corpus of Peirce's work can one realize how critical Peirce became towards Kant and how he drew closer to a Hegelian turn in his philosophy.[4] Only then can one understand Peirce's particular take on the realist-nominalist debate, according to which realism is a continuity between reality and knowledge while nominalism is any sort of discontinuity including a mirroring idea of representation, and which is at the heart of any sort of classic and neo-pragmatism.[5] Rorty's critiques on representation do not affect Peirce's philosophy: continuity between reality and knowledge means continuity between reality and representation. But it is a representation which is also an evolution and a transformation of reality.[6] This transformation or mediation goes far beyond the usual description of realism and constructivism and becomes one of the main characteristics of the overall project of pragmatism along with continuity, the pragmatic maxim as method, consequentialism and evolutionism, the intertwining among normative sciences, namely, the relevance

---

4   Vincent Colapietro, "Portrait of an Historicist: An Alternative Reading of Peircean Semiotic", *Semiotiche* 2 (2004), 49-68; Giovanni Maddalena, *Metafisica per assurdo. Peirce e i problemi dell'epistemologia contemporanea* (Soveria Mannelli: Rubettino, 2009) and Maddalena 2015; Chris Barnham, *The Natural History of the Sign: Peirce, Vygotsky and the Hegelian Model of Concept Formation* (Mouton, Amsterdam: De Gruyter, 2022).

5   Paul Forster, *Peirce and the Threat of Nominalism* (Cambridge: Cambridge University Press, 2011), Robert Lane, *Peirce on Realism and Idealism* (Cambridge: Cambridge University Press, 2018).

6   On Rorty see Rosa Maria Calcaterra, *Contingency and Normativity: The Challanges of Richard Rorty* (Lanham: Brill-Rodopi, 2019), Giovanni Maddalena, "Rorty as a Legitimate Member of the Pragmatist Family", *European Journal of Pragmatism and American Philosophy* 12 (1) (2020), and *The Ethics, Epistemology, and Politics of Richard Rorty*, ed. by Giancarlo Marchetti (London: Routledge, 2021).

of aesthetics and ethics to a strict technical consideration of logic. The ensemble of these topics makes pragmatism unitary insofar as it subsists at the intersection between humanity, with all its purposes and ideals, and reality, whether physical, mental, ideal.[7] The second route that reveals the unity of the pragmatist project is philosophical. Pragmatists themselves did not realize how much their anti-Kantianism went towards a different sort of philosophy, one potentially far removed from the rationalist project of modernity.[8] They worked towards a new version of synthesis that could include all human interests within the gnoseological adventure, without any prejudices. This is why pragmatism is still alive. It does not exclude either theology or technology, either feminism or biology. The pivotal idea that the pragmatic maxim represents is that knowledge works, reality changes, truth happens. These characteristics cannot be thought of if one does not challenge the Kantian conception of synthesis and analysis. Kant ties his rationalist project to synthesis understood as the way in which we can also reach universality and necessity in our empirical knowledge. He did that by intertwining intellectual intuitions and concepts in a powerful way. In order to get out from his rationalism we have to provide a different picture of the way in which we can reach certainty in our scientific endeavors. Pragmatists did not challenge the definition of analysis and synthesis explicitly but moved hard in that direction by finding new instruments of reasoning and new ways of describing their activity such as Peirce's abduction, James's stream of thought, Dewey's instrumental logic, and Mead's gestures.[9] Even neo pragmatists such as Rorty, Putnam, Brandom, and Margolis proposed new epistemologies that go in

---

7   *Il pragmatismo. Dalle origini agli sviluppi contemporanei*, ed. by Rosa Maria Calcaterra, Giovanni Maddalena and Giancarlo Marchetti (Roma: Carocci, 2015).

8   Fernando Zalamea, *Peirce's Logic of Continuity: A Conceptual and Mathematical Approach* (Boston: Docent Press, 2012).

9   John Dewey, *Logica sperimentale. Teoria naturalistica della conoscenza e del pensiero*, ed. by Roberto Frega (Macerata: Quodlibet, 2008), Guido Baggio, *La mente bio-sociale. Filosofia e psicologia in G. H. Mead* (ETS: Pisa, 2015), Matteo Santarelli, *La vita interessata. Una prospettiva a partire da John Dewey* (Macerata: Quodlibet, 2019).

the same direction. I am convinced that all of them did not realize how much their attempts were focused on attacking the Kantian distinction yet they forged new tools to grapple with it and, in doing so, indicated a path that crosses various discoveries in contemporary mathematics and other sciences.[10] Stango's own very interesting reading of the pragmatic maxim, which is deepened in chapter one, is another example of this synthetic move which is the mark of this movement of thought. Stango successfully shows how the synthesis of the ideal and the empirical, the normative and the descriptive, is the core of the maxim. He notes that this idea is in fact a classic one and more closely tied to medieval philosophy than scholars usually acknowledge.

The reading of pragmatism as a classical philosophy, from both an epistemic and a moral point of view, is at the core of Stango's reading. He shows how much the new tools of pragmatism re-establish the classical notion of purposefulness in an Aristotelian way and, contrary to what the majority of scholars maintain, re-propose the necessity of metaphysical elements. On this point, Stango's book opens another interesting debate. The mainstream reading of pragmatism lists anti-foundationalism as a given. Stango shows that, at least as far as Peirce and Dewey are concerned, it is easier to read their arguments as a reworking of ancient philosophical thought, which includes its foundationalist aspirations, rather than as a revolution against medieval metaphysics. On a philological ground, this conclusion follows from all the known premises about pragmatism, but it has not attracted much attention. Indeed, pragmatists criticized Descartes and the modern philosophical tradition as sources of the dualism they rejected from the very beginning. The fruit of this rejection could not be totally at odds with what preceded the modern, rationalist project.

10 Fernando Zalamea, *Filosofía sintética de las matemáticas contemporáneas* (Bogotá: Editorial Universidad Nacional de Colombia, 2008), Moreno Andreatta, François Nicolas, and Charles Alunni, *A la lumière des mathématiques et à l'ombre de la philosophie. Dix ans de séminaire* mamuphi *'Mathematiques, musique et philosophie* (Paris: Delatour-IRCAM, 2012), Giseppe Longo, "Le conseguenze della filosofia", in *A Plea for Balance in Philosophy*, ed. by Roberta Lanfredini e Alberto Peruzzi (ETS: Pisa, 2015), 17-44.

Here, Stango's work recalls some of the best pieces of Peirce's scholarship such as those from Fisch, Potter, Smith, Colapietro, and De Tienne.[11] However, while these authors often linked some part of Peirce's work to classical philosophy, Stango ascribes the entire philosophy of Peirce and what is of value in pragmatism to those philosophical experiences.

On a more theoretical ground Stango rejects the contemporary attempts to find a different foundationalism in pragmatism. In fact, all serious scholars have understood how present the metaphysical claims are in pragmatist epistemology and how much the supposed anti-foundationalism is more a refusal of an "a priori", or a "wrong", "fake", or "anti-scientific" metaphysics rather than a definite rejection of a metaphysical foundation.[12] Certainly, many scholars have proposed different ways out of this stalemate of refusal and non-refusal. Foundherentism, analytic metaphysics, refashioned transcendentalism, transactionalist metaphysics, a posteriori metaphysics – these are all examples of such proposals.[13] Stango takes a bolder position by refusing them all and accepting that pragmatism, above all in his preferred Peircean terms, simply needs a classical, metaphysical foundation which is deepened by appealing to the similarity between pragmatism and ancient philosophy.

---

11   John E. Smith, "Religion and Theology in Peirce", in *Studies in the Philosophy of Charles S. Peirce*, ed. by Philip P. Wiener and Frederic H. Young (Cambridge: Harvard University Press, 1952), 251-267; Vincent G. Potter, *Charles S. Peirce on Norms and Ideals* (Amherst: University of Massachusetts Press, 1967); Max H. Fisch, *Peirce, Semiotics, and Pragmatism*, ed. by Kenneth L. Ketner and Christian J. W. Kloesel (Bloomington: Indiana University Press, 1986), Vincent M. Colapietro, *Peirce's Approach to the Self: A Semiotic Perspective on Human Subjectivity* (Albany: State University of New York Press, 1989), and André De Tienne, "Peirce on the Symbolical Person", in *Semiotica e fenomenologia del sé*, ed. by Rosa Maria Calcaterra (Torino: Aragno, 2006), 91-109.

12   Girel 2021.

13   Susan Haack, *Evidence and Inquiry* (Cambridge: Blackwell Publishers, 1993), Claudine Tiercelin, *La pensée-signe: ètudes sur C. S. Peirce* (Nîmes: J. Chambon, 1993), Maddalena 2009, Zalamea 2008.

His original reading proposes a cooperation between pragmatism, understood in a strict Peircean way, and Thomism. Pragmatism would become a way to ameliorate Thomism considered as an apex of medieval and classical philosophy. Here again, I think that the pragmatist attempt showed more originality than it could fully work out. However, it is impossible not to accept Stango's challenge that sees in this incompletion not the hint of new metaphysical discoveries but a lack of conscience about what metaphysics had already achieved. The reader will tell whether Stango is right or wrong, but he would miss a sophisticated and defiant challenge if he did not take his position seriously.

INTRODUCTION

The essays collected in this volume grew out of the work done on the pragmatism of Charles S. Peirce and John Dewey during the years of my doctoral studies as a Ph.D. student at Università degli Studi di Macerata and as a Visiting Scholar at the Pennsylvania State University. The title of the doctoral dissertation that I defended in 2014, *Agency and Normativity: A Study in the Philosophy of Peirce and Dewey*, reflects the philosophical interests I had at that time: my concern back then was to articulate a non-reductive view of human agency and normativity which relied upon and opened to a non-naïve version of realism. Such realism – about human values and norms, about logical, ethical, and aesthetical ideals, about the embodied self and his agency, etc. – could be defined as 'non-naïve' insofar as it always emerged from the mediation of human interpretation of and active engagement with the world – Peirce's semeiotics, on the one hand, and Dewey's theory of inquiry, on the other.

Already at that point, however, it was clear to me that the problems relative to the so-called philosophy of action and metaethics could not be properly addressed without a concomitant engagement with more foundational issues in semantics, philosophy of mind, and metaphysics. What is 'meaning' and how do we clarify it in order to navigate our moral lives and the world? What is the nature of the 'self'? What is 'consciousness'? Does it still make sense to speak of 'substance' today? Or is it even possible to speak of 'substances' from a pragmatist point of view? What is the concept of 'truth' proposed by the pragmatists, and how does it relate to more traditional approaches? All these questions animated the original concerns of my doctoral dissertation and found partial and inchoative treatment in it. The essays collected here constitute the fruit of my work on the same questions, now offered in a more explicit and mature form than was possible then.

This volume does not aim at providing an overall interpretation of pragmatism. For one, the essays deal almost exclusively with Peirce and Dewey and not much is said of the other great pragmatists, both classic and contemporary. Moreover, their main concern is to shed some light on specific issues rather than to draw a picture of the pragmatist movement as a whole in its historical significance.[1] The problem of the identity and historical significance of pragmatism remains for me an open question. First, although I see the reasons of those scholars who defend a unitary reading of pragmatism – at least, the classical pragmatism of Peirce, James, Dewey, and Mead – I myself feel more and more inclined to see a deeper metaphysical discontinuity within the continuity of the fathers of pragmatism, a discontinuity represented by the radical nominalist drift away from the extreme realism of Peirce, as we find, for instance, in the nominalist tendencies of Dewey and Mead and in their more recent glorified version, the rhetorical poetic pragmatism of Rorty. Second, while the serious study of the pragmatists would lead any careful reader – and led me, I hope – to see that there is very little truth, if any at all, in the customary dismissal of classical American pragmatism as anti-theoreticism, as utilitarianism turned into a metaphysical system, or as the industrialist and capitalist spirit of the United States made into a philosophical worldview – it is also true that the version of pragmatism that has had the greatest fortune at the broader cultural level is the worst and almost caricatural version of

---

1   For competing or mutually enriching interpretations of American pragmatism as a whole, see Richard J. Bernstein, *The Pragmatic Turn* (Cambridge MA: Polity, 2010); Cornel West, *The American Evasion of Philosophy: A Genealogy of Pragmatism* (Madison, WI: University of Wisconsin Press, 1989); Cheryl Misak, *The American Pragmatists* (Oxford: Oxford University Press, 2013); John E. Smith, *Purpose and Thought: The Meaning of Pragmatism* (New Haven: Yale University Press, 1978); *Il pragmatismo. Dalle origini agli sviluppi contemporanei*, ed. by Rosa Maria Calcaterra, Giovanni Maddalena and Giancarlo Marchetti (Roma: Carocci, 2015); *Su Peirce. Interpretazioni, ricerche, prospettive*, ed. by Massimo A. Bonfantini, Rossella Fabbrichesi, and Salvatore Zingale (Milano, Bompiani, 2015).

pragmatism – pragmatism as anti-foundationalism, pragmatism as a progressive critique of the Western "Platonic" tradition, pragmatism as a crass political opportunism, pragmatism as the voice of those who believe in change over the "fixism" of the old philosophical, scientific, economical, pedagogical systems, etc. So, what is the true historical significance of American pragmatism? One has a hard time trying to answer this question because, despite the subtlety and sophistication of most pragmatist texts, one can hardly disjoin the textual evidence from the reality of its *Wirkungsgechichte*. To me, the historical significance of American pragmatism must remain an unsolved problem.

Since the very beginning of my engagement with the pragmatists, however, I have always believed that the reading of pragmatism that is popular among both its advocates (e.g. Rorty[2]) and detractors (e.g. Horkheimer[3]), namely, that pragmatism must be an anti-metaphysical philosophy, or more precisely, a philosophy whose metaphysics cannot be any form of realism, is flatly wrong.[4] Some scholars have recently done tremendous work in rectifying this view[5] but even those who study the problem of realism within pragmatism seem to remain suspicious of more traditional forms of metaphysical realism. The hope is that the essays that follow can stir the scholarship in a different direction – a direction in which the mutual diffidence between pragmatism and classical philosophy can be at least in part be overcome. The final essay, "Can Thomism and Pragmatism Cooperate?", tackles this issue directly and explicitly, with surprising results, I think. In particular, I try to show the implications of Peirce's metaphysical "ideal-realism" for a more

---

2   See e.g. Richard Rorty, *Philosophy and Social Hope* (New York: Penguin Books, 1999).

3   See Max Horkheimer, *Eclipse of Reason* (New York: Continuum, 2004).

4   The case of the neopragmatist Hilary Putnam is more complex and cannot be discussed here. For a recent treatment of Putnam's engagement with realism, see Antonio Lizzadri, *Dal realismo scientifico al realismo interno. Putnam verso il pragmatismo* (Sesto San Giovanni: Mimesis International, 2022).

5   See especially Robert Lane, *Peirce on Realism and Idealism* (Cambridge UK: Cambridge University Press, 2018).

traditional, Thomistic 'correspondence' doctrine of truth and how Peirce's metaphysical categories can and should work together with a more traditional metaphysics of substance.

The first essay, "The Pragmatic Maxim and the Normative Sciences: Peirce's Problematical 'Fourth' Grade of Clarity," contains the semantic and logical heart of what I take "pragmatism" to be. Although I do not use this language in the essay, I would characterize this semantic and this logic as a 'dramatic' semantic and logic. In other words, the logic of pragmatism is not a linear, one-directional logic, in which the conclusion simply follows from the premises. On the contrary, the conclusion 'retroactively' acts on the premises and cast them in a different light, just as in a well-crafted drama the conclusion gives new meaning and sheds new light on all the parts of the plot that preceded it and eventually led to that conclusion. More deeply, the logic of meaning that Peirce unpacks in trying to articulate his famous "pragmatic maxim" and the different degrees of clarity of meaning is a logic in which meaning eventually reveals not only practical expectations 'developed from below,' but also normative ideals 'demanded from above.' And while the normative ideals from above cannot be accessed apart from the practical expectations from below, it is these normative ideals demanded from above that give final significance also to the practical expectations from below and thus orient and shape meaning as such when meaning is treated pragmatically as "purpose." In other words, the 'real" from below is only fulfilled in the 'ideal' from above, the *Summum Bonum* or Reasonableness, through a sort of logical-semantic reversal. This is the basic sense of the "fourth" grade of clarity vis-à-vis the third grade, and this is the significance of what I call the pragmatic-normative task of the maxim vis-à-vis the pragmatic-explicating task.[6] One could see the same logic at work in the very idea of sign: while the "object" of a sign can only be accessed through

---

6   The tenet that meaning is 'dramatic' has received an interesting recent development, though in a different direction from the one that I have proposed, in the pragmatic philosophy of gesture of Giovanni Maddalena, see his *The Philosophy of Gesture: Completing Pragmatists' Incomplete Revolution* (Montreal & Kingston – London – Chicago: McGill-Queen's University Press, 2015).

the "representamen," it is the manifestation of the "object" in the "interpretant" that casts the "representamen" itself in a new light and turns it into the permanent threshold for the never-exhausted manifestation of reality, for the always-growing semeiotic process. The reader should thus take this essay, together with chapter 5, as the closest thing to a general interpretation of pragmatism that the book makes available.

In a sense, the fourth essay, "Dewey, Semiotics, and Substances," tries to apply the same logic, now assumed in its semiotic version, to the insidious problem of the possibility of talking about substances in Dewey's philosophy. As I have said, I believe that the philosophy of Dewey constitutes a radical departure from the ideal-realism of Peirce and eventually leads to undesirable versions of logical and metaphysical nominalism, which might be considered a problem analogous to the psychologism and naturalism Peirce himself saw in Dewey's logic understood as a theory of inquiry. Nevertheless, if one reads Dewey's treatment of substance carefully, one can also find in his work the elements that point in the direction of a different metaphysical path, one in which the rejection of realism actually means the invocation of a more careful, more patient semiotic doctrine of experience and thus of substances. Contrary to my overall reading of pragmatism, I stress here an element of continuity between Peirce and Dewey, and one which is not always taken sufficiently seriously in Deweyan studies: the role that semiotics plays in Dewey's theory of experience and metaphysics. Thus, Dewey's partial suspicion towards the notion of substance turns out to be the mark of a form of sign- and experience-based metaphysics in which a "substance" can be accessed and manifests itself only according to the growth of the signs that flourish within experience. In particular, the unexplored notion of "indexical residuum" plays in Dewey's proposal the role of that reversal that I spoke of in relation to Peirce's pragmatic account of meaning: the growing meaning of the signs within experience – signs which slowly gather around and give birth to the apprehension of substances – are illuminated by the apprehension of reality as inexhaustible in meaning when the "indexical residuum" implicit in our cognition becomes "emphatic" in experience. If the 'top-down' metaphor is maybe misplaced to describe the onto-logical reversal in the case of Dewey, it is nevertheless true that Dewey's semiotic theory of substances relies on an understanding of experience as deep, and therefore relies on an understanding of onto-logical meaning as 'coming forth' and illuminating those very signs through which such depth is always already probed. While Dewey's overall metaphysical framework remains in my view unacceptable – "inquiry" cannot be the ultimate horizon of being because this inevitably leads to a sort pragmatist version of post-Hegelian problematicism – his semiotic account of experience and substance remains valuable and worth considering.

The second essay, "I Who? A New Look at Peirce's Theory of Indexical Self-Reference," was born out of the frustration with those readings of Peirce's metaphysics and philosophy of mind according to which Peirce's system underplayed and almost denied the existence of individuals and thus the reality of the human self. Other works have already settled the issue, I think conclusively, regarding Peirce's semeiotic account of the self and its real import, which is not a denial but a semiotic deepening of the reality of the self.[7] Peirce's greatest contribution on this topic is that of having rescued the self from a too quick identification with a substance as well as from its treatment as a merely 'psychological' reality, while by the same token treating the self as a logical reality and thus giving real ontic weight to logic – again in line with his ideal-realism. What the essay provides, thus, is a semiotic account of a particular aspect of Peirce's approach to the self, one that I take to be somewhat foundational for all the others. The self originates as a capacity for self-reference, a capacity that is 'inborn' only in the sense that the human being, understood as a living growing sign, is naturally inclined, due to his constitutional endowment and his environing conditions, to take experience as the "index" of his life. While there is no need to repeat the argument developed in the essay here, what matters in this introduction is that the logic of "reality" and "ideality" seems to be at work also when we come to Peirce's theory of the self. In other words, in order to be genuinely real, the

---

7   See Vincent M. Colapietro, *Peirce's Approach to the Self: A Semiotic Perspective on Human Subjectivity* (Albany: SUNY, 1989).

human self, has to be identified neither with the human substance, nor does it have to be something inborn; rather, it can be a "destined" outcome for the human sign. On this point, Peirce's Aristotelianism becomes manifest more than ever: teleology means growth, and the historical destined growth of the capacity for indexical self-reference – in short, the self's capacity to say "I" – is the manifestation of the natural teleology governing the human sign.

One last essay completes this volume, this one devoted to a Deweyan engagement with contemporary philosophy of consciousness. Thus, in the third essay, "A Deweyan Assessment of Three Major Tendencies in Philosophy of Consciousness," I analyze three major proposals on the nature of consciousness, namely, "naturalistic dualism," the "phenomenal concept strategy," and "a priori physicalism," and I conclude that Dewey's account of consciousness and experience has the resources to address the same problems that these theories have without falling into their mistakes. Besides the many technical arguments put forth in this essay, the crux of my interest for Dewey's "naturalist" account of consciousness is motivated by the fact that, according to Dewey, one neither has to 'transcend' the material world in order to speak of consciousness, nor does one have to find a way to 'deflate' the reality of consciousness in order to take the material world seriously. The 'cash value' of Dewey's proposal is that it is reasonable to have a broad enough view of nature to find a place for consciousness within it (against all mechanistic-functionalistic reductions of nature), so that human consciousness, instead of being considered an oddity, can actually be taken to be the highest expression of the material world. Whether Dewey would put the issue this way and accept a language that almost sounds like that of the 'great chain of being' or reject it as naively metaphysical, I cannot tell. What is certain is that he resisted any view that reduced nature to mechanism and which therefore could not be hospitable to the riches of human consciousness. The reader should note that consciousness here means neither onto-logical intentionality, nor the human capacity for meaning but, as the current wisdom in philosophy of mind teaches, "phenomenal consciousness." The problems related to a Deweyean approach to the other issues are not discussed in this essay.

***

I would like to thank Prof. Francesco Botturi, under whose advice as a Master's student I ventured into the study of American pragmatism at the Catholic University of the Sacred Heart of Milano and from whom I have received uninterrupted guidance and support from the very beginning of my studies; Prof. Luigi Alici and Prof. Francesco Totaro, my dissertation director and internal reader at the Università degli Studi di Macerata respectively; Prof.ssa. Rosa Maria Calcaterra and Prof. Mario De Caro, both external readers of my dissertation.

During the years of my doctoral work, I had the opportunity to spend two years as a Visiting Scholar at the Pennsylvania State University, where I had the privilege to study first and to start my career as a teacher later. I can only recall with immense gratitude the endless hours of discussion with Prof. Vincent M. Colapietro, whose direction, insights, and generosity over the years have allowed me to understand 'from the inside,' as it were, the spiritual and philosophical adventure of American pragmatism. I owe him, among many other things, the luxury of having worked not only on American pragmatism, but with an American pragmatist. Thus, my sincere thankfulness goes to him, as well as to many others, in particular Drs. David W. Agler and Francesco Poggiani, who were engaged in similar studies at PennState around the same time and with whom I shared, among other things, the desire to understand and the thrill of the discovery.

I am also especially indebted to Prof. Giovanni Maddalena, who has followed and partly guided my geographical, professional, and philosophical adventures since the time of my MA thesis, always with patience, philosophical acumen, and his distinctive capacity to take philosophy very seriously without ever succumbing to ideological seriousness. I owe him much over the years, and I owe him in this particular case the support necessary to make the publication of these essays possible.

I am also grateful to the many scholars I have met through three different philosophical associations devoted to the promotion of American philosophy – Pragma, the Society for the Advancement of American Philosophy, and the Charles S. Peirce Society – with whom I have often had illuminating discussions.

Thanks to my parents, to whom this volume is dedicated. *Dulcis in fundo*, many thanks to Dr. Ursula L. Roessiger, who has always patiently read and corrected my work in English, who has patiently discussed with me many of the ideas contained in these essays and many others, and who teaches me what patience and kindness look like every day.

Finally, I am grateful to Miss Anne Kraft, who has helped with the editing process, and to the editors and publishers of the following articles who granted permission for them to be re-printed, with minor changes, in the present volume:

Ch. 1
"The Pragmatic Maxim and the Normative Sciences: Peirce's Problematical 'Fourth' Grade of Clarity", *Transactions of the Charles S. Peirce Society* 51 (1) (2015), pp. 34-56.

Ch. 2
"I Who? A New Look at Peirce's Theory of Indexical Self-Reference", *The Pluralist* 10 (2) (2015), pp. 220-246.

Ch. 3
"A Deweyan Assessment of Three Major Tendencies in Philosophy of Consciousness", *Transactions of the Charles S. Peirce Society* 53 (3) (2017), pp. 466-490.

Ch. 4
"Dewey, Semiotics, and Substances", *The Pluralist* 14 (3) (2019), pp. 26-50.

Ch. 5
"Can Thomism and Pragmatism Cooperate?", *International Philosophical Quarterly* 59 (4) (2019), pp. 467-484.

M.S.
Hancock, Massachusetts, July 2022

CHAPTER 1
THE PRAGMATIC MAXIM AND THE NORMATIVE SCIENCES
Peirce's Problematical 'Fourth' Grade of Clarity

One of the crucial debates within pragmatism concerns the import of Charles S. Peirce's "pragmatic maxim." My claim is that for Peirce the maxim has a twofold, problematical nature, which I explain in terms of two different tasks that the maxim is supposed to perform: a pragmatic-explicating task (PET) and a pragmatic-normative task (PNT). After a clarification of the two tasks, I discuss the link between PNT and what could be called the "fourth" grade of clarity in the interpretation of a sign. I conclude by reflecting on the reasons why Peirce is committed to the "purity" of PET and find a possible solution in his modal realism.

Introduction

One of the crucial debates within pragmatism concerns the import of Charles S. Peirce's "pragmatic maxim." The aim of this chapter is to show that Peirce maintains a twofold attitude toward his maxim. I would call this twofold approach 'problematical,' not because it is the origin of inconsistencies within Peirce's thought, but because the collocation and use of the pragmatic maxim constitutes a genuine problem upon which Peirce continued to reflect throughout his life.[1] This problem concerns the relationship among semantics,

---

1   This chapter does not address the vexed problem of Peirce's "proof" of pragmatism. For this, see e.g. Max H. Fish, *Peirce, Semeiotic, and Pragmatism*, ed. by Kenneth L. Ketner and Christian Kloesel (Bloomington, IN: Indiana University Press, 1986), ch. 2; Richard S. Robin, "Classical Pragmatism and Pragmatism's Proof", in Jacqueline Brunning and Paul Forster (eds.), *The Rule of Reason: The Philosophy of Charles Sanders Pierce* (Toronto-Buffalo-London: University of Toronto

metaphysics, and what Peirce called the "Normative Sciences," i.e., the inquiry into the correct normative criteria for human self-control. On the one hand, Peirce stresses repeatedly that his version of pragmatism takes the form of a "logical principle" and laments that pragmatism is too often transformed into a "philosophical attitude" by other thinkers (CP 5.415, 1905). On the other hand, however, Peirce maintains that his pragmatism, "simply a maxim of logic," also involves "a whole system of philosophy" (CP 8.191, 1904). What does this tension mean? My claim is that for Peirce the pragmatic maxim has two different, but complementary, tasks. I will call the first the *pragmatic-explicating task* (PET), and the second the *pragmatic-normative task* (PNT). Generally speaking, PET coincides with the use of the maxim as a mere tool of semantic disambiguation of any proposition in its "third" grade of clarity. In contradistinction, PNT coincides with the use of the maxim as a tool for obtaining the pragmatic meaning of only those propositions that fit the normative ideal of the "development of concrete reasonableness" (CP 5.3, 1902). Peirce refers to this latter case as a grade of clarity higher than the third grade. Following W. P. Krolikowski,[2] I call this "the fourth grade of clarity." While PET aims to bring about the semantic disambiguation of any proposition by showing its nature of conditional practical maxim, PNT intends to produce only true propositions and therefore unconditioned prescriptions.

As I will show, the shift from the first to the second approach is marked by the role and weight that Peirce attributes to the connection

---

Press, 1997); Vincent M. Colapietro, "The Proof of the Pudding: An Essay in Honor of Richard S. Robin*," Transactions of the Charles S. Peirce Society*, 48(3) (2012), 285-309; Christopher Hookway, *Truth, Rationality and Pragmatism. Themes from Peirce* (New York: Oxford University Press, 2002); Christopher Hookway, *The Pragmatic Maxim: Essays on Peirce and Pragmatism* (Oxford: Oxford University Press, 2012); and Cornelis de Waal, *Peirce: A Guide for the Perplexed* (London: Bloomsbury, 2013), pp. 116-120.

2   W. P. Krolikowski, "The Peircean *Vir*", in *Studies in the Philosophy of Charles Sanders Peirce. Second Series*, ed. by Edward C. Moore and Richard S. Robin (Amherst: The University of Massachusetts Press, 1964), pp. 257-270.

between the pragmatic maxim and the Normative Sciences.[3] Many interpreters have acknowledged the development of the maxim as a normative "principle of logic" once logic became for Peirce the first of the Normative Sciences. Richard S. Robin describes Peirce's shift from his psychologizing pragmatism to his more mature and semantically- and normatively-aware pragmaticism in the following way:

> Apart from the reversal of the justificatory roles of logic and psychology, what basis was there in psychology for thinking that all human beings ever want are sensible or practical results? Doesn't science in the pure practice of it aim at something else? Doesn't ethics demand a loftier ideal? . . . Precisely this kind of questioning forced the reconsideration that eventually led Peirce to a reformulation of pragmatism. Originally, the pragmatic maxim was a logical rule for the clarification of concepts in terms of conceivable practical bearings . . . . The new formulation mentions a higher grade of clarity [the fourth level of clarity]. This reformulation of the original maxim avoided earlier psychologizing, . . . and articulated a higher ideal for human motivation than personal satisfaction. Peirce effectively transformed pragmatism into pragmaticism. (Robin, p.141)[4]

Although Robin is insightful for acknowledging the role played by the doctrine of normative ideals (i.e., Normative Sciences) in Peirce's understanding of the maxim, I think there is evidence against the idea of a definitive shift from an early conception of the maxim ("the pragmatic maxim *was* a logical rule for the clarification of concepts," emphasis added) to a later, normative one ("the *new* formulation mentions a higher grade of clarity," emphasis added). Rather, I believe that PET and PNT are *two approaches to the maxim*

---

3   See e.g. Vincent G. Potter, S. J., "Normative Science and the Pragmatic Maxim", *Transactions of the Charles S. Peirce Society* 5 (1) (1967), 41-53.

4   Cf. Charles G. Conway, "The Normative Sciences at Work and Play", *Transactions of the Charles S. Peirce Society* 48 (3) (2008), 288-311 (p. 290). A more recent account of Peirce's anti-psychologism and pragmatic maxim is Paul Forster, *Peirce and the Threat of Nominalism* (New York, Cambridge University Press, 2011), in particular pp. 78-80.

that Peirce develops over time without eliminating the tension between them.

I find three flaws in the standard readings of the link between the pragmatic maxim and the Normative Sciences:

(i) First, the link between the maxim and normativity is usually considered to be only *external*, in the sense that it is limited to the fact that the maxim attains the status of a normative principle of "logic" and inquiry as a tool of semantic disambiguation.[5] PET clearly displays this aspect of the maxim. However, I claim that Peirce's mature use of the maxim tends to include also an *internal* link to normativity, as displayed by PNT and the fourth level of clarity. In PNT, the maxim becomes a tool for obtaining the pragmatic meaning of *only* those propositions that fit the normative ideal of the "development of concrete Reasonableness."

(ii) Second, it is usually claimed either that a mix of the normative and the explicating approaches has always been present in Peirce's understanding of the maxim[6], or that after 1902 Peirce takes a normative turn that represents a radical novelty in respect to his

---

5   See Misak, p. 92; *The Rule of Reason: The Philosophy of Charles Sanders Peirce*, ed. by Brunning and Forster (Toronto-Buffalo-London: University of Toronto Press, 1997), p. 9; Hookway, *Truth*, p. 60.

6   See Bent Sørensen, "The Pragmatic Maxim of the Mature Peirce Regarding its Special Normative Function", *Semiotica* 177-1/4 (2009), 177-188 (pp. 178-179); Thomas M. Olshewsky, "Realism and Semiosis", in *Proceedings of the C. S. Peirce Bicentennial International Congress*, ed. by Kenneth L. Ketner (Lubbock: Lubbock Graduate School, Texas Technical University Press, 1983), p. 200; Kelly Parker, *The Continuity of Peirce's Thought* (Nashville and London: Vanderbilt University Press, 1998), p. 196; Michael Shapiro, "History as Theory: One Linguist's View", in *Peirce and Contemporary Thought*, ed. by Kenneth L. Ketner (New York, Fordham University Press, 1995), p. 305; Karl O. Apel, *Charles S. Peirce: From Pragmatism to Pragmaticism* (Amherst: University of Massachusetts Press, 1981), p. 72; Karl O. Apel, "Transcendental Semiotic and Hypothetical Metaphysics of Evolution: A Peircean or Quasi-Peircean Answer to a Recurrent Problem of Post-Kantian Philosophy", in *Peirce and Contemporary Thought*, ed. by Kenneth L. Ketner (New York: Fordham University Press, 1995), p. 383.

earlier understanding of the maxim.[7] Against these interpretations, I believe that there is evidence to show that even after 1902 Peirce does not want the main task of the maxim to become PNT but instead to remain faithful to the 'purity' of PET. Why is Peirce interested in maintaining the priority in pragmaticism of the pragmatic-explicating task of the maxim? As I will show, the reason is the following: while PNT aims to clarify potentially *all* the meanings of *exclusively* those representations which further the development of concrete Reasonableness, it is only PET that is potentially able to unpack *all* the possible meanings of *all* the possible representations of reality. In other words, Peirce remains faithful to a semantic perspective that guarantees the clarification of all the possibilities of meaning of all signs, including those representations that are bad or 'unreasonable.'

(iii) Third, Peirce scholarship has often stressed the difference between Peirce's maxim and the verificationism of logical positivism.[8] Moving from this concern, interpreters have argued that what mainly distinguishes Peirce from the logical positivists are his modal metaphysics articulated as "scholastic realism," with particular reference to the reality of 'universals' understood as laws and general dispositions, and his broad conception of "experience."[9] Although this is a crucial aspect of Peirce's pragmatism, this

---

7   See Robin; Conway, p. 290; Vincent G. Potter, S. J., *Charles S. Peirce on Norms and Ideals* (Amherst: The University of Massachusetts Press, 1967), pp. 54-55.

8   For a neo-positivist reading of Peirce, see e.g. Willard V. O. Quine, *From a Logical Point of View* (Cambridge: Harvard University Press, 1961); Alfred J. Ayer, *The Origins of Pragmatism: Studies in the Philosophy of Charles Sanders Peirce and William James* (San Francisco: Freeman, Cooper, 1968), p. 44 and p. 49.

9   See Richard Rorty, "Pragmatism, Categories, and Language", *The Philosophical Review* 70(2) (1961), 197-223; John J. Fitzgerald, *Peirce's Theory of Signs as Foundation for Pragmatism*, ed. by Kenneth L. Ketner and Christian Kloesel (Bloomington, IN: Indiana University Press, 1966), p. 96; Cheryl J. Misak, *Verificationism: Its History and Prospects* (London and New York: Routledge, 1995), p. 91 and p. 104; Harold Moore, "Ayer and the Pragmatic Maxim", *Transactions of the Charles S. Peirce Society* 7(3) (1971), 168-175; Shapiro, p. 25; Richard Smyth, "The Pragmatic Maxim in 1878", *Transactions of the Charles S. Peirce Society* 13(2) (1977), 177-188.

interpretative tendency has caused the importance of *possibility* to be overlooked in the understanding of what the pragmatic maxim brings about. In other words, while focusing on generality, the anti-positivist interpretation has lost sight of how the pragmatic maxim leads to realism about not only generals, but also about different *subclasses of possibilities.* What I claim is that for Peirce the class of possibility unpacked by the pragmatic maxim includes both *what could happen if certain conditions C occurred* and *what ought to happen unconditionally*, and that, of course, the two subclasses do not coincide. If we look at meaning in a Peircean way, in the first case we speak of "practical possibility," while in the second case we deal with "normative practical possibility." The latter is clearly a subclass of the former. While PET highlights the first subclass of possibility, PNT brings to light the second one.

The present chapter tries to overcome these flaws and to cast new light on the pragmatic maxim. I will proceed as follows. First, I present the pragmatic-explicating task of the maxim (PET) and its two formulations, viz., the conditional-mood formulation and the imperative-mood formulation (§1). Second, I introduce the pragmatic-normative task of the maxim (PNT) and show in what sense PNT can be considered an outgrowth of PET (§2). Third, I clarify the inner connection between the pragmatic maxim and the Normative Sciences and discuss the link between PNT and what could be called a 'fourth' grade of clarity in the interpretation of a sign (§3). Finally, I reflect on the reasons why Peirce is committed to the 'purity' of PET and connect this to his modal realism (§4).

1. *The Pragmatic-Explicating Task of the Maxim and Its Two Formulations*

In its more basic use, the pragmatic maxim is a tool of semantic disambiguation of a proposition *p*. This is the use of the maxim for a pragmatic-explicating task (PET). In this vein, Peirce writes that "pragmatism" is "a mere maxim of logic instead of a sublime principle of speculative philosophy" (EP 2:134, 1903). As a tool for the identification of the meaning of a proposition, PET aims to distinguish meaningless propositions, which are simply "metaphysical rubbish" or "gibberish," from meaningful propositions, which have a "plain, practical definition" (CP 8.191, c.1904).[10] In order to explain this point, I will mainly draw upon two different formulations of the maxim, the first appearing in 1878's "How to Make Our Ideas Clear," the second presented in 1903's "The Maxim of Pragmatism." The first formulation is the *conditional-mood formulation*; the second is the *imperative-mood formulation*. Let us start with the conditional-mood formulation.

As is well-known, the 1878 formulation of the pragmatic maxim reads: "Consider what effects, which might conceivably have practical bearings, we conceive the object of our conception to have. Then, our conception of these effects is the whole of our conception of the object" (EP 1:132; W 3:266). We can harmlessly extend the notion of "conception" to the idea of a proposition, taking it to mean a representation of an object.[11] The first two grades of clarity described in "How to Make Our Ideas Clear" are the "familiarity" with p and the capacity of logical analysis of p. In other words, in order to grasp the meaning of a proposition in the first grade of clarity, an interpreter must be able to pick out at least one instance of the object signified by that proposition ("familiarity," EP 1:124-125, 136; W 3:258, 271), while to know p at the second grade of clarity, she must be able to give a verbal definition of the content of the same proposition (EP 1:125-126, 136; W 3:258-259, 271). The maxim yields the third grade of clarity, the pragmatic understanding of p (EP 1:132, W 3:266; see also CP 3.457, 1897).[12]

---

10   See also EP 2:338-339; CP 5.423, 1905.

11   Here I follow Christopher Hookway's suggestion that we clarify "concepts" or terms by clarifying propositions that contain them (*The Pragmatic Maxim*, p. 9 and footnote 7). See also EP 1:22.

12   We can talk of different "levels" or "grades" of clarity as long as we do not understand them in a hierarchical or axiological way (one is more valuable then the other) or in a temporal way (one 'comes' before or after the other). The different "grades" might be more opportunely called "Kinds" of clearness, but never "Stages." See R 649:3, 1910; R 647. Cf. Cheryl J. Misak, *Truth and the End of Inquiry: A Peircean Account of Truth* (Oxford: Clarendon Press, 1991), p. 14.

Peirce's own understanding of the maxim develops over time. As early as 1893, Peirce voices his perplexities about the "materialistic" and nominalistic tendencies of his first formulation (CP 5.402n.2), which are explicitly corrected in the following years, as the last formulation of the maxim in 1913's "An Essay toward Improving Our Reasoning in Security and in Uberty" (EP 2:463-474) shows. Peirce's correction of his early formulation can be summarized in the following three points. First, the "practical bearings" of a proposition and "what is tangible and practical" (EP 1:131, W 3:265) are not limited to instances of empiricistically understood sense-data and observations, but include a very broad notion of "experience," which admits also mathematical, aesthetical, moral, and religious "perceptions."[13] Second, the practical bearings should not be understood as merely individual instances of action, tokens or 2ndnesses, but as general resolutions and dispositions to act, types or 3rdnesses (e.g., EP 2:341, 347, 1905). Accordingly, the meaning of *p* is given by the total sum of the *contextual, specific but general resolutions to act* that would result from an agent's endorsement of *p*, not simply in conditions that are likely to occur but in all possible conditions (see EP 2:241, CP 5.3, 1903). Peirce's pragmaticism, as opposed to other forms of pragmatism, refuses to make "Doing" the "Be-all and the End-all" of human life and thought (EP 2:341, 1905). Third, the meaning of a proposition, once explicated in its logical nature as a subjunctive conditional, covers counterfactual situations. In other words, the richness of the meaning of a sign does not refer only to the actual interpretations of that sign that have taken place or will take place ("will-be"); it also refers to *all* the possible interpretations of a sign of an object ("may-be" or "might-be") that would follow from the general dispositions of that object ("would-be") if counterfactual conditions C occurred (EP 2:401-402, CP 5.467, 1907; EP 2:354, 1905), among which we should include unlikely environmental conditions and human desires.[14] In

---

13 Misak speaks of Peirce's "extremely generous construal of experience" (*Truth and the End of Inquiry*, p. 21).

14 Although the tenets of Peirce's mature understanding of the maxim have become clearer over the years, he was already cultivating them in 1878. A single quotation captures the core of these tenets: "To develop its meaning

short, *the "total meaning" of* p *is given by the total sum of all the possible practical resolutions which would ensue in the context of all possible environmental conditions and all possible purposeful desires* (see EP 2:401-402, 1907).

I would formulate the conditional-mood version of the maxim in the following way:

Given all the possibilities of an object O, which depend upon its general dispositions, (P1) if an agent were to assume a representation *p* of O in a belief B (B*p*), and (P2) if the same agent were to pursue one of *all* the possibilities of purpose that she could endorse, (C) then the meaning of *p* would coincide with the specific resolution to act that the agent would have in this context.

There are two aspects of Peirce's understanding of the maxim that this formulation makes explicit. The first is that the "belief" in *p*, whether it be genuine or assumed for the mere sake of the argument, is a necessary condition for the application of the maxim to *p*, as it is displayed in P1. Simply put, if *p* is not believed by the agent (or assumed as true, which is the same thing), there can be no "practical bearing" of *p* on that agent. Peirce clarifies this when he points out the difference between two different propositional states or acts, "apprehending" *p* and "believing" that *p*.[15] The nature of a belief, B*p*, is a disposition to act or readiness to act upon *p* when the right circumstances occur, so that *p* performs the function of a "maxim

---

[the meaning of an object], we have, therefore, simply to determine what habits it produces, for what a thing means is simply what habits it involves. Now, the identity of a habit depends on how it might lead us to act, not merely under such circumstances as are like to arise, but under such as might possibly occur, no matter how improbable they may be" (EP 1:131, 1878). Cf. Rossella Fabbrichesi, "From Gestures to Habits: A Link Between Semiotics and Pragmatism," in *The Bloomsbury Companion to Contemporary Peircean Semiotics*, ed. by Tony Jappy (London: Bloomsbury, 2020).

15   See Christopher Hookway, *Peirce* (Boston and London: Routledge and Kegan Paul, 1985), pp. 128ff.; Giovanni Maddalena, "Peirce's Theory of Assent", in *Ideas in Action*, ed. by M. Bergman (Helsinki: Nordic Studies in Pragmatism, 2010), 211-223.

of conduct" (EP 2:139, 1903). But this disposition traces back to the "act of judgment," which is in turn essentially connected to the act of "assertion" (EP 2:140) or "acceptance" of *p*. In fact, "a judgment is an act of formation of a mental proposition combined with an adoption of it or act of assent to it" (EP 2:191, 1903). Since assent implies self-control, it also entails that epistemic, ethical, and ultimately aesthetical standards are involved in the 'responsible' endorsement of *p*. In asserting *p*, the inquirer is "betting," at least for the mere sake of the argument, on the truth of *p* (EP 2:140; see also EP 2:200, 1903), and is committing herself to normative criteria.

The above considerations concerning the conditional-mood formulation of the maxim help us avoid a misunderstanding about the difference between PET and PNT. For Peirce, semantics is inextricably normative, in the sense that judgments and beliefs unavoidably require a commitment to certain criteria. Therefore, PET also necessarily deals with norms to some extent. However, when I say that PET is not concerned with 'normativity,' I am simply pointing out that PET can be applied to all beliefs, including unreasonable make-believes, in order to unpack their "third" grade of clarity, while PNT, as will become clear later, has a narrower scope.

The second aspect that the conditional-mood formulation manages to display is present in P2 and is the purposeful nature of the semeiotic process. Interpretation of "intellectual concepts" (EP 2:402) is a teleological process, at least in the sense that the interpreter is always guided by a specific goal in interpreting a sign.[16]

Before moving to the imperative-mood formulation of the maxim, it is important to stress a further point. To be sure, the pragmatic unpacking of the meaning of *p* is not an enhanced verbal definition of *p* that admits only the vocabulary of human action. As Kelly Parker underscores, the "third" level of clarity is not provided by a "super-dictionary" in which objects are described in practical concepts (p. 182). On the contrary, the revolutionary import of the pragmatic maxim is to reveal that when an interpreter commits

---

16   Cf. Thomas L. Short, "Peirce's Concept of Final Causation." *Transactions of the Charles S. Peirce Society* 17(4) (1981), 369-382.

herself to *p*, the meaning of *p* in its third grade of clarity is the interpreter's "readiness" to behave in a determinate way, wherein the ability to pick out instances of *p* and to articulate verbal definitions of *p* are only sectorial cases. For instance, Cheryl Misak is right in saying that "the pragmatic maxim is, roughly, that a person does not have a complete grasp of a predicate F if she is unable to say what would be the consequences of hypotheses of the sort '*a* is *F*'" (*Truth and the End of Inquiry*, p. 4). But the problem emerging from Misak's interpretation is the following: if the third level of clarity is obtained simply by explicating *p* using the vocabulary of possible experiences and actions ("... to *say* what ..."), then the third grade of clarity is just a specialization of the second grade of clarity, i.e., a specialization of the verbal definition yielded by the use of a specific type of vocabulary. However, as Parker says, this is hardly the case. The third level of clarity, produced by the application of the pragmatic maxim, is closer to the world of practical resolutions, prescriptions, and readiness to act than to the world of descriptions based on a practical vocabulary.[17]

This point is also supported by the development of Peirce's semeiotic, with particular reference to the classification of interpretants. Peirce comes to the conclusion that the "ultimate" meaning or interpretant of a sign is not a further sign but is a habit of interpretation (e.g., EP 2:430). When he speaks of the "living definition" of a sign, Peirce refers to the habits of interpretation that a sufficient consideration of that sign would produce in the interpreter. As late as 1908, Peirce writes that the third level of clarity in the interpretation of a sign is its "living comprehension" (EP 2:448), i.e., an interpreter whose semeiotic dispositions allow her to correctly interpret that sign every time the occasion to do so occurs. Therefore, the third level of clarity of a proposition brought about by the maxim is not a super-definition obtained through a special vocabulary (viz.,

---

17   However, Peirce himself might have been hesitant about this point. For instance, at CP 2.330, a passage rightly discussed by de Waal (p. 112), Peirce applies the maxim to the concept of lithium and provides a "definition" of it through the mere use of practical vocabulary. At the same time, however, he calls the third-grade meaning of the concept of lithium a "precept", "more serviceable than a definition."

the vocabulary of human action), but coincides rather with the semeiotic habits themselves developed by the interpreter and the specific resolutions to act that would spring from them in different contexts.

The 1903 formulation of the maxim introduces the imperative mood. It highlights in a clearer way that the pragmatic grade of clarity of meaning coincides with a contextual resolution to act. It reads:

> Pragmatism is the principle that every theoretical judgment expressible in a sentence in the indicative mood is a confused form of thought whose only meaning, if it has any, lies in its tendency to enforce a corresponding practical maxim expressible as a conditional sentence having its apodosis in the imperative mood. (EP 2:134-135)

Now, the prescriptive language used here by Peirce, although rigorous if correctly understood, might be misleading. Does the apodosis of the conditional represent a genuine norm, such as the ones elaborated by the Normative Sciences? I do not believe so. In this formulation of the maxim, Peirce makes use of prescriptive language only to show that being ready to act in a determinate way implies that the interpreter has a certain purpose or resolution to act. In other words, the pragmatic meaning of a proposition can be expressed in the language of *practical knowledge*, which is *prescriptive* in nature. Once highlighted in its fundamental connection to human action, the meaning of a proposition is what guides the agent's deeds and therefore 'prescribes' (where prescription = a piece of knowledge in its action-guiding function). This is the typical logical structure of every practical judgment, as well as of those practical judgments that are bad from the viewpoint of the Normative Sciences. Compared to the indicative mood, the ought-to formulation has the advantage of spelling out that the "third" grade of clarity of a proposition is not an enhanced verbal definition (where the 'enhancement' component is the use of a practical vocabulary), but is the real readiness to act in such-and-such a way when the opportune circumstances occur. I would express the imperative-mood formulation of the maxim in the following way:

Given all the possibilities of an object O, which depend upon its general dispositions, (P1) if you assume a representation p of O in a belief B (Bp), and (P2) if you pursue an end E, where E is one of all the possibilities of purpose you could pursue, (C) then you ought to do X (= you have created in yourself the specific resolution to do X in this context and potentially a corresponding practical disposition for similar circumstances). X is the meaning of p in this context.

It is fundamental here to stress that the imperative-mood formulation is still a rendition of the pragmatic maxim understood as a mere tool of semantic disambiguation. Therefore, it corresponds to the pragmatic-explicating use of the maxim, PET. This formulation simply brings about a better explication of the action-guiding function of the meaning of p when it is revealed in its practical import. The conditional-mood and the imperative-mood formulations are equivalent in content and change only in the way in which they highlight the pragmatic level of meaning.

2. The Tension and Continuity between the Pragmatic-Explicating Task and the Pragmatic-Normative Task of the Maxim

The foregoing is far from a complete picture of Peirce's view on the maxim. In fact, the maxim, understood as a mere pragmatic-explicating tool (PET), tends to grow a more specific task. I call this the pragmatic-normative task (PNT). In some sense, the pragmatic maxim gets its life from an internal instability in the uses it can serve. Such instability is well-expressed in the following 1907 passage:

Suffice it to say once more that pragmatism is, in itself, no doctrine of metaphysics, no attempt to determine any truth of things. It is merely a method of ascertaining the meanings of hard words and of abstract concepts. All pragmatists of whatsoever stripe will cordially assent to that statement. As to the ulterior and indirect effects of practicing the pragmatistic method, that is quite another affair.

All pragmatists will further agree that their method of ascertaining the meanings of words and concepts is no other than that experimental method by which all the successful sciences (in which number nobody in his senses would include metaphysics) have reached the degrees of certainty that are severally proper to them today;–this experimental method being itself nothing but a particular application of an older logical rule, "By their fruits ye shall know them" (EP 2:400-401).

Peirce introduces here the distinction between (1) "pragmatism in itself," that is PET, and (2) the practice of the "pragmatistic method," that is something "ulterior and indirect" if compared to PET. Peirce adds that the pragmatistic method corresponds to the experimental method and that this method is a type of verificationism in which the consequences of a hypothesis should be tested through "experience."[18] Appealing to experience is, in Peirce's view, the ground for producing "true" beliefs and ascertaining what is "real" (EP 1:120-123) in the long run. It is clear from the passage that the maxim is a part of the scientific method, although the scientific enterprise is broader than the mere use of the maxim. The question is therefore: when used in the context of scientific inquiry, is the maxim only used in a pragmatic-explicating fashion or does it tend to a further, normative task?

I take the pragmatic-normative task of the maxim to mean something very precise. The necessary and sufficient condition for PNT is that a *genuine norm* appears as one of the conditions expressed in the protasis. Here "norm" means one of the ethically good and aesthetically admirable purposes established in the Normative Sciences (NS). The *Summum Bonum*, which Peirce identifies with all the purposes that contribute to the "development of concrete Reasonableness," is unconditionally normative for human action. As I will detail in the following section, only PNT has the specific scope of clarifying the *meaning of a proposition in the light of concrete Reasonableness*, which corresponds to the 'fourth' grade of clarity of that proposition.

PNT is formulable in the conditional mood and in the imperative mood. The conditional-mood formulation reads as follows:

Given all the possibilities of an object O, which depend upon its general dispositions, (P1) if an agent believed p, where p is a representation of O (Bp), and (P2) if the same agent pursued one of

---

18   Cf. the "scientific method" presented by Peirce in 1878 "Fixation."

the *good* purposes established in the NS, then (C) the meaning of *p* coincides with that specific resolution to do X that the agent would have in that context.

While formulated in the imperative-mood, PNT is:

Given all the possibilities of an object O, which depend upon its general dispositions, (P1) if you believe *p*, where *p* is a representation of O (B*p*), (P2) since you *ought to* pursue E, where E is one of the normative possibilities of purpose you could pursue established in the NS, (C) then you ought to do X. In this context, X is the meaning of *p*.

Peirce's two approaches to his maxim are therefore determined by the way in which the normative concern affects its use. I am referring not only to the fact that the use of the maxim is claimed to be normative for scientific inquiry. As I mentioned earlier, normativity relates to the pragmatic maxim in two ways: (1) in an *external* way, if the *use* of the maxim, also simply as PET, is normative; (2) in an *internal* way, if genuine normativity appears as a *component* of the maxim. Now, PNT requires the occurrence of a genuine norm in the protasis as a necessary condition, so that in this case normativity does not merely affect the use of the maxim, but also its structure. In the case of PET, the pragmatic maxim *does not require* genuine norms among its conditions. We have therefore:

(1) PET does not put any limit on the conditions under which the meaning of *p* is made explicit.

On the contrary,

(2) PNT puts some restraints on the conditions under which the meaning of *p* is made explicit.

In particular, the essential restraint in PNT is a practical one: the purposes of the agent involved in the hypothetical conduct upon B*p* cannot be *all* the possible purposes that an agent can endorse, but *only* ends that are 'good' from a normative viewpoint.[19]

---

19   While Peirce is explicit in saying that there are "moral facts" and therefore morally good ends as opposed to bad ones, he is quite reluctant to provide

Let us think about the following example. Peirce sometimes claims that the genuine man of science is not guided in his inquiry by practical or applicative concerns.[20] What we see here is not a pragmatic clarification of the idea of "science" through PET (what a given conception of "science" *means* at its third grade of clarity), but an unpacking of the same notion through PNT (what the notion of "science" *ought* to mean, or what the scientific life *ought* to be, i.e., the 'fourth' grade of clarity of the idea of '"science"). If we were to formulate in an extended form the idea of "science" through PNT, the norm that would occur in the protasis would be: "You simply ought to pursue the truth" (indeed, pursuing merely applicative results turns the practice of inquiry into something totally different from "science"), and the apodosis would be a prescriptive application of that norm and other contextual beliefs. If this reading is correct, we can also guess at a bolder consequence of Peirce's approach. We have defined "science" as the total sum of all the possible, contextual practical resolutions of an inquirer truly governed by the ideal of the pure pursuit of truth. But if we accept this, we should also accept that *everything that falls into the content of such resolutions obtains a normative clarification*. Let us take the example of lithium used by Peirce (CP 2.330). While the word "lithium" is explicated in its third grade of clarity when it is seen as a rule "prescribing what you are to do in order to gain a perceptual acquaintance with the object of the word," its 'fourth' grade of clarity is obtained only when this rule is put to service, so to speak, within the contextual resolution of a devout inquirer who has made of himself an instrument of "Truth." In a case where the meaning of "lithium" were unpacked through

---

examples of what kinds of morally good ends we ought to pursue, apart from the overarching goals of the development of concrete Reasonableness and the pursuit of truth. As a consequence, since the aim of this chapter is merely interpretative, I must leave my reference to 'good ends' empty. However, we can still appreciate the crucial theoretical point that Peirce is making in distinguishing PET from PNT, and hope that further moral inquiry will expand upon Peirce's mainly formal insight.

20 See, e.g., "the investigator who does not stand aloof from all intent to make practical applications, will not only obstruct the advance of the pure science, but what is infinitely worse, he will endanger his own moral integrity and that of his readers" (EP 2:29, 1898).

the resolution of a scientist completely enslaved by his desire for immediate gratifications, such meaning could not be granted the 'fourth' grade of clarity. In this light, we get a glimpse of what the "development of concrete Reasonableness" is in relation to the 'fourth' grade of clarity. As a First[21], the development of concrete Reasonableness is a merely *undifferentiated ideal*. As a Second, it is each one of all the *actual good events and deeds* resulting from a resolution to act expressed in PNT. As a Third, it is the *evolving set of the good resolutions to act* (including their corresponding habits) expressed in PNT, in which the ideal is differentiated and re-comprehended into a richer unity.

The Kantian distinction between a hypothetical "practical maxim" and the "categorical imperative" serves as a helpful analogue.[22] Peirce remarks that "the instant that an esthetic ideal is proposed as an ultimate end of action, at that instant a categorical imperative pronounces for or against it" (EP 2:202). If PET translates into a hypothetical imperative, only PNT corresponds to a contextual, categorical imperative. Christopher Hookway gets the philosophical meaning of the imperative-mood formulation of the pragmatic maxim exactly right when he explains the shift from the indicative-mood to the imperative-mood formulation. According to him, in the indicative-mood formulation Peirce refers to "laws" and "regularities" but does not "make much attempt to spell out the implications for practice that the use of the concept has" (Hookway, *The Pragmatic Maxim*, p. 179). Instead, the normative-mood formulation spells out "the inseparable connection between rational cognition and rational purpose" (*The Pragmatic Maxim*, p. 167) and, for this reason, constitutes an improvement on the indicative-mood formulation. The imperative language shows the action-guiding, practical function of meaning, which is equivalent, in Peirce's terms, to the role played by the proposition in determining self-control in one way or another (CP 8.191, c.1904; CP 5.477, 1907). So, "it is likely that Peirce thought

---

21 Both First and Second here are degenerate forms of Third.
22 Notice that Peirce sometimes uses the same terminology, but in a different and somewhat misleading way, cf., e.g., CP 5.517n. This use, however, does not change the fact that the Kantian terminology can help to clarify Peirce's point.

that pragmatic clarifications aided rational self-control by equipping us to make such efforts, by equipping us to issue imperatives to our future selves" (Hookway, *The Pragmatic Maxim*, p. 180). However, what Hookway does not see is that when the pragmatic maxim is used to make the 'fourth' grade of clarity explicit, it yields a prescription of a different type, something of the nature of a categorical imperative rather than a conditional maxim. As a matter of fact, only if a genuine norm occurs in the protasis is the prescription that is produced in the apodosis an unconditioned, "categorical" prescription. The shift from PET to PNT is not only in the conditions (a good purpose must appear among C), but also in the result, that is, in the nature of what the apodosis prescribes. In the former case, it is *any* purpose whatsoever, expressed in prescriptive language, which would result from C if we were to believe *p*; in the latter case, it is only the good and admirable purposes, always expressed in prescriptive language, which would result from C if we were to believe *p*.

Some passages betray Peirce's twofold approach to his maxim. In what follows, I consider four of these passages, which I take to be good examples of what I would call the 'tension' between PET and PNT.

Example 1. Consider the tension present in the following passage: "[S]ince pragmaticism makes the purport [of a concept] to consist in a conditional proposition concerning conduct, a sufficiently deliberate consideration of that purport will reflect that the conditional conduct ought to be regulated by an ethical principle, which by further self-criticism may be made to accord with an esthetical ideal" (CP 5.535, 1905). In this quotation Peirce alludes to the process through which, from the mere apprehension of certain rules of conduct resulting from a representation, the mind is teleologically led to assess these rules and develop "normative" criteria. A "sufficiently deliberate consideration" is the condition under which the agent gradually "grows" an ideal, which is at the same time ethical and aesthetical. The shift from the mere explication of a purpose to the identification of the purposes that we ought to follow marks the insertion of a normative perspective within the use of the maxim.

Example 2. There is an essential difference between how a sign *could* be translated and how a sign *ought to* be translated. This distinction is expressed in another passage, where Peirce speaks of the translatability of a sign without stressing the shift from an explicating paradigm to a normative one. "[If] the meaning of a symbol consists in *how* it might cause us to act, it is plain that this 'how' cannot refer to the description of mechanical motions that it might cause, but must intend to refer to a description of the action as having this or that *aim*. In order to understand pragmatism, therefore, well enough to subject it to intelligent criticism, it is incumbent upon us to inquire what an ultimate aim, capable of being pursued in an indefinitely prolonged course of action, can be" (EP 2:202, 1903). The same undeclared shift is displayed in the following passage: "[I]f, as pragmatism teaches us, what we think is to be interpreted in terms of what we are prepared to do, then surely *logic*, or the doctrine of what we ought to think, must be an application of the doctrine of what we deliberately choose to do, which is Ethics" (EP 2:142, 1903). In particular, there is a difference between the habits that could spring out of a sign in the human mind or those that ought to be developed, namely, the "ultimate" logical interpretants (not merely because of a truly "general description," that is, habits, [see CP 5.3, 1902], but because they are the realization of the "immediate interpretants" of a sign, of its *correct* interpretability). This is displayed by the two uses of the maxim.

Example 3. In "Issues of Pragmaticism" (1905), we read that "Pragmaticism makes thinking to consist in the living inferential metaboly of symbols whose purport lies in conditional general resolutions to act" (CP 5.403n3). Peirce then mentions the "aesthetic ideal" ("the share which God permits him to have in the work of creation") and the way in which the "*vir* is begotten," showing again the tension between a merely explicating task in approaching symbols (so that the meaning is given by "conditional general resolutions to act") and a normative task (so that the meaning is given only by those general resolutions to act that are consistent with the ideal). It is the human being who enters the realm of normativity by growing an aesthetical ideal in herself, almost as a conversion which gives new life, and starts to interpret signs and symbols in light of this new normative vocation toward the development of concrete Reasonableness. PNT is the result of this transformation.

Example 4. I claimed at the outset that Peirce's approach to the pragmatic maxim is problematical. The problematical tension between PET and PNT is displayed by the ambiguity of the notion of "rational." For instance, Peirce explains that pragmatic meaning "consists in the total of all general modes of rational conduct which . . . would ensue upon the acceptance of the symbol" and "upon all the possible different circumstances and desires" ("Issues", EP 2:346, CP 5.438, 1905). The problematical aspect resides in how we interpret the meaning of "rational." "Rational" can be taken in the basic sense of a general disposition or in the more specific sense of what is normative and good:

(1) If the meaning is what is obtained through the pragmatic-explicating use of the maxim, "rational" means *all* the general modes of conduct resulting from a deliberate acceptance of the symbol. It is obviously possible that the representation we have is false and that our goal is wicked, so that the consequence of its acceptance is indeed a general resolution to act, but a bad one. If it is bad, it is not "rational" in a normative way. If "rational" is meant to be a normative concept, the pragmatic-explicating use of the maxim cannot account for it.

(2) If the meaning is what is obtained through the pragmatic-normative use of the maxim, "rational" means all the *normative* and *good* general modes of action resulting from the deliberate acceptance of the symbol.

In the former case, "rationality" = generality; in the latter, "rationality" = normative generality.[23] While PET produces the former type of rationality, the latter can be only produced by PNT.

Although not identical, PET and PNT are "continuous." In other words, PNT should be considered as a "destined" outgrowth, or natural development, of PET. Why does the pragmatic-normative approach to meaning (PNT) emerge from the merely pragmatic-explicating one (PET)? We should remember that the pragmatic maxim is a tool

---

23   Even Potter, *Charles S. Peirce on Norms and Ideals*, pp. 54-55, p. 58, and
      pp. 60-63 mistakenly merges together "generality," as the principle that
      governs individuals, and "normativity."

for scientific inquiry. Now, in Peirce's view, all the purposes held by agents are teleologically subject to a developmental process of normativity under the amending stubbornness of "experience" (CP 5.564, c.1906). Also in science, then, inquirers grow a capacity for critical assessment that enable them to become aware of the difference between the norms to which they are *actually* committed and the genuine norms they *ought to* endorse.

A brief critical history of 1877's "The Fixation of Belief" can be helpful here. In this essay, Peirce maintains that the need for inquiry springs out of the "irritation of doubt," so that its task becomes the removal of the doubt through the fixation of a belief. This epistemological framework shows a difficulty that Peirce recognized later on (EP 2:140, 1903). In fact, the statements contained in "Fixation" might lead to a psychologistic understanding of "logic" and its sustaining goal, the pursuit of truth: "truth" would coincide with whatever is able to remove the "irritation of doubt," independently of any further consideration. However, if Peirce's psychologism-flavored statements in "Fixation" are interpreted in the light of the more mature developments of his thought, we get a different picture. Accordingly, the need for agency compels us, as an efficient cause, to the fixation of a "determinate" belief, whatever this belief might be, just to fulfill the need to act consistently (see, e.g., EP 1:114, CP 5.374-375, 1877; EP 1:131, CP 5.400, 1878). But, at the same time, this need grows, first, into the 'suspicion' of the truth, then into a 'desire' for the truth, and eventually into the pursuit of truth as a genuinely normative "ideal" for science.[24]

---

24 The stubbornness of experience corresponds to the teleological "power" of "Reason" operating in semeiosis. As Thomas L. Short, "Peirce on the Aim of Inquiry: Another Reading of 'Fixation'", *Transactions of the Charles S. Peirce Society*, 36 (1) (2000), 1-23 (p.7) has convincingly stated, the "social impulse," which according to "Fixation" plays against the non-scientific methods of determining a belief, turns out to be the inchoative manifestation of Reason and need for truth. Robert B. Talisse, *A Pragmatist Philosophy of Democracy* (New York: Routledge, 2007), pp. 56ff provides an insightful reading of "Fixation" as the description of different competing epistemic practices, but he misses the point of the developmental emergence of the normative perspective from the pre-normative one. The movement from point (1) to point (2) is highlighted

Now, when we come to "methodeutic," we have to acknowledge that the alethic ideal of science can affect the use of the maxim in a twofold way. First, it simply prescribes that we use the maxim as a tool of scientific inquiry. We can speak in this case of an *external normativity* of the alethic ideal for the maxim. Here, the maxim is not subject to any restriction, since all the purposes are admitted among the conditions of its application to a belief. Second, the alethic ideal can also become one of the logical conditions of the application of the maxim. In this case, we speak of an *internal normativity* attached to the maxim. As it should be clear at this point that only in this second case do we have PNT. The important point here is that the shift from external to internal normativity in the use of the maxim–i.e., the appearance of PNT–is a "destined" and continuous process. In fact, external normativity is grounded in the fact that PET furthers the development of concrete Reasonableness. Now, since the development of concrete Reasonableness has an absolute value, inquirers should also accept it in each and every application of the maxim. Thus, the normativity of the *Summum Bonum* tends to *slide* into the logical conditions of the maxim and to produce PNT.

3. *The Pragmatic Maxim, the Normative Sciences and the 'Fourth' Grade of Clarity*

In the 1902 definition of "Pragmatic and Pragmatism" written for Baldwin's *Dictionary of Philosophy and Psychology*, Peirce comments on the use of the maxim and introduces something that might be called a 'fourth' grade of clarity:

> [We] would venture to suggest that it [the Pragmatic Maxim] should always be put into practice with conscientious thoroughness, but that, when that has been done, and note before, a still higher grade

---

by Peter Skagestad, "C. S. Peirce on Biological Evolution and Scientific Progress", *Synthese* 41(1) (1979), 85-114, although he does not explicitly recognize the role of teleology in it. Finally, Hookway's concern that Peirce has a psychologistic conception of thinking (*Peirce*, pp. 52-58) should be corrected in the light of Short's developmental interpretation.

of clearness of thought can be attained by remembering that the only ultimate good which the practical facts to which it directs attention can subserve is to further the development of concrete reasonableness; so that the meaning of the concept does not lie in any individual reactions at all, but in the manner in which those reactions contribute to that development. (CP 5.3, 1902)

We find here the seeming dichotomy previously highlighted between the use of the maxim in its purity (which corresponds to PET) and the method of discovery of true beliefs (which corresponds to PNT), here individuated in those beliefs and purposes that contribute to the development of concrete Reasonableness. For Peirce, then, only "reasonable" beliefs and purposes can attain the 'fourth' level of clarity.

While a dichotomy between PET and PNT is untenable, their distinction in terms of function is absolutely legitimate. The essential difference is that in the case of PNT the application of the maxim is 'bounded.' The "third" grade of clarity corresponds to the pragmatic-explicating use of the maxim and its concern is expressible in the question: "Does B*p* have a pragmatic meaning?" The 'fourth' grade of clarity corresponds to the pragmatic-normative use of the maxim and its concern is: "Does B*p* fit in the development of concrete Reasonableness? How so?" Clearly, the passage from PET to PNT shows a normative shift in the problem addressed. The purpose of action prescribed in the apodosis of the pragmatic-normative use of the maxim is not "rational" merely in the sense that it is the general prescription that would follow in general conditions (even if *p* were false and the purposes of the agent were evil; here "rationality" = "generality"), but it is "rational" in the sense that it is the ethically good and aesthetically admirable purpose which would result from the endorsement of a proposition in a particular context.

To make this point clearer, I would formulate PNT in order to display *two different levels* in obtaining the fourth grade of clarity. Let us begin with the first level. As we already know, the imperative-mood formulation of PNT reads: given all the possibilities of an object O, which depend upon its general dispositions, (P1) if you believe *p*, where *p* is a representation of O (B*p*), (P2) since you *ought to* pursue E, where E is one of the normative possibilities of purpose you could pursue established in the Normative Sciences, (C) then you ought to do X. In this context, X is the meaning of p. I call this the *first level of the attainment of the 'fourth' grade of clarity* because the attainment of the fourth grade of clarity is only partial. Consider the case in which p is a false proposition. Even though p is false, if the premises of the maxim are genuine scientific attitudes (such as the task of knowing the truth), the apodosis of the conditional will be a contextual prescription in which X is genuinely good and admirable for *that* agent in *that* context. In other words: even though p is false, if the agent in a particular context acts according to the best of her epistemic, moral, and aesthetical beliefs, the prescriptive outcome of the application of the maxim will be at the same time contextually good and admirable. It will be the necessary, intermediate step in order to get at a fuller realization of the development of concrete Reasonableness (in which p must also be true). As Peirce stated over and over again, an authentic scientific service to the cause of truth is not made only of achievements and successes.

The *second level of the fourth grade of clarity* is obtained through the application of PNT in which a further condition, P3, occurs:

Given all the possibilities of an object O, which depend upon its general dispositions, (P1) if you believe p, where p is a representation of O (Bp), (P2) since you *ought to* pursue E, where E is one of the normative possibilities of purpose you could pursue established in the NS, (P3) if p is the result of an "investigation carried sufficiently far" into O (W 3:274, 1878), (C) then you ought to do X. In this context, X is the meaning of p.

In this case, P3 introduces the truth of p as a condition for the attainment of the second level of the fourth grade of clarity. In this case, the agent not only acts in accordance with the best of her epistemic and moral beliefs, but she also acts in accordance with a true proposition. As a consequence, X is the contextual meaning of p that, limited to that context, fully develops concrete Reasonableness or, as Peirce sometimes puts it, the "drama of creation."

Peirce's concern about the "ultimate" meaning of a concept intersects with this problem. As we have seen, the "ultimate" interpretant of a sign cannot be a sign itself but has to be something different, namely, a habit. If this is true, we also see that the account of the pragmatic maxim at its highest level of clarity becomes: the "ultimate" interpretant of a sign is not the habit that an agent would happen to develop in certain conditions, but that "destined" habit in which anthropologically destined habits and objectively destined habits come to coincide, so to speak. The interpretant would result from a set of conditions in which *p* is true and in which the agent is actually adopting the development of concrete Reasonableness as the ultimate ideal of her conduct. In short, we conceive an object (i.e., we interpret a sign) in its 'fourth' grade of clarity only when we think it in its truth, goodness and beauty, and when we understand that this endeavor is unavoidably intertwined with the reasonableness (in a normative sense) of our conduct. The example of the lithium in the scientific practice can be seen now in its full clarity.

4. Why Is Peirce Committed to the Pragmatic-Explicating Task of the Maxim? Possibility and Moral Truth

What remains to be answered is the question: why is Peirce so interested in keeping the purity of PET even when the "secret" of his pragmaticism reveals an essential connection of the pragmatic maxim with the Normative Sciences (EP 2:200, 1903)? I believe that there are at least two reasons here.

The first reason is the most important and is related to Peirce's modal metaphysics.[25] The reality of possibility is broader than what is actual (what "exists") and what is normative (what "ought-to be"). The subclass of possibilities that are genuinely normative emerges in the field of what is possible in general. What is "practically normative" is a subclass of what is "practically possible." In other words, moral truth is only a case of what can be done. While PET unpacks the latter, only PNT reveals the former. As we have seen, PNT limits the range of possibilities in at least two ways: on the one hand, the protasis of the

---

25 See Robert Lane, "Peirce's Modal Shift: From Set Theory to Pragmaticism", *Journal of the History of Philosophy* 45(4) (2007), 551-576.

conditional cannot be any purpose whatsoever, but must contain one genuine norm; on the other hand, the apodosis of the conditional does not produce just any practical resolution, but only an unconditionally normative purpose, a good and admirable prescription in a certain context. In other words, PNT cannot cover *all* the possibilities of interpretation of *p* that could emerge from the application of the pragmatic maxim to *p*. Only PET can describe *all* the real possibilities, including those possibilities that should not be pursued. Only PET has the capacity to clarify at the third grade of clarity what belongs to the broad metaphysical class of possibility without being at the same time either normative or actual.

In 1905's "Issues of Pragmaticism," Peirce claims that one of the most important doctrines entailed by pragmaticism is the reality of "possibilities." The complete outcome of a modal metaphysics, enlightened by the application of the maxim, is not only the acceptance of real generals (beyond the mere existence of real individuals), but also the linked reality of "real vagues" and "real possibilities". Peirce writes:

> Another doctrine which is involved in Pragmaticism as an essential consequence of it, but which the writer defended (*Journal of Speculative Philosophy* 1868, and *North American Review* 1871) before he had formulated, even in his own mind, the principle of pragmaticism, is the scholastic doctrine of realism. This is usually defined as the opinion that there are real objects that are general, among the number being the modes of determination of existent singulars, if, indeed, these be not the only such objects. But the belief in this can hardly escape being accompanied by the acknowledgment that there are, besides, real *vagues*, and especially, real *possibilities*. For possibility being the denial of necessity, which is a kind of generality, is vague like any other contradiction of a general. Indeed, it is the reality of some possibilities that pragmaticism is most concerned to insist upon. (EP 2:354, 1905)

The reality of "some possibilities" upon which "pragmaticism is most concerned to insist" coincides with a realist interpretation of the pragmatic meaning of a sign displayed by PET.[26] Clearly,

---

26 For a taxonomy of types of possibility, see CP 6.371, 1902, from "Notes on Metaphysics." It is highly instructive that in this passage Peirce

the normative is only one subclass of the possible interpretations that a sign carries with it. Peirce remains faithful to PET because it displays the semeiotic nature of reality in all its breadth, while PNT only focuses on a subclass of the possibilities of reality. The "kernel of pragmatism" is PET because only the pragmatic-explicating task of the maxim can unpack "the *total* meaning of the predication of an intellectual concept," or "the whole meaning of an intellectual predicate," which consists "in affirming that, under all conceivable circumstances of a given kind, the subject of the predication would (or would not) behave in a certain way,–that is, that it either would, or would not, be true that under given experiential circumstances (or under a given proportion of them, taken *as they would occur* in experience) certain facts would exist" (EP 2:402). Peirce also spells out the fact that obtaining the "total meaning" of a proposition should leave unbounded the conditions of the protasis as far as human purposes are concerned. He writes that for the pragmaticist "[t]he rational meaning of every proposition" is the "form in which the proposition becomes applicable to human conduct, not in these or those special circumstances, nor when one entertains this or that special design, but that form which is most directly applicable to self-control under every situation, and to every purpose" (EP 2:340, CP 5.427, 1905)[27].

If it is true that in Peirce's terms the pragmatic meaning of p is always and essentially tied to the "purpose" of an agent/interpreter of p, it follows that the perspective on p can be twofold. The first perspective displays an attitude in which p is considered in all its possible "practical bearings," i.e., all the possible consequences that

---

laments that "moral possibility" is not usually taken to mean "something reasonably free from extreme improbability," but rather "morally permissible", showing that the perspective provided by PET on possibility, even in the field of human agency, should be left free from normative considerations.

27   Also "under all conceivable circumstances of a given kind" (EP 2:402, 1907). "The entire intellectual purport of any symbol consists in the total of all general modes of rational conduct which, conditionally upon all the possible different circumstances and desires, would ensue upon the acceptance of the symbol" (EP 2:346, 1905).

would follow if an unrestrained set of conditions occurred. This is the attitude related to PET. This perspective is complete on one side but partial on the other side. On the one side, it is complete insofar as it is concerned with *all* the possible practical bearings of p given all the possible conditions. However, on the other side, PET is partial because it does not consider the aspect of normativity (logical, ethical, and aesthetical) that according to Peirce is naturally related to the purposes of the semeiotic process. In light of Peirce's theory of normativity, only some of all the possible purposes are good and ought to be pursued. The second perspective displays a different attitude, explicitly concerned with the dimension of normativity. This is the case of PNT. From this perspective, the conditions of the application of the maxim are restricted only to the good and admirable purposes that an agent ought to pursue in her life. Also in this case, the perspective is complete on one side but partial on the other side. It is complete insofar as the concern with the ultimate interpretants of p allows for a broad consideration of Bp, which does not exclude the normative perspective. However, it is also partial, insofar as from this viewpoint it is not possible to make explicit *all* the possible practical bearings of p, but only those that follow "purposes" which are good and admirable from the normative viewpoint. While PET and PNT are irreducible to each other (hence the tension and their problematical treatment), they are also complementary.

The second reason for Peirce's concern for the priority of PET is that it is in the light of the logically false, the ethically bad, and the aesthetically repugnant that the normativity of what is true, good and admirable emerges. Hence, possibility plays a crucial role here because it has a fundamental function in the development of the Normative Sciences: it is in contrast to possible instances of deformity of what is normative and "rational" (the false, the morally evil, the aesthetically repugnant), what Peirce calls sometimes the "perversity of thought" (EP 2:342, CP 5.430, 1905), that the possibilities of the development of concrete Reasonableness take shape and are perceived. Although Peirce never explicitly articulates his thoughts on this point, a Peircean argument would sound like this. What is genuinely normative is found in contrast to what is a deformity of concrete Reasonableness. Moreover, what is genuinely normative is only a subclass of all the possibilities of the meaning of a sign, since all the possibilities of the meaning of a sign include also that which is a deformity of concrete Reasonableness. Since the discovery of what is genuinely normative emerges in contrast to what is a deformity of concrete Reasonableness, the Normative Sciences require an approach to the pragmatic meaning of a sign that is maximally broad. In conclusion, the Normative Sciences also require the purity of PET.

CHAPTER 2
'I' WHO?
A New Look at Peirce's
Theory of Indexical Self-Reference

The present chapter focuses on Charles S. Peirce's treatment of self-referential statements in order to develop a Peircean, semeiotic theory of personal self-consciousness. After providing a sketch of Peirce's semeiotic theory of the first-person pronoun "I," I defend the claim that Peirce maintains that "I" has a real, non-fictional referent and that we have to focus on the perceptual conditions of self-referential statements in order to appreciate how the personal "self" comes to birth.

1.

The aim of this chapter is to address the problem of what is usually called 'self-consciousness' by studying Charles S. Peirce's semeiotic treatment of self-referential statements. Peirce believes that an adequate study of the mind requires "to reduce all mental action," including "self-consciousness," "to the formula of valid reasoning" (W2: 214, EP1: 30, 5.267, 1868) and its semeiotic nature. While Peirce makes frequent use of the notion of "consciousness," he is at the same time distant from the understanding of the 'conscious mind' that Descartes invented and made canonical (e.g. W1: 491, 1866), and which from the modern epoch stretches out to the contemporary discussion on, as David Chalmers put it, the 'hard problem' of the mind.[1] In what follows, I argue that Peirce puts forth a powerful

---

1   Cf. David J. Chalmers, "Facing Up to the Problem of Consciousness", *Journal of Consciousness Studies* 2(3) (1995), 200-219. While in the present chapter I will be mainly concerned with Peirce's theory of indexical self-referential statements, I will also relate Peirce's theory to

theory of self-consciousness based on his semeiotic understanding of self-reference and indexicality.[2] To the question, 'How can we elucidate the phenomenon of self-consciousness?', we shall answer, with Peirce, 'What we call self-consciousness corresponds to the practice of narratives and descriptions ultimately based on indexical self-referential statements, which are in turn rooted in very specific dimensions of human experience.' It is also important to underscore from the outset that the problem of indexical self-reference cannot be separated from Peirce's concept of experience, which is one of the most interesting insights of Peirce's philosophy and classical American pragmatism. In particular, it will be essential to see what are the experiential-perceptual conditions under which indexical self-referential statements can work as such.[3]

---

contemporary debates and positions in the philosophy of mind in order to show how such debates are still victim of a radical Cartesian prejudice and could benefit from a Peircean philosophical framework. Of course, a full-fledged assessment of contemporary Cartesianism goes beyond the limited scope of the present chapter. For a convincing critical account of the Cartesian roots of contemporary analytic philosophy of mind, see Richard Rorty, *Philosophy and the Mirror of Nature* (Princeton: Princeton University Press, 1979).

2   In this chapter, "self-reference" is not the logical property of a statement that refers to itself (e.g. "this proposition is true"). Rather, I take "indexical self-reference" to be the description of the semeiotic structure of human self-consciousness. Peirce's attempt to deal with self-consciousness in logical, or semeiotic terms, antedates the work of Hector-Neri Castañeda, who boldly stated in 1966 that his logical treatment of self-consciousness was "almost brand new." Hector-Neri Castañeda, "'He': A Study in the Logic of Self-Consciousness" *Self-Reference and Self-Awareness*, ed. by Andrew Brook and Richard C. DeVidi (Amsterdam and Philadelphia: John Benjamins Publishing Company, 2001), 51-79.

3   Galen Strawson has recently stressed the (already Peircean) tenet that a study of the self should be based on the notion of "experience." This is what he calls the "thin" or "live" conception of the subject of experience, according to which "no subject of experience exists unless experience exists for it to be the subject of." Galen Strawson, "I and *I*: Immunity to Error through Misidentification of the Subject", *Immunity to Error through Misidentification*, ed. by Simon Prosser and François Recanati (Cambridge: Cambridge University Press, 2012), p. 208. This is the "synergy self," "something that is essentially experientially live,

Peirce scholarship has usually seen the problem of self-reference as a chapter in the broader metaphysical problem of individuation and has consequently dwelt with it in light of this latter. It has been long claimed that Peirce's theory of human individuality is somehow troublesome. In a famous comment, Richard J. Bernstein writes that "the nature of human individuality always seemed to be a source of intellectual embarrassment for Peirce."[4] Although partially insightful, I take this statement to be highly problematical in two ways. What does "human individuality" mean here? Bernstein's commentary does not say. His assessment exemplifies in fact an (unfortunate) tendency present in (some) readings of Peirce. Was Peirce interested in denying human individuality or was he interested in finding a deeper sense of individuality than the caricatures of human subjectivity that even the best of philosophy has managed to produced? Second, once we have made clear what that phrase means, is there any conclusive evidence in Peirce's thought for such interpretation? Let us leave the two questions open for now. There are three standard interpretations of Peirce's philosophy that take Peirce to put forth a nihilistic doctrine of human individuality. One of these is provided by Bernstein, according to whom Peirce's metaphysics cannot account for the originality and spontaneity, stemming from an "individual I," that characterizes human agency.[5] Similarly, Paul Weiss maintains that for Peirce there are no real "individuals" and that what we call individuals are actually

something that exists only in the act or activity of experience" ("I and I'', p. 209). This picture of the self must be preferred to an idea of the self as a structure opposed to or different from the course of experience itself. Though interesting for its experiential approach, G. Strawson's contribution seems in the end to put forth an associationist, Humean conception of the self ("I and I'', pp. 212-214), which I believe Peirce would have strongly criticized as nominalistic. For a brief and clear sketch of Peirce's rejection of Hume, see Robert J. Roth, "Did Peirce Answer Hume on Necessary Connection?", *The Review of Metaphysics* 38(4) (1985), 867-880.

4   Richard J. Bernstein, "Action, Conduct, and Self-Control", *Perspectives on Peirce: Critical Essays on Charles Sanders Peirce*, ed. by Richard J. Bernstein (New Haven: Yale University Press, 1965), 66-91.

5   Bernstein, "Action, Conduct, and Self-Control", pp. 90-91.

only the parts of bigger wholes.[6] Finally, John F. Boler concludes from a compared study of Duns Scotus's and Peirce's metaphysical systems that Peirce cannot produce a genuine notion of "individuality" because he weds himself to a sort of Scotistic metaphysics but rejects at the same time Scotus's notion of "contraction."[7] These three nihilistic interpretations rely on a series of famous passages in which Peirce *prima facie* seems to claim that (1) self-consciousness is not an original and intuitive power, or that (2) the existence of the human individual is not real apart from the social organism, or finally that (3) the metaphysical status of the individual self is nothing more than that of an error and ignorance bearer (e.g. 1.673; W2: 200-204, EP1: 18-21, 1868; W2: 241-242, EP1: 55, 1868).

A great deal of work has been done in order to show that Peirce does not hold such a nihilistic view. In particular, Vincent M. Colapietro's 1989 study is commonly considered the first groundbreaking work on this topic.[8] Further studies on Peirce's notions of individuality and selfhood have shown that the nihilistic interpretation of the self is a misunderstanding of Peirce's thought.[9] The common conclusion of

---

6   Paul Weiss, "Charles S. Peirce, Philosopher", *Perspectives on Peirce: Critical Essays on Charles Sanders Peirce*, ed. by Richard J. Bernstein (New Haven: Yale University Press, 1965), 120-140.

7   John F. Boler, *Charles Peirce and Scholastic Realism: A Study of Peirce's Relation to John Duns Scotus*. Seattle: University of Washington Press, 1963), pp. 142-144; p. 160.

8   Short and Lane explicitly acknowledge this point. Thomas L. Short, "Hypostatic Abstraction in Self-Consciousness", ed. by Jacqueline Brunning and Paul Forster, *The Rule of Reason: The Philosophy of Charles Sanders Peirce* (Toronto-Buffalo-London: University of Toronto Press, 1997), 289-308; Robert Lane, "Persons, Signs, Animals: A Peircean Account of Personhood", *Transactions of the Charles S. Peirce Society* 45(1) (2009), 1-26.

9   See Vincent M. Colapietro, "Toward a Pragmatic Conception of Practical Identity", *Transactions of the Charles S. Peirce Society* 42(2) (2006), 173-205; Cornelius F. Delaney, "Peirce's Critique of Foundationalism", *The Monist* 57(2) (1973), 240-251; Cornelius F. Delaney, "Peirce's Account of Mental Activity", *Synthese* 41(1) (1979), 25-36; Cornelius F. Delaney, *Science, Knowledge, and Mind: A Study in the Philosophy of Charles S. Peirce* (Notre Dame and London: Notre Dame University Press, 1993), pp. 130-156; Jeffrey R. DiLeo, "Peirce's Haecceitism",

these works can be summed up in the three following statements: (i)

Transactions of the Charles S. Peirce Society 27(1) (1991), 79-109; Ilona Kemp-Pritchard, "Peirce on Individuation", *Transactions of the Charles S. Peirce Society* 14(2) (1978), 83-100; Stanley M. Harrison, "Peirce on Persons", *Proceeding of the C.S. Peirce Bicentennial International Congress*, ed. by Kenneth L. Ketner (Lubbock: Texas Technical University Press, 1981), 217-221; Larry Holmes, "Prolegomena to Peirce's Philosophy of Mind", *Studies in the Philosophy of Charles Sanders Peirce. Second Series*, ed. by Edward C. Moore and Richard S. Robin (Amherst: The University of Massachusetts Press, 1964), 359-381; Gresham Riley, "Peirce's Theory of the Individuals", *Transactions of the Charles S. Peirce Society* 10(3) (1974), 135-165; Giovanni Maddalena, "Esperienza e soggettività. Un confronto tra Peirce e Dewey", *Semiotica e fenomenologia del sé*, ed. by Rosa M. Calcaterra (Torino: Nino Aragno Editore, 2006), 111-122; Emily Michael, "Peirce on Individuals", *Transactions of the Charles S. Peirce Society* 12(4) (1976), 321-329; Patricia A. Muoio, "Peirce on the Person", *Transactions of the Charles S. Peirce Society* 20(2) (1984), 169-181; Helmut Pape, "A Peircean Theory of Indexical Signs and Individuation", *Semiotica* 31(3/4) (1980), 215-243; Kory S. Sorrell, "Peirce and a Pragmatic Reconception of Substance", *Transactions of the Charles S. Peirce Society* 37(2) (2001), 257-295; Kory S. Sorrell, *Representative Practices: Peirce, Pragmatism, and Feminist Epistemology* (New York: Fordham University Press, 2004), pp. 33-75; Lynn G. Stephens, "Peirce on Psychological Self-Knowledge", *Transactions of the Charles S. Peirce Society* 16(3) (1980), 212-224; Pierre Thibaud, "Peirce on Proper Names and Individuation", *Transactions of the Charles S. Peirce Society* 23(4) (1987), 521-538; Richard Menary, "Our Glassy Essence: Pragmatist Approaches to the Self", *The Oxford Handbook of the Self*, ed. by Shaun Gallager (Oxford: Oxford University Press, 2011), 609-632; Haci-Halil Uslucan, "Charles Sanders Peirce and the Semiotic Foundation of Self and Reason", *Mind, Culture, and Activity* 11(2) (2012), 96-108; Mary Magada-Ward, "'As Parts of One Esthetic Total': Inference, Imagery, and Self-Knowledge in the Later Peirce", *The Journal of Speculative Philosophy* 17(3) (2003), 216-223; Andrew Robinson, *God and the World of Signs: Trinity, Evolution, and the Metaphysical Semiotics of C.S. Peirce* (Leiden and Boston: Brill, 2010). I would like to spend a few words here on the most important recent essay on Peirce's understanding of the self, namely André De Tienne's "Peirce on the Symbolical Person", *Semiotica e fenomenologia del sè*, ed. by Rosa M Calcaterra (Torino: Nino Aragno Editore, 2006), 91-109. De Tienne's essay has several merits. First, it stresses that for Peirce the correct method in philosophy of mind is semeiotic (and not psychological, neurophysiological, etc.). the correct method in philosophy of mind.

Peirce's alleged negative claims about the "self" intend to undermine a Cartesian, intuitionist conception of self-consciousness, and to

---

Second, De Tienne correctly stresses the developmental origin of the "person." Third, he shows that Peirce, since his early writings, rejects Kant's idea of the transcendental unity of apperception as the ground for accounting for the "consistency" of representations. (See on this also Zachary M. Gartenberg, "Intelligibility and Subjectivity in Peirce: A Reading of his 'New List of Categories'", *Journal of the History of Philosophy* 50(4) (2012), 581-610.) However, it seems to me that De Tienne overlooks the problem of the origin of self-consciousness, as if talking of the symbolic nature of "personality" could solve the problem of self-consciousness: : the claim that the human being is an evolving sign and that his mental life ought to be studied semeiotically does not constitute an explanation of how that particular inference which is self-consciousness comes into being. That De Tienne overlooks this problem is proved by the fact that he focuses on "personality," including higher-order personalities, without addressing the problem whether for Peirce higher-order personalities have something like self-consciousness (I would answer negatively; however, I cannot address this point here). In addition to this, De Tienne, in addressing the problem of self-conscious personality, puts the cart before the horse. He writes: "The general indetermination of a person refers to the very quality of its internal manifold. Let's remember again the "New List of Categories" of 1867, in which Peirce described the manifold of substance in terms of "it," in terms of "present in general," and we shall have a beginning idea of the generality that characterizes every person as a representational agent. A person experiences itself at any moment as a present in general, that, as a general (this symbolical) representation of that connexity which is internal to its own manifold of more or less defined possibilities" ("Peirce on the Symbolical Person", pp. 105-106). Now, as De Tienne knows perfectly, the confused unification of the phenomenon at the mere level of the "it" excludes any reflexive reference to a self; on the contrary, De Tienne uses here phrases such as: "a person experiences *itself* at any moment as a present in general" (italics added). Now, either we experience "a present in general" without any reference to us at the level of the "IT" (that could be eventually referred to us), or we attribute to us what was before experienced as a mere present in general, in which case we are attributing a description to ourselves. In the first case, the simple unification of experience is wrongly conceived as implying self-consciousness, while in the second case self-consciousness is only assumed, without explaining what its genesis is. It is for this reason, I believe, that new attention should be devoted to Peirce's treatment of self-consciousness.

replace it with a full-fledged inferential account of the operations of the mind; (ii) the same claims underscore the developmental origin of the individual self-consciousness, which relies mainly (although not exclusively) upon social and linguistic dynamics; (iii) finally, the apparently ambiguous place of individuality in Peirce's metaphysics is due to his conception of individuality as a limit-case within continuity and as ultimately indivisible from continuity.

Although all these studies provide essential insights into Peirce's doctrine, I believe that they all rely on an *ambiguous* use of the notion of individuality. My overall interpretation is that Peirce's doctrine of the human individuality, or individual selfhood, is a complex one and has to be understood in a threefold way, so that every reference to only one of these three ways is a form of reduction of Peirce's perspective:

(1) "Individuality" is the law-like continuity of a unique series of instantiations that constitutes the reality of every human being.

(2) "Individuality" means the constant possibility in the mental life of adult human beings to refer to their empirical "I" through acts of self-reference and self-ascription of mental states.

(3) "Individuality" also refers to the unique mission to which a human being is called in the ongoing process of creation.

In this chapter, I focus only on the second point, i.e., the problem of self-reference, to which only an unsystematic attention has been given so far.[10] Can Peirce really be included in the list of philosophers

---

10 To be fair, Stephens deals explicitly with the problem of "psychological self-ascriptions" in Lynn G. Stephens, "Peirce on Psychological Self-Knowledge", *Transactions of the Charles S. Peirce Society* 16 (3) (1980), 212-224. However, Hookway claims: "It is rather surprising that Peirce does not offer an account of our ordinary first-person avowals." Christopher Hookway, *Peirce* (London: Routledge, 1985), p. 26. Although challenging, Hookway's statement is wrong if it is taken to entail that Peirce did not address the topic of what we call self-referential statements. A striking example of the massive presence of this topic in Peirce's thought is his constant reflection on self-control as one of the essential dimensions of human rationality. On human rationality, deliberation and self-control, see Vincent M. Colapietro, "Peirce's Guess at the Riddle of Rationality: Deliberative Imagination as the Personal Locus of Human Practice", *Classical American Pragmatism: Its Contemporary Vitality*,

who maintained what Peter Strawson called a "no-ownership" or "no-subject" doctrine of the self?[11] As I will show, a nihilistic interpretation of Peirce's view on human individuality is untenable also from the perspective of self-reference. I take this to be an important endeavor, since it has also been claimed recently that Peirce holds a nihilistic understanding of the individual self. In particular, Cornelis de Waal writes that according to Peirce the individual human being is "wholly defined in terms of imperfections".[12] As I will show, although de Waal's interpretation relies on the genuine anti-individualistic tendency of Peirce's theory of inquiry and metaphysics, a nihilist interpretation of Peirce's doctrine of the self is partial and in the end misleading.

Peirce's often-quoted definition of the human being as a "sign developing according to the laws of inference" is already found in his 1868 "Some Consequences of Four Incapacities" (W2: 240; EP1: 53) and expresses a belief that will be maintained until his late writings. However, an analysis of his manuscripts shows that Peirce developed these ideas even before the publication of that essay, as the 1865 Harvard Lectures and 1866 Lowell Lectures clearly prove. In particular, in Lowell Lecture XI, Peirce, at the end of his series of lecture on the "Logic of Science," explicitly asks the question: "What is man?" and articulates the same answer that he will include in "Some Consequences." The problem of self-reference is a part of the anthropological question and the anthropological question is first and foremost, in Peirce's terms, a logical question about the nature and classification of thinking.[13] The fact that Peirce in his

---

ed. by Sandra Rosenthal, Carl R. Hausman, and Douglas R. Anderson (Chicago: University of Illinois Press, 1999), 15-30.

11   Peter F. Strawson, *Individuals: An Essay in Descriptive Metaphysics* (London and New York: Routledge, 2003), pp. 95ff.

12   Cornelis de Waal, "Science Beyond the Self: Remarks on Charles S. Peirce's Social Epistemology", *Cognitio* 7(1) (2006), 149-163; Douglas Browning, *Act and Agent: An Essay in Philosophical Anthropology*, Coral Gables: University of Miami Press, 1964).

13   This methodological point is particularly clear in Corrington: "The semiotic reconfiguration of methods of inference has direct implications for philosophical anthropology. ... we can almost derive our anthropology from semiotics." Robert S. Corrington, *An Introduction to C.S. Peirce:*

early writings defines logic as the science of the conditions of the relation of symbols to their objects and that he concludes his 1866 lectures on the logic of science with a thorough meditation on the symbolic nature of the human being should make us realize that Peirce stands on a somewhat unconventional ground in addressing the problem of the nature of the human mind. In other words, Peirce's method of inquiry in philosophy of mind mainly coincides with his semeiotic logic right from his first steps.[14] Therefore Peirce, while trying to give a "thoroughly unpsychological view of logic" (W1: 164), was at the same time settling a study of the mental life of the human being (and of self-consciousness, interpreted as self-reference, as a case of it) in semeiotic terms. This reading is confirmed by Peirce's further inquiries, as it is witnessed, for instance, by his 1893 "Immortality in the Light of Synechism," in which we read that the human being's "spiritual consciousness" has the same nature of those "eternal verities" embodied in the rest of the universe as a whole (EP2: 3). "Verity" is first and foremost a logical notion, and is outside the epistemic boundaries of what is usually considered to be the adequate subject-matter of philosophy of mind. On the contrary, Peirce thinks that the subject-matter of logic overlaps with the subject-matter of philosophy subject-matter of philosophy of mind. In fact, Peirce believes that human thinking is not reducible to its material instantiations and supports, that is, to its replicas, or to merely physical and biological semeiotic processes. For these reasons I believe that an analysis of the logic of indexical self-referential statements, as the one provided in this chapter, is the best way to develop a philosophy of self-consciousness in a Peircean mood.

Peirce's theory of indexical reference can have a fundamental role in answering the problems arising from a Cartesian approach to self-reference. In particular, the presence of an indexical component in self-reference could very likely account for the directness of self-reference without resulting into a form of intuitionist introspectivism

---

Philosopher, Semiotician, and Ecstatic Naturalist (Lanham: Rowman and Littlefield, 1993), p. 76.

14   F. Bellucci, *Peirce's Speculative Grammar: Logic as Semiotics* (New York and London: Routledge, 2018).

(Peirce's theory of indexical reference does not entail intuitionism). At the same time, indexicality avoids the widespread assumption that a full-fledged descriptive knowledge is the only way in which the term "I" can refer to the individual self. The question is therefore whether self-referential statements are descriptive all the way through or if on the contrary indexicality plays some role in them. I will argue that in Peirce's view self-referential statements include an irreducible and non-descriptive indexical component.

I proceed as follows. After providing a sketch of Peirce's theory of the first-person pronoun "I" understood as a "rhematic indexical legisign," I defend the claim that Peirce maintains that "I" has a real, non-fictional referent and that this referent coincides with a specific type of perception related to our consciousness of the present and our sense of effort in agency (the present&effort-perception).

2.

Although self-referential statements resort to different terms (i.e. the personal pronoun "I," the possessive adjective "my," or the possessive pronoun "mine"), I focus throughout this chapter on the use of the first-person pronoun "I" and I take it as an example of what goes on also in the other cases. My claim is that an analysis of Peirce's account of the meaning and the use of "I" is the best way to approach the study of self-reference in a Peircean mood. This approach coincides with Peirce's externalist methodology in the study of mental phenomena.[15] The linguistic production of self-

---

15   Delaney, "Peirce's Account of Mental Activity", pp. 25-36 and *Science, Knowledge, and Mind*; Short, "Hypostatic Abstraction in Self-Consciousness"; Stephens, "Peirce on Psychological Self-Knowledge", 212-224. For contemporary externalist approaches in philosophy of mind see e.g. Gareth Evans, *The Varieties of Reference* (Oxford: Oxford University Press, 1982) pp. 225-235; Jordi Fernandez, "Priviledged Access Naturalized", *The Philosophical Quarterly* 53 (2003), 352-372; Fred Dretske, "Introspection", *Proceeding of the Aristotelian Society* 94 (1993), 263-278. However, a clarification is needed here. Although I follow Delaney in characterizing Peirce's method in philosophy of mind as "externalist," it is necessary to remember that Peirce does not assume

referential statements is such a public and external phenomenon. However, it is important to make clear that, according to Peirce, the phenomenon of self-consciousness is *not* reducible to linguistic performances, even though the linguistic practice of self-reference represents a big part of it; on the contrary, Peirce develops a broad semeiotic approach to the mental life, for which the signs implied in the phenomenon of self-consciousness also include non-linguistic signs, such as qualities of feelings and perceptions. As it should be clear at the end of this chapter, the phenomenon of self-consciousness also entails experiential non-linguistic components. However, the importance of the focus on self-referential statements (exemplified in this chapter) results from Peirce's cautiousness to adopt a naïve introspective method of inquiry in philosophy of mind and his consequent preference for an externalist approach.

According to Peirce's taxonomy, "I" falls under the class of "rhematic indexical legisigns."[16] As some scholars have shown (see

---

as epistemically prior or intuitive the distinction between the "internal" dimension of selfhood and the "external" world. As Peirce shows as early as 1865 in the first of the Harverd Lectures (W1: 167-168), the classification as "internal" or "external" of what is given is the hypothetical product of inquiry, so that the distinction between the "internal" and the "external" world is more blurred that we usually believe. I believe that Wilson and Almeder are simply wrong in attributing to Peirce the naïve assumption of the "external" world of physical objects as immediately given in experience, while I agree with Riley in attributing to Peirce an inferential understanding of "internal" and "external" as class-concepts. Aaron B. Wilson, "The Perception of Generals", *Transactions of the Charles S. Peirce Society* 48(2) (2012), 169-190; Robert F. Almeder, "Charles Peirce and the Existence of the External World", *Transactions of the Charles S. Peirce Society* 4(2) (1969), 63-79; "Peirce's Theory of the Individuals", 135-165. The same "externalist" method is used in the logical manuscripts collected in W1, in which a classification of the arguments is pursued with no appeal to "introspection." Therefore, it is in the light of this philosophical caution that we can use the notion of methodological "externalism," which turns out to have here the simple meaning of a caveat in appealing to intuitive introspection as a method in philosophy of mind.

16 Obviously, "I" can also be used as a common noun, or "rhematic symbolic legisign." See e.g. R668: 16-17; R649: 36.

in particular Agler; also Boersema; Goudge; Pietarinen; Hilpinen; Maddalena; Lizska; Pape; Short; Thibaud; Weber), a rhematic indexical legisign (1) is a non-descriptive sign (e.g. EP2: 342, 1905), (2) incorporates but does not reduce to the background or collateral factors necessary to the fixation of the reference (e.g. EP2: 494, 1909), and (3) is directly referential.[17] Moreover, (4) personal pronouns are indexical artificial types or legisigns and are therefore governed by social and linguistic conventions (e.g. EP2: 274; 297, 1903). In addition, (5) the singular object to which a rhematic indexical legisign refers does not need to be a real object but can also be a mere logical object, i.e. it can have a merely "logical" existence (e.g. R280: 36-37) or membership to a Logical Universe whatsoever. From the first four points it follows that "I" does not need to be a descriptive term in order to enable self-referential statements. Nevertheless, we could still wonder, is the referent of "I" real merely in a "Universe of Discourse"? Indeed, point (5) entails that the referent of a rhematic indexical legisign can be a logically real object and nothing more. In addition to this, Peirce admits as real also the world of fictional objects, such as the heroes of literature, whose existence and features depend upon the deliberate creative activity of their authors (see e.g. EP2: 209; 5.152, 1903; see Forster

---

17   David W. Agler, "Peirce's Direct, Non-Reductive Contextual Theory of Names", *Transactions of the Charles S. Peirce Society* 46(4) (2010), 611-640; David Boersema, "Peirce on Proper Names and Reference", *Transactions of the Charles S. Peirce Society* 38(3) (2002), 351-362; Thomas A. Goudge, "Peirce's Index", *Transactions of the Charles S. Peirce Society* 1(2) (1965), 52-70; Ahti-Veikko Pietarinen, "Peirce's Pragmatic Theory of Proper Names", *Transactions of the Charles S. Peirce Society* 46(3) (2010), 341-363; Hilpinen, "Peirce on Language and Reference"; Maddalena, "Esperienza e soggettività"; James J. Liszka, *A General Introduction to the Semeiotic of Charles Sanders Peirce* (Bloomington and Indianapolis: Indiana University Press, 1996); Pape, "A Peircean Theory of Indexical Signs and Individuation"; Thomas L. Short, *Peirce's Theory of Signs* (New York and Cambridge: Cambridge University Press, 2007); Thibaud, "Peirce on Proper Names and Individuation"; Eric T. Weber, "Proper Names and Persons: Peirce's Semiotic Consideration of Proper Names", *Transactions of the Charles S. Peirce Society* 44(2) (2008), 346-362.

[2011: 100-101]) and are logically localized in the Universe of artistic creation (and not in the Universe of non-fictional objects). In what follows, I argue that Peirce attributes to the referent of "I" (what is eventually identified as the "private self") a stronger, not merely logical or fictional reality. In particular, I want to show that Peirce acknowledges a *specific* type of perception that constitutes the fundamental collateral experience, and therefore the fundamental condition, for the indexical functioning of "I" as a truly referring term. This specific type of perception is what I call the present&effort-perception.[18] It follows that it is this specific, complex perception that constitutes, in Peirce's terms, the experiential ground on which self-reference can develop as pointing at a non-fictional reality. In this sense, the phaneroscopic givenness and unavoidableness of the present&effort-percept is crucial for the development of the private self and its characterization as a real, non-fictional object.

Let me introduce my overall understanding of the present&effort-perception. It seems to me that according to Peirce the perceptual condition of self-reference has at least two forms. The first is what Peirce in his 1905 "Issues of Pragmaticism" calls the "conative externality of the Present." In this light, a fundamental aspect of Peirce's doctrine of the "I" is his phenomenology of time as an essential phenomenon for the constitution of personal experience. I will simply call this perception, following Peirce, the 'insistence of the present.' Although the structures of human "inwardness" have not been overlooked by Peirce scholarship,[19] they have not been connected explicitly to the flow of time. However, in Peirce's view the insistence of the present is not the only perceptual basis for self-reference. The second experience is the perception of an initiative and causal efficacy in agency. Peirce identifies it with

---

18 Admittedly a clumsy phrase, 'present&effort-perception' has the advantage of clarity. Moreover, it avoids the introduction of a neologism to explain Peirce's already idiosyncratic terminology.

19 See in particular Vincent M. Colapietro's "Inwardness and Autonomy: A Neglected Aspect of Peirce's Approach to Mind", *Transactions of the Charles S. Peirce Society* 21(4) (1985), 485-512 and DiLeo's "Peirce's Haecceitism" on this point.

that part of the free will that is the "sense of effort."[20] I will call this second perception simply 'sense of effort in agency.' Such position is understandable if we recall that Peirce puts forward a broad notion of "perception," which is not limited to sense-organ perceptions and proprioceptive experience, and which relies on a broad phaneroscopic approach rather than assuming the viewpoint of the special sciences.[21] Self-reference hits an existent target (what is hence called the 'individual self') in virtue of a composite act of perception based on the insistence of the present and the sense of effort in agency. The 'individual self' has its birth *contextually* to the growth of the logical possibility of self-referential statements and finds its original, non-fictional ground in the present&effort-perception. Against any type of Cartesian intuitionist, immediatist, and innatist approach to the self, Peirce renews Fichte's insight that the 'self' poses itself by thinking, on the basis a more original unity (in this case, the phenomenon of the insistence of the present and the sense of effort), the distinction between an 'Ego' and a 'Non-Ego.'[22]

---

20   The "sense of effort" (2ndness) is only one dimension of the free will because the free will also entails self-control and therefore genuine knowledge (3rdness).

21   Peirce reserves the same treatment to the notion of "experience," as Cheryl Misak has amply shown. See e.g. Cherly Misak, "A Peircean Account of Moral Judgment", *Peirce and the Value Theory: On Peircean Esthetics and Ethics*, ed. by Herman Parret (Philadelphia: John Benjamins Publishing Company, 1994), pp. 43-45; Misak, *Verificationism: Its History and Prospects* (London and New York: Routledge, 1995), pp. 99-108; and "C.S. Peirce on Vital Matters", *The Cambridge Companion to Peirce*, ed. by Cheryl J. Misak (New York and Cambridge: Cambridge University Press, 2004), pp. 152-158.

22   Although Corrington, following Colapietro's idea of the "mind-as semeiosis" ("Inwardness and Autonomy", p. 493), gets Peirce exactly right when he interprets the "self" in semeiotic terms as a "sign-using organism" of a special type (*An Introduction to C.S. Peirce*, p. 76), he fails to explain how such self comes into being contextually or together with that form of inferential indexical self-reference that I am presenting here. The fact that all the interpreters of the "Cognitive Series" agree that "self-consciousness" is not intuitive but inferential does not imply, unfortunately, that they have made clear that for Peirce the self to which we inferentially get is not 'already there' before the growth of indexical self-reference. On

Let me put my thesis in the following way by using the terminology of Peirce's theory of perception (see below): there is a composite "percept," the present&effort-percept, which is at the origin of our perception of ourselves and which constitutes the existent referent of our indexical self-referential statements. All the narratives and descriptions of ourselves, in which we find the self-mediation of the person in the light of a growing reasonable ideal,[23] are ultimately rooted in this indexical self-reference. In what follows, I simply articulate this idea in greater detail.

One of the clearest examples of Peirce's account of time is found in 1905 "Issues of Pragmaticism." After providing a metaphysical account of the past and the future in modal terms, Peirce details a phaneroscopic and metaphysical theory of the present, according to which the consciousness of the present is the "conative externality" (something that presses and pushes) of the "Nascent State of the Actual" (EP2: 359, 5.462). This experience is the "living present" or the "Living Death" (EP2: 358) of what is actual. It coincides with the continuously perceived point in experience in which from the inevitable transformation of the present moment into a past event a new present emerges, in which "we are born anew" (EP2: 358, 5.459). In this context, Peirce observes:

> What is the bearing of the Present instant upon conduct? Introspection is wholly a matter of inference. One is immediately conscious of his Feelings, no doubt; but not that they are feelings of an ego. The self is only inferred. (EP2: 359, 5.462)

---

the contrary, the "self" is constituted together with the development of indexical self-reference and the intelligence of its perceptual conditions. This is why in this chapter I prefer to talk of "self-reference" rather than simply of the "self." Therefore, Corrington, among the others, does not follow through his own insight that "the self is temporal in its self-constitution" (*An Introduction to C.S. Peirce*, p. 96).

23   Colapietro ("Inwardness and Autonomy"), Corrington (*An Introduction to C.S. Peirce*) and Robinson (*God and the World of Signs*) all stress the evolutionary dynamic through which the self comes to embody more and more reasonable ideals. Unfortunately, they do not anchor this dynamic in a clear semeiotic account of self-reference.

As we know, while the belief in the individual self, or the ego, is inferred (and therefore takes time and a whole set of conditions), the immediate "feeling" of the instantaneous coming to being of a new actuality (= present) is not. I believe that Peirce's seemingly random association of "introspection" and "Present" in this passage suggests that we have to look at the consciousness of the present in order to have a better grasp of Peirce's understanding of self-reference.

Let me now turn to the second crucial instance of perception, the sense of effort in agency. Whereas the insistence of the present has a more passive connotation, the sense of effort in agency is more of the type of an active experience.[24] When I speak of the sense of effort in agency I mean that specific percept that arises from the human individual's initiative, in which the immediate experience of one's causal efficacy on something can be considered more crucial than the other experiential factors involved. It is the essentially dyadic experience that Peirce describes as "the sense of an opposing resistance then and there," which is "entirely different from purpose, which is the idea of a possible general" (R283: 76; see also R614: 3; EP2: 383, 1906).[25] This experience occurs at least in a twofold way. The first instance of the sense of effort in agency resides in the dialogic nature of semeiosis. In Peirce's words, "the person is not absolutely an individual," since "his thoughts are what he is saying to himself" or "what [he] is saying to that other self that is just

---

24 Peirce foreshadows this point when he describes the "first" in human agency: "The first is agent, the second is patient, the third is the action by which the former influences the latter. Between the beginning as first, and the end as last, comes the process which leads from first to last" (W6: 173, EP1: 250, 1887-1888).

25 Sometimes Peirce seems to deny that the sense of effort in agency and the consciousness of the present are compatible. If this were true, my entire reading would be jeopardized. For instance, in 1885 he writes that "volition," which is the "consciousness of duality or dual consciousness," "does not involve the sense of time (i.e. not of a continuum) but it does involve the sense of action and reaction" (W5: 225). However, a deeper understanding of this statement shows that what Peirce is claiming is that "volition" is a 2ndness and not a 3rdness. Similarly, the consciousness of the present does not entail a 3rdness insofar as it is the tense manifestation of the mode of actuality, which is 2ndness.

coming into life in the flow of time" (EP2: 338, 1905). In this case, thought has the nature of a "conversation" (EP2: 402, 1907) between an old, critical self and a new, emergent self, where the former tries to determine and persuade the latter to give its assent to something. This thesis, which *prima facie* seems to contradict the thesis that there is something like an *individual* self, simply points out the *dialogical* nature of the self, whose *entire* reality has an inferential and semeiotic structure. What is important to acknowledge here is that it is this dialogical structure that makes the sense of effort in agency possible, at least in one of its most basic forms. In this case, part of the self performs paradoxically (but interestingly) the function of that opposing "non-Ego" (EP2: 154, 1903; EP2: 195, 1903; EP2: 268, 1903) against which the sense of effort is born. The second instance of the sense of effort in agency is more closely related to the bodily nature of the self. As an organism, the self can initiate a new movement and produce changes through a muscular effort in itself (the "central body") and in the surrounding environment (EP2: 412-413, 1907).[26] Also in this second case, the experience is an internal reaction against an X, which is identified in its function of being a "non-Ego." I quote at length a passage in which Peirce spells out what the sense of effort in agency is:

> It may be said that there is no such phenomenon in the universe as brute force, or freedom of will, and nothing accidental. I do not assent to either opinion; but granting that both are correct, it still remains true that considering a single action by itself, apart from all others and, therefore, apart from the governing uniformity, it is in itself brute, whether it show brute *force* or not. I shall presently point out a sense in which it does display force. That it is possible for a phenomenon in some sense to

---

26   Certainly, the acquaintance with that particular body that we end up considering "our" body plays an incredibly important function in the development of self-referential capacity. In other words, it constitutes part of the experiential collateral condition for the development of the use of "I" (see how crucial is the "central body" in Peirce's treatment of self-consciousness, W2: 202, EP1: 19-20, 1868). However, the fact that the acquaintance with one's central body is crucial for the human mind does not imply that the referent of self-ascriptions is first and foremost, or essentially, the body.

present force to our notice without emphasizing any element of law, is familiar to everybody. We often regard our own exertions of will in that way. ... It is not pretended that what is here termed is the whole phenomenon, but only an element of the phenomenon – so much as belongs to a particular place and time. That when more is taken into account, the observer finds himself in the real of law in every case, I fully admit. (1.428)

For Peirce, these two phenomena exemplify the most fundamental moments in which the human "force" or brute will is immediately perceived in initiating a new action (see 5.520).[27]

But, we might ask, why should Peirce need to appeal to the present&effort-perception in order to ground the possibility of self-reference? In particular, hasn't Peirce made clear in his 1868 "Questions Concerning Certain Faculties Claimed for Man" that at least the experience of ignorance and error is sufficient to give the start to the development of self-reference?[28] In order to answer these questions, I will focus now on Peirce's 1868 treatment of the development and nature of self-consciousness. If my reading is correct, the conclusion is that the phenomena considered in 1868 are not *conclusive* in order to grant that the referent of self-referential statements is a real, non-fictional object. If we are seeking for a

---

27 The obvious objection to my reading is that Peirce's remarks about human "force" and "brute will" are usually extremely harsh. For instance, in 5.520 Peirce refers to the force of an agent as "sham" if compared to the "power" of agency, which is ultimately identifiable with "reasonableness," "knowledge," and "love." In 1.673 Peirce mentions the need to "annihilate" our "blind will" (see also 8.81). Although from a general viewpoint it is probably true that Peirce believes that the reasonable growth (3rdness) of the individual human beings in mutual communion is the *most important point* to make about the human condition, it is also true that overlooking the aspect of indexical self-reference (2ndness) in Peirce's account of the self results in a partial and less convincing interpretation of his theory as a whole. Although not central, Peirce's theory of indexical self-reference is integral to the architecture of his conception of the self.

28 In the manuscript "Questions on Reality" (W2: 162, 1868) Peirce claims that "error" and "ignorance" are what distinguish our empirical ego from the "absolute ego." See also W2:169; 192.

Peircean conclusive argument for the reality of the individual self, we have to look elsewhere.

Let me consider the two phenomena at stake in "Questions Concerning Certain Faculties." The first phenomenon is the experience of ignorance and error. This case is crucial for the appearance of "self-consciousness," namely, for the semeiotic process that leads to the development of the power of self-reference. Peirce's idea is that from a number of instances of error 1, 2, 3, ..., n, the child abductively infers the existence of a private self, at first abstractly grasped as "X responsible for ignorance and error." In this case, the external facts from which the belief in the private self is inferred by a child are, on the one hand, the agreement between people's linguistic testimony about a certain state of affairs and the perception of that state of affairs, and, on the other hand, the previous ignorance or different belief about the same state of affairs. "Abduction" is here an instance of creative formulation of a hypothesis of explanation, which is then deductively explicated and inductively confirmed through further experiences (e.g. W2: 218-219, EP1: 34-35, 1868). To my knowledge, Peirce does not mention explicitly what are the further experiences that corroborate the belief in the private self. However, it follows from what he says that these experiences are *at least* further experiences of ignorance and error. The repeated contrast between the public "evidence of fact," conveyed in linguistic testimony about a certain state of affairs, and (one's) contrasting beliefs about the same state of affair, keeps pointing at the reality of something like a "private" self and strengthens the probability of this conclusion. However, why cannot it be simply an abstract object, a product of the human mind's tendency to seek for an explanation at all costs? As a matter of fact, the mere *logical* existence of the private self in a highly probable explanatory hypothesis would still ground the possibility of the indexical use of the "I" in self-referential statements.

The second phenomenon considered by Peirce is that the manifold of mental activity can be reduced to some sort of unity. In this case, perception refers first to different external facts and second to the subjective, mental powers that the human being can infer from those external facts. At a higher inferential level, the human being can also infer a further unitary mental power from the multifold "objects" of consciousness manifested in experience and their corresponding subjective modalities. In this case, abduction functions as a process of reduction of a manifold to a higher-order conceptual unity (e.g. W2: 217, EP1: 33). As in the first case, also in this case the validity of the conceptual reduction requires inductive evidence, which is partially provided by the fact that this abductive operation of unification is always possible to the human being (at least, in normal conditions of mental development). In this sense, by questioning the arguments in favor of an "intuitive self-consciousness," Peirce makes clear that it is because the individual self can be inferred from "every other fact" that the belief in its existence is close to certainty, and not because we have an intuitive power of self-knowledge (W2: 203-204, EP1: 20-21, 1868).[29] This constant inferential possibility counts as an

---

29   Peirce provides here an extremely interesting argument against the Cartesian idea of an immediate and privileged access that the human being would have to the knowledge of his mind. That we can refer to our selves moving from *"every other fact"* (EP2: 21) does not imply that we have, in principle, a privileged access to the mind (a special type of immediate knowledge of it, as the Cartesian tradition would say), but only the *empirical truth* that every fact can virtually become the premise for inferring self-referential statements. This point is very important given the Cartesian legacy that seems to characterize the philosophy of mind in the analytic tradition. For instance, from a general viewpoint, there is a basic conviction that "self-knowledge is importantly different from the knowledge of the world external to one's self", which is to say that we have a privileged access to the knowledge of the mind, so that the knowledge of the 'extra-mental world' and the knowledge of the 'mind' are different in principle. See Brie Gertler, "Self-Knowledge", *Stanford Encyclopedia of Philosophy* (2008).
     In the case of self-knowledge, the knower has a uniquely privileged epistemic access to the object, as it is exemplified by the "acquaintance" we have with ourselves in everything that is in a relation of presentation with us, e.g. Bertrand Russell, "Knowledge by Acquaintance and Knowledge by Description", *Proceedings of the Aristotelian Society*, 11 (1910-1911), 108-128. As in the case of Descartes's reduction of the mind to conscious 'ideas,' some claim that the self *is* its conscious states and that some type of self-reference is always implied in each kind of content of consciousness, e.g. Roderick Chisholm, "On the Observability of the Self", *Philosophy and Phenomenological Research* 30 (1969), 7-21; Richard Moran, *Authority and Estrangement: An Essay on Self-Knowledge*

inductive validation of the hypothesis in the existence of a private self. Furthermore, it is possible to say that the two types of evidence that support the two cases of abduction work conjointly, so that the first abductive conclusion to the existence of a private self is supported by and supports in turn the second one. However, it still remains true that insofar as only these two phenomena are considered, we can take the referent of indexical self-ascriptions to be a merely logically real object represented in a highly probable hypothesis.

The two cases just highlighted constitute a collateral experience sufficiently strong to fix the self as a *logically* real object and to make of it the referent of the first-person pronoun "I." However, insofar as the two phenomena are the only background for the belief in the private self, it is still possible that the private self is *only* a logically real object, whose existence is limited to a specific Universe of Discourse (i.e., the explanatory context in which we seek for an explanation of

(Princeton: Princeton University Press, 2001); Richard A. Fumerton, *Metaepistemology and Skepticism* (Lanham: Rowman and Littlefield, 1996); François Recanati, "Immunity to Error Through Misidentification: What It Is and Where It Comes From", *Immunity to Error through Misidentification*, ed. by Simon Prosser and François Recanati (Cambridge: Cambridge University Press, 2012), pp. 180-201. Our privileged access to our minds has also the epistemic consequence that in our grasp of our minds we reach a level of "certainty" which is precluded to us in any other domain of knowledge. One recent version of this special epistemology of mind is represented by the claim that at least some self-referential statements (i.e., present tense self-ascriptions of psychological states) are immune to the error of reference through misidentification (Sidney S. Shoemaker, "Self-Reference and Self-Awareness", *The Journal of Philosophy* 65(19) (1968), 555-567; Evans, *The Varieties of Reference*; Prosser and Recanati, *Immunity to Error through Misidentification*). It seems to me that the "Cartesian" approach is so rooted in the majority of the contemporary debates on self-knowledge that also those authors who refuse an intuitionistic account of self-knowledge tend to think that only a direct introspection can grasp something like a stable "ego." Singularly, Elizabeth Anscombe has come to the conclusion that the term "I" is not a referring term because in order to be so it would need an unmistakable referent and therefore would presuppose a "Cartesian Ego" immediately known in its essence as a *res cogitans*. G.E.M. Anscombe, "The First Person", *Mind and Language*, ed. by Samuel Guttenplan (Oxford: Clarendon Press, 1975), 45-65.

the experiences of ignorance and error and the ubiquity of reflection in the mature mental life of human beings). In other words, these two phenomena justify the conclusion that the referent of the term "I" is an existent object in the real, non-fictional world only in a weak sense. In an important essay, Thomas L. Short shows that the individuation of the self in the mental development of the child occurs as a hypostatic abstraction. Short addresses the question whether the object represented in the hypostatic abstraction, i.e. the "self," is real or not. For Short, the Peircean "self" is "no more than a harmony of parts".[30] He adds that "one cannot dismiss such as self as unreal, since every entity of any degree of complexity whatsoever is itself real only insofar as its parts are organized by and subordinated to some law".[31] In addition, Short explains that for Peirce "the self is not a single, simple, stable entity, but is constantly in the process of being formed".[32] Short has the merit to avoid a nihilistic interpretation of Peirce's theory of the self and to show its experiential and developmental nature. Nevertheless, it seems to me that Short's interpretation does not grasp a core feature of Peirce's account of self-reference. In fact, although Short refers to "self-consciousness" as a necessary condition for self-controlled behavior and growth, he seems to deny that self-consciousness displays an irreducible element of singularity. On the contrary, in the very act of ascribing to oneself the more or less integrated harmony of one's character, the human being is referring to a point of singularity. For Peirce, the indexical component in self-referential statements is precisely what accounts for this phenomenon. I believe that the present&effort-perception provides the perceptual ground on the basis of which self-reference refers to an existent object in the real, non-fictional world. If my interpretation is correct, the two cases treated in 1868 are not the *only* ways in which genuine self-referential statements develop. In order to understand how "I" refers to a real, non-fictional object, the two 1868 theses must be read together with a third set of phenomena, i.e. the consciousness of the present and the sense of effort in agency. If it is the conjunction of these three phenomena that constitutes the complete collateral experience on

---

30   Short, "Hypostatic Abstraction in Self-Consciousness", p. 307.
31   Short, "Hypostatic Abstraction in Self-Consciousness", p. 307.
32   Short, "Hypostatic Abstraction in Self-Consciousness", p. 305.

which the existent referent of indexical self-ascriptions is fixed, it is only the present&effort-perception that plays the crucial role of a genuine indexical experience. The belief in one's private self is introduced not only as the explanatory hypothesis of the experience of ignorance, or as the unitary condition of possibility of the ubiquity of reflection, but also as the natural interpretation of a recurrent perceptual experience.

3.

Before tackling the analysis of the present&effort-perception, we have now to consider some elements of Peirce's theory of perception and phaneroscopy.[33] Let me start with perception. According to Peirce, perception is in a sense the epistemically fundamental operation. In fact, all concepts are acquired through it. Peirce acknowledges in perception three different factors, which are irreducible to each other even though they can only perform their function in connection, i.e., the "percept," the "percipuum" (sometimes also called "perceptual fact," see 2.146) and the "perceptual judgment." The percipuum is in turn a particular instance of perceptual judgment, being the immediate interpretative judgment of the percept (7.643, 1903). According to Peirce's analysis, the percept is the moment of immediate determination of the human consciousness,

33 The best overview of Peirce's theory of perception is still Richard J. Bernstein, "Peirce's Theory of Perception", *Studies in the Philosophy of Charles Sanders Peirce*, Second Series, ed. by Edward C. Moore and Richard S. Robin (Amherst: The University of Massachusetts Press, 1964), 165-189. Also, Robert F. Almeder, "Peirce's Theory of Perception", *Transactions of the Charles S. Peirce Society* 6(2) (1970), 99-110, Delaney, *Science, Knowledge, and Mind*, pp. 118-129, and Sandra Rosenthal, "Peirce's Pragmatic Account of Perception: Issues and Implications", *The Cambridge Companion to Peirce*, ed. by Cheryl J. Misak (New York and Cambridge: Cambridge University Press, 2004), 193-213 are enlightening analyses. Rosenthal's "Peirce's Theory of Perceptual Judgment" focuses on some distinctions within perception, viz. "antecept," "ponecept," "antecipuum" and "ponecipuum," which are not discussed in this chapter since they do not add essential elements to my analysis of the present&effort-perception. See Sandra Rosenthal, "Peirce's Theory of the Perceptual Judgment: An Ambiguity", *Journal of the History of Philosophy* 7(3) (1969), 303-314.

in which something is already affecting the capacity of feeling but is not yet a content of cognition (e.g. EP2: 4). Hence, "a percept contains only two kinds of elements, those of firstness and those of secondness" (7.630). The percept is a "quality of feeling," or a "quale-consciousness" (1stness) actualized as a modification of the human consciousness and hence acting as a compulsion (2ndness). Thus, "the percept is a single event happening *hic et nunc*. It cannot be generalized without losing its essential character. For it is an actual passage at arms between the non-ego and the ego" (2.146). On the other hand, the perceptual judgment (including in this sketch also the percipuum) represents the emergence of the element of generality implied in cognition (3rdness) right from its beginning. All the elements implied in perception follow a non-controlled dynamic:[34] although perception can be educated over time and is susceptible of criticism within certain limits, it is not controlled *while it occurs*. Furthermore, the perceptual judgment has the formal structure of an abductive inference in which a general predicate synthesizes a manifold matter and has therefore a variable hypothetical logical force.[35] The fundamental point to stress here is that although the perceptual judgment is an abductive inference, its logical force is particularly strong or "nearly approximating to necessary inference" (4.541, 1906) as far as the attribution of "existence" is concerned. Indeed, "existence" is for Peirce the first conception that performs the unifying function operating in perception. In a striking 1906 passage, Peirce links together the perceptual judgment and the abduction to the existence of an object. He writes:

> how then is the Perceptual Judgment to be explained? In reply, I note that a percept cannot be dismissed at will, even from memory.

---

34 See e.g. "If one *sees* one cannot avoid the percept; and if one *looks* one cannot avoid the perceptual judgment" (7.627).

35 While in this chapter I am stressing the indexical component of self-reference, we might still wonder what type of knowledge of ourselves is provided by the mere present&effort-perception, independently from further narratives and descriptions. The answer is explicitly (although succinctly) given by Peirce when he talks of "pure self-consciousness" as an instance of the "most degenerate Thirdness" (EP2: 161, 1902): we know ourselves as a promise of growth and intelligibility, or, as Peirce puts it, "a mere feeling that has the dark instinct of being a germ of thought."

... Moreover, the evidence is overwhelming that the perceiver is aware if this compulsion upon him; ... Now existence means precisely the exercise of compulsion. Consequently, whatever feature of the percept is brought into relief by some association and this attains a logical position like that of the observational premiss of an explaining Abduction, the attribution of Existence to it in the Perceptual Judgment is virtually and in an extended sense, a logical Abductive Inference nearly approximating to necessary inference. (4.541, 1906)[36]

Let me note two things about this passage. First, the "percept" does not have a cognitive status. We can have access to the percept as an isolated element and talk about it only through an act of prescision. Technically speaking, the percept coincides with an instance of brute experience and not with knowledge (see 6.336, 1906).[37] Second, the concept of existence is attributed to the "percept" through an abductive inference that has an almost necessary logical force. This constitutes the first moment of the percipuum, in which, although a perceptual judgment has not been fully developed yet, the percept has already entered the realm of cognition through an almost necessary abductive inference that states that *there is* something. Now, in considering the experiential conditions of self-referential operations, is there anything that resembles a perception of a self?

I believe that the present&effort-perception plays this function in human life. In the two cases discussed in the 1868 article, the percepts involved are always withdrawn from the external, public world and do not refer directly to something like the self. In the first case, the percept is most likely the experience of the clash between an expectancy and someone's linguistic testimony. However, in this case it is still unclear why such experience should generate a new type of awareness, that is, self-awareness ('I am wrong'), instead of a mere increase of information ('Someone or something is wrong'). In the second case, the percept is each one of the qualities of feeling actually present in our experience of "facts." Nevertheless, this case only proves that reflection is inferential,

---

36   This analysis could be furthered through a study of the category "IT (also called "present in general" and "substance") in Peirce's "On a New List of Categories" (W2: 49-59).

37   See Delaney, *Science, Knowledge, and Mind*, p. 50.

while it is still possible that the higher-level process of abduction that gathers our mental faculties into unity is responsible for the creation of a "self" in the same way in which a novelist creates the main character of a novel (that is, the self would simply be "logically" real). As a consequence, the self to which the personal pronoun "I" seems to refer on the basis of those two cases could be the product of a wrong or merely artistic hypothesis, although even at this level the belief in the private self is supported by some evidence. On the contrary, if something such as the present&effort-perception is really occurring in experience, the percepts of that perception constitute a specific class of signs on the basis of which indexical self-reference can be grounded more strongly. As a consequence, not only the "private" self in its indexical dimension is something real, but it is also non-fictionally real, as distinct from what is the product of an artistic or literary act of creation: roughly put, while a fictional object becomes real as it is constructed by the regularities that the constructing mind puts into it deliberately, the present&effort-perception is unavoidably (= non-fictionally) occurring in experience as having certain phaneroscopic characters. When the present&effort-perception is put in connection with other experiences (first and foremost, the experience of error and ignorance and the ubiquitous possibility of reflection, the two cases discussed in 1868), it is finally fixed as the real, non-fictional object, the 'individual self,' to which self-referential statements refer.

It follows from this picture that two main aspects characterize the present&effort-perception, namely, "compulsion" and "inwardness." The first character, compulsion, is an immediate experience of effort, resistance and reaction against an X (which Peirce calls generically "non-Ego"). Peirce's analysis shows that the *concept* of "individuality" is derived contextually with the concept of "relation" and that they are derived in turn from the dyadic, immediate *experience* of relation in its "dumb" force, or pure 2ndness. It is important to stress that at this level of analysis we cannot say that the existence of two individual reagents is prior and that the dyadic experience of connection is secondary. On the contrary, Peirce's phaneroscopic insight shows that the dyadic and "dumb" experience of compulsion, effort, and reaction is at the origin of the concept of individual reagents and is therefore phaneroscopically prior. We could say that the *concepts* of individuality and relation are contextually derived from a previous dumb *experience* of compulsion, effort, or reaction, occurring as an undifferentiated whole. This point is even more instructive if we reflect on the fact that the object of the indexical self-reference must have some kind of individuality. Furthermore, Peirce often connects the notion of individuality to the notion of existence (e.g. EP2: 270-271, 1903; 1.432; 1.456; 1.457; 3.613). As a consequence, I am inclined to say that it is mainly from the compulsiveness of the present&effort-perception that human beings grow the notion of their existential individuality.

The second characteristic of the present&effort-perception is inwardness. According to Peirce, although a perception brings with itself an almost immediate attribution of existence to the object perceived, the classification of the origin of the percept as "external" or "internal" is the less immediate inferential result of a series of experiential tests (6.333-335). Peirce observes that "we are conscious of hitting and of getting hit, of meeting with a *fact*. But whether the activity is within or without we know only by secondary signs and not by original faculty of recognizing fact" (W5: 246, 1.366, 1885). In fact, the experience of compulsion and reaction could simply refer to the mere external contrast between a part of the environment and my body. On the contrary, the present&effort-percept results from the experience of a radical initiative in conduct, not from the reactive contact of the external physical environment with my body. For example, by describing an imaginary "dreamer" moving from sleep to wake, Peirce writes about the pure "sense of Reaction" occurring in experience as 2ndness:

> imagine our dreamer suddenly to hear a loud and prolonged steam whistle. At the instant it begins, he is startled. He instinctively tries to get away; his hands go to his ears. It is not so much that it is unpleasing, but it forces itself so upon him. The instinctive resistance is a necessary part of it: the man would not be sensible his will was not borne down, if he had no-assertion to be borne down. It is the same when we exert ourselves against outer resistance; except for that resistance we should not have anything upon which to exercise strength. This sense of acting and of being acted upon, which is our sense of the reality of things, – both of outward things and of ourselves, – may be called the sense of Reaction. … It essentially involves two things acting upon one another. (EP2: 4-5, c. 1894; see also the case of "surprise," EP2: 195, 5.57-58, 1903)

In this passage there is no explicit reference to an experience of inward compulsion of reaction. From a general point of view, although the "sense of acting and being acted upon" can include something like an *inner* compulsion, it does not entail it necessarily. The sense of compulsion taken in its pureness can invariably refer to the resistance performed by the items of the internal world (such as in the case of the present&effort-perception) and by those of the external, physical world (such as in the case of the reaction between my body and the bodies around me). Similarly, in a 1906 passage, Peirce develops the phaneroscopic analysis of the notion of "action" which echoes what he says about the "sense of Reaction." He observes that "Action," as a "surd dyadic relation," entails an agent and a patient and can occur in the form of either an "active effort" or a "passive surprise" (EP2: 382-385, 1906), but does not mention the problem of the external or internal origin of the compulsion. According to Peirce's theory of perception, then, the classification of the percepts as "external" or "internal" pertains to the percipuum and the perceptual judgment and is not present at the level of the mere quality-feeling.[38] One must subject his perceptual experience to "various tests in order to ascertain whether it be of internal or of external provenance" (6.333). Peirce proposes three tests. The first test is the test by "physical concomitance." If the object that I infer from my percept (e.g., a tree) is also represented by a recording device (e.g., a camera that reproduces the tree in a picture), then there is an extremely high probability that the origin of the percept is external and consequently a very low probability that the origin is internal. The second test is the test by "experience of other observers," including oneself at different times. In this case, if the object that I infer from my percept is also acknowledged by other observers or by myself at different times, then the reality of the percept is certified in its public nature, although the probabilities that its origin is internal or external are even. The third test is the test by "criticism of all the circumstances of apparition" of the percept, which also takes the form of "making a direct inward effort to suppress the apparition." Let me apply the three tests to the present&effort-perception. If we have to recur to a "direct inward effort" in order to test any percept

---

38   See DiLeo, "Peirce's Haecceitism", pp. 96-97

(third test), it follows that the effort to suppress the percept should also be directed to the present&effort-percept. According to Peirce, the consciousness of the present and the sense of effort in agency have an invincible insistency on us. Philosophically speaking, this fact is even more striking in the case of the sense of effort, because the direct effort performed to suppress the apparition of the percept coincides in this case with the percept itself that is the target of the suppressing effort. The reality and insistency of the present&effort-percept is also confirmed by its unavoidability in each and all moments of our lives (second test). At the same time, it is neither possible to other observers to have experiential access to the same present&effort-percept (second test), nor to record it through an external device (first test). In conclusion, the present&effort-percept should be classified in Peirce's terms as deriving from an internal origin.

4.

I would like to conclude by summing up the elements involved in the present&effort-perception and indexical self-reference from a logical, phaneroscopic, and metaphysical standpoint. This will stress once again the richness of Peirce's semeiotic approach to self-reference. From a logical viewpoint, the quality-feeling ("percept") of present&effort, as an actual determination of human consciousness, is a pure, genuine index, while the perceptual judgment that *emerges* from it brings with itself an element of generality that turns the pure index into a degenerate index (e.g. 8.266).[39] The unifying function of the perceptual judgment is an instance of the synthesizing role of "conception" introduced by Peirce as early as 1867 in his "On a New List of Categories." As in any other cognition, also in the case of perceptual judgment the cognitive unification is imposed on a percept (the "manifold" of the impression) only because

---

39   What Delaney says about the relation between "perception" and "science" can be said about the relation between indexical self-reference, on one side, and the growth of one's self and one's self-knowledge on the other side. Delaney, *Science, Knowledge, and Mind*, p. 129.

the percept teleologically calls for a certain type of unification.[40] The possibility of self-reference through the personal pronoun "I" emerges therefore from the conjunction of the present&effort perception and the ability to master patterns of use of a natural language. According to my interpretation, the present&effort-percept is a "rhematic indexical sinsign" that grows into a "dicentic indexical sinsign" and eventually grounds the possibility of self-reference by the use of the "rhematic indexical legisign" "I."[41] In other words, the present&effort-percept is the *"Informational* index" on the ground of which the *"Monstrative* index" "I" grows up and stands (see EP2: 172, 1903) as referring to a real, non-fictional singular object.[42] From a phaneroscopic viewpoint,

---

40   Peirce's understanding of semeiosis as teleological cannot be presented here. For a discussion of this point (which however seems sometimes to reduce the teleological nature of semeiosis to the fact that the individual interpreter has always a purpose in interpreting X), see at least Menno Hulswit, "A Guess at the Riddle of Semiotic Causation", *Transactions of the Charles S. Peirce Society* 34(3) (1998), 641-688 and Short, *Peirce's Theory of Signs.*

41   See Liszka, *A General Introduction*, pp. 49-50.

42   The importance of the present&effort-perception for Peirce's theory of self-referential statements can be highlighted by contrasting it to John Campbell's recent account of how the pronoun "I" refers. John Campbell, "On the Thesis that "I" Is not a Referring Term", *Immunity to Error through Misidentification*, ed. by Simon Prosser and François Recanati (Cambridge: Cambridge University Press, 2012), pp. 1-21. Campbell focuses on Anscombe's thesis that "I" is not a referring term. He accepts the non-referring thesis only within certain limits, as an inevitable stage in the developmental process of self-reference. "Usually, we use a term the way we do because it stands for something. In the case of "I," the use comes first and we look for a reference afterwards; the use may even drive us to find a new kind of object, such as a soul, to act as reference for the term, rather than having the use grounded in a prior conception of the reference of the term" ("On the Thesis that "I" Is not a Referring Term", p. 1). That is, at first the word "I" does not refer at all and its use is made possible a corresponding "token-reflexive rule," for which "Any token of "I" refers to whoever produced it" ("On the Thesis that "I" Is not a Referring Term", p. 7). Although not-referring, the term "I," used on the basis of the token-reflexive rule, works as a "regulatory idea for the idea of reference of the first person, in directing us to find the thing – the self – that is dealt with by all our narratives of memory, by all out self-ascriptions of physical and

the present&effort-percept is a brute experience of compulsion, effort and contrast, and is therefore an instance of pure 2ndness. In it, the mere possibility of consciousness (1rstness) has become actual. The perceptual judgment grows out of the percept as a synthesis of general traits (3rdness) and is characterized by a corresponding sense of specialization in one's mental habits (e.g. EP1: 327-329, 6.145, 1892). From the logical and phaneroscopic standpoint, we see that the attribution of the concept "existence" to the present&effort-percept corresponds to the first moment in the development of the perceptual judgment and plays the role of an almost necessary logical quantification on that pure

---

psychological properties and so on" ("On the Thesis that "I" Is not a Referring Term", p. 18). I think that this account of the use of "I" is highly questionable for at least two reasons. First, it has the hardly believable implication that a child would start to use the term "I" in a conscious way without referring at all. Second, it works on the unjustified assumption that the referent of a term can be only grasped in a descriptive fashion, as Campbell's appeal to the role of the "narratives" and descriptions of our lives seems to indicate. In his account, Campbell substitutes the possibility of an indexical self-reference with the view according to which in the early stages of our mental development we follow the linguistic pattern for the conscious use of "I" without referring to any experience. Why does Campbell commit himself to such a claim? The answer has to be found in his analysis of indexical reference and its perceptual conditions. According to the "model of perceptual demonstratives" endorsed by him, a genuine use of demonstrative terms (indices) always involves not only the application of linguistic patterns but also the "perceptual identification of the object" to which the demonstratives refer. The perceptual experience performs the function of "singling out" the object "as figure from ground" ("On the Thesis that "I" Is not a Referring Term", p. 11). What is missing in the use of "I" is a similar perceptual experience, so that only the linguistic pattern remains in the early instances of self-referential statements ("On the Thesis that "I" Is not a Referring Term", pp. 16-18). The reason why "introspection" as "sensory modality" does not work is that there is "no ground" against which the self can emerge as a "figure." In my view, this idea of perception is a reduction of the perceptual experience to some sort of sense-organ perception and represents a strong reduction in comparison to Peirce's perspective, which includes what I have called the present&effort-perception. As shown, Peirce's acknowledgment of the present&effort-perception offers the "ground" (in Campbell's terminology) on which our indexical self-referential statements can find their individual, existent referent right from the dawn of self-consciousness.

index or percept, so that its undifferentiated quality is already seen in the light of a promise of intelligibility. Finally, from a metaphysical viewpoint, the percept corresponds to an instantiation (actuality) of a mere possibility of instantiation (possibility or might-be), which grows into the general tendency and disposition (generality or would-be) of a perceptual judgment and eventually of a habit, which is in this case the habitual capacity of saying "I."[43]

---

43   There are three objections that could be addressed to my interpretation. (1) The first is: "Why," one might say, "does Peirce claim that self-consciousness develops in virtue of the experience of error if the "feelings" of the present&effort-perception accompany the human being most likely right from the start of his conscious life?". I accept the objection as a further question on which more work is needed. However, let me just point out that Peirce's perspective allows for an account of self-consciousness and private self that avoids both the extreme positions according to which, on the one side, self-consciousness is an original structure of the mental life which does not undergo any development; and, on the other side, self-consciousness and the private self are a fictional or social construction. The immediate "feeling," or the present&effort-percept, is a phenomenon already present in the mental life of babies, but at that stage it is not interpreted as the minimum referent of indexical self-referential statements until the organism has undergone a certain process of growth and social interation, the nature of which I have tried to described in this chapter. The second and third objections are objections of partiality. In fact, a full analysis of Peirce's doctrine of self-reference should also take into account (2) Peirce's rejection of the Kantian "*I* think" and (3) Peirce's belief that "corporate personalities" or higher-order consciousnesses are real. For reasons of space, I have to cut short with the discussion of points (2) and (3), on which however I believe that my reading casts some light. On point (2), see Masato Ishida, *A Philosophical Commentary on C. S. Peirce's "On a New List of Categories": Exhibiting Logical Structure and Abiding Relevance*, Doctoral Dissertation (Pennsylvania State University, State College PA, 2009); André De Tienne, "Peirce's Revolution: Semiotic VS. Transcendental Unity", *Semiotics Around the World: Synthesis and Diversity. Vol. 1*, ed. by Irmengard Rauch and Gerald F. Carr (Berlin: Mouton de Gruyter, 1996); Colapietro, "Toward a Pragmatic Conception of Practical Identity"; Karl O. Apel, *Charles S. Peirce: From Pragmatism to Pragmaticism* (Amherst: University of Massachusetts Press, 1981); Karl O. Apel, "Transcendental Semiotic and Hypothetical Metaphysics of Evolution: A Peircean or Quasi-Peircean Answer to a Recurrent Problem of Post-Kantian Philosophy", *Peirce and Contemporary Thought*, ed. by Kenneth L. Ketner (New York: Fordham

CHAPTER 3
A DEWEYAN ASSESSMENT OF THREE MAJOR TENDENCIES IN PHILOSOPHY OF CONSCIOUSNESS

In this chapter I suggest that John Dewey's approach to the problem of consciousness is both methodologically and metaphysically superior to those found in contemporary debates. Dewey advances a picture of consciousness that avoids the mistakes present in the three major tendencies in contemporary philosophy of consciousness, namely, David J. Chalmers's Naturalistic Dualism, the Phenomenal Concept Strategy, and Daniel C. Dennett's A Priori Physicalism. I argue that Dewey's philosophy of consciousness shows that Naturalistic Dualism is wrong, that the Phenomenal Concept Strategy could be better, and that A Priori Physicalism goes too far.

1. *Introduction*

In recent years, philosophy of mind has been concerned primarily with consciousness. Despite technical differences and minutiae, the problem of consciousness is widely identified today with that of subjective experience. Philosophers recur to different characterizations of subjective experience, including qualia, phenomenal or experiential properties, and what-it's-like-nesses, in the attempt to clarify what makes our conscious life what it is beyond the underlying machinery of neurophysiology. Most of the debate hinges upon whether subjective experience can be accommodated within a purely materialist worldview.

University Press, 1995), 366-397; Harrison, "Peirce on Persons"; Giovanni Maddalena, "Peirce's Incomplete Synthetic Turn", *The Review of Metaphysics* 65(3) (2012), 613-640. On point (3), see Lane, "Persons, Signs, Animals" and de Waal, "Science Beyond the Self".

What I want to suggest in this chapter is that John Dewey's approach to the problem of consciousness, what he calls "psycho-physical" consciousness or "feeling," is both methodologically and metaphysically superior to those found in contemporary debates. Why superior? Because, as I will try to show, Dewey proposes a convincing and empirically-minded picture of consciousness that avoids the mistakes present in the three main tendencies in contemporary philosophy of consciousness, namely, David J. Chalmers's Naturalistic Dualism (ND), the Phenomenal Concept Strategy (PCS), and Daniel C. Dennett's A Priori Physicalism (APP). In short, Dewey's still mostly unexplored philosophy of consciousness[1] offers a valuable methodological and metaphysical framework for thinking about the qualities of experience without incurring in what I take to be deep flaws in those three tendencies.

ND is puzzled by subjective experience to the point of deeming it necessary to stretch its naturalistic ontology to include *special, non-physical properties*. PCS, while sticking to a purely materialist ontology, introduces *concepts with special properties* to cope with the epistemic difficulties of a world in which the qualities of experience seem to add something substantial to what an even perfect purely

---

1   See however John Stuhr, "Dewey's Notion of Qualitative Experience", *Transactions of the Charles S. Peirce Society* 15 (1) (1979), 68-81; Barry D. Smith, "John Dewey's Theory of Consciousness", *Educational Theory* 35 (3) (1985), 267-272; Thomas C. Dalton, *Becoming John Dewey: Dilemmas of a Philosopher and Naturalist* (Bloomington and Indianapolis: Indiana University Press, 2002) for an exegetical account of Dewey's approach to mind and consciousness, and Teed Rockwell, *Neither Brain nor Ghost: A Nondualist Alternative to the Mind-Brain Identity Theory* (Cambridge: MIT Press, 2005) and Tibor Solymosi, "Neuropragmatism, Old and New", *Phenomenology and the Cognitive Sciences* 10 (3) (2011), 347-368 for a development of Dewey's pragmatism in relation to contemporary neurosciences, which Solymosi has termed "neuropragmatism." Neuropragmatism provides a pragmatist account of embodied cognition and consciousness that departs from the contemporary neuroscientific understanding of consciousness as something that goes on 'inside our brain,' similar to Alva Noë, *Out of Our Heads* (New York: Hill and Wang, 2009). However, none of these works deal with the hard problem of consciousness extensively while also failing to address the ND, PCS, and APP approaches to it.

physical knowledge is able to capture. Finally, APP sees *nothing exceptional in subjective experience*, thinking on the contrary that a sufficiently powerful physical knowledge is enough to bring about that subjective experience that the first two tendencies find baffling. I shall argue that Dewey's philosophy of consciousness shows that ND is wrong (§3), that PCS could be better (§4), and that APP goes too far (§5).

Before doing that, however, let's investigate Dewey's understanding of psychophysical consciousness.

2. *Dewey on Psychophysical Consciousness*

Following contemporary classifications, Dewey's position on consciousness could be characterized as a form of physicalism.[2] This is not to say that for him a living, sentient being has the same complexity of inorganic matter. Maybe, he would prefer to label his theory *psychophysicalism* rather than physicalism.[3] Nevertheless, the contemporary idea of physicalism still applies to Dewey. For consciousness is for him simply a com- plex organization of the physicochemical and does not require anything mental that is not

---

2   Cf. Daniel Stoljar, "Physicalism", *Stanford Encyclopedia of Philosophy* (2015). Dewey's rejection of a dualism of "mind" and "matter" in nature is sometimes framed in terms very close to neutral monism, for instance: "Nothing but unfamiliarity stands in the way of thinking of both mind and matter as different characters of natural events, in which matter expresses their sequential order, and mind the order of their meanings in their logical connections and dependencies" (LW1: 66). Nevertheless, for Dewey, consciousness (in the contemporary sense of phenomenal consciousness) would be a manifestation of matter and not of mind, for feeling does not involve in itself any "logical connections and dependencies." This is why it is expedient to characterize Dewey's account of consciousness as a version of physicalism. It is also why, given the scope of this chapter, the neutral monist metaphysical framework can remain in the background as a chapter in Deweyan philosophy of nature. Thanks to an anonymous reviewer for raising this question.

3   "If we identify . . . the physical as such with the inanimate we need another word to denote the activity of the organisms as such. Psycho-physical is an appropriate term" (LW1:195).

capable to result from the potentialities of matter.[4] Thus, Dewey's psychophysicalism is a kind of emergentism, one in which it is the proper organization of lower-level components to determine the emergence of a higher-level whole with its systemic properties (LW1:207- 208). It is for the presence of these properties that Dewey introduces the idea of the "psycho-physical": a physical system is "psychic" when it has the capacity to act *psychically*—namely, when it manifests a behavior based on need-demand-satisfaction (LW1:195-196).

Consciousness is thus a dimension of psychophysical existence. In order to distinguish psychophysical consciousness from logical awareness, Dewey identifies the former with *sentiency* or *feeling*. Feeling is the capacity that an organism has to respond to its environment not simply selectively, but more strongly "discriminatively" (LW1:197). As Peter Godfrey-Smith has recently rehashed, for Dewey psychophysical consciousness and homeostasis are tightly connected.[5] So, feeling is what makes possible that sort of biological scorekeeping through which the organism learns from its environment the varying conditions within which it has to perpetuate its patterns of organized activity.

To contemporary qualia theorists, however, the Deweyan ideas presented so far will sound hugely naïve and in a certain sense out of target. Isn't at least *prima facie* evident that there is a *gap* between the what-it's-likeness*less* reality of the physical, purely functional machinery that governs our behavior, and our subjective life, so full of qualities? It is these qualities that a philosophy of consciousness is called to explain, not exclusively nor primarily the underlying machinery. As Chalmers sees it, the "hard problem of consciousness" is *hard* precisely because it seems to remain intact also after all the "easier" neurophysiological problems have been explained. Until Dewey describes feeling simply as the condition for the biological scorekeeping of the organism, he has dwelt only with the machinery

---

4   Sometimes Dewey follows this use: "The *quality* occurs exactly ... as any natural event, say a thunder-shower. There is no passage from the physical to the mental" (LW14:81).

5   Peter Godfrey-Smith, "John Dewey's Experience and Nature", *Topoi* 33 (1) (2014), 285-291.

of discriminative behavior, but not with subjective experience. So at least the contemporary complaint would go. The motivating principles of ND and PCS depend upon a concern about this gap. In particular, ND believes that if the world were made only of physical properties, subjective experience could not be possible. And since we *do have* subjective, qualitative experience, our ontology should include also nonphysical, qualitative properties. PCS's is more epistemological in focus than ND. According to PCS, the world is purely physical, but if we only had third-person, functional-physical concepts, we would not be able to account for the epistemic novelty represented by the qualities of experience, as Frank Jackson's "knowledge argument" and Joseph Levine's "explanatory gap" show so well.[6] For this, first-personal "phenomenal concepts" are also required. PCS is also committed to further thesis, the "conceptual isolation" thesis regarding phenomenal concepts. In order to make sense of the fact that our qualitative experiences constitute a true epistemic addition to any amount of functional-physical knowledge, PCS claims that phenomenal concepts are conceptually closed with respect to functional-physical concepts.

The third major tendency, APP, is not worried about the gap between the physical and the qualitative, neither metaphysically, nor epistemically. APP is committed to a view in which the qualities of experience are so completely dominable by physics that physical knowledge is in principle capable of deriving those qualities, just as it can derive any other information about the universe.

I will deal with ND, PCS, and APP individually in the rest of the chapter, but it is important to stress already at this point how Dewey's methodological and metaphysical framework has the resources to put the problems with which NC, PCS, and APP deal in a totally different light. So, is there a gap, either metaphysical or epistemic (or both) between neurophysiological functions and qualities? Dewey's overarching approach is to look for a "solution" of the problem

---

6   Frank Jackson, "Epiphenomenal Qualia", *Philosophical Quarterly* 32 (1982), 127-136; Joseph Levine, "Materialism and Qualia: The Explanatory Gap", *Pacific Philosophical Quarterly* 64 (1983), 354-361. I present and discuss these arguments in the following sections.

through "a revision of the preliminary assumptions ... which generate the problem" (LW1:202). In one crucial passage from *Experience and Nature*, Dewey explains how the qualitative traits of life, i.e. "feelings," should be seen with respect to physical properties:

> Red differs from green for purposes of physical science as that which gives specific meaning to two sets of numbers applied to vibrations, or to two different placements of lines in a spectrum. The difference is proleptically qualitative; it refers to a unique difference of potentiality in the affairs under consideration. But as far as calculation and prediction are concerned these differences remain designable by non-qualitative indices of number and form. But in an organic creature sensitive to light, these differences of potentiality may be realized as differences in immediate sentiency. To say that they are *felt*, is to say that they come to independent and intrinsic existence on their own account. The proposition does not mean that feeling has been extraneously superadded to something else, or that a mode of extrinsic cognitive access to a purely psychical thing has entered intrusively into a world of physical things. (LW1:204)

Dewey is saying that there are *different ways in which a physical property can be identified* in experience. A first way is to identify a physical property through scientific experimentation and inquiry. This mode identifies the physical as an "object of knowledge" (LW1:202). However, experience is not limited to knowledge. For this reason, a physical property can also be identified simply by its being "had" (LW1:198) thanks to the interaction between our neurophysiological structures and the world. This might reasonably imply a further, crucial claim: when the right set of neurophysiological properties and environing conditions are had conjointly in the appropriate way, they amount to an episode of subjective experience, quality, or feeling, so that feeling is *nothing more than this lived having* of the interaction of organic and extra-organic physical factors. At this level of experience, no "concept" is needed to the organism to undergo a qualitative experience. The feeling of red is not a cognitive operation requiring a corresponding concept in order to be singled out in experience: the quality in its experiential "emphasis" (LW3:56-57) surprises the organism, so to speak, by its happening as feeling.

Dewey's point can also be put in the following way. The same mixture of frequencies of electromagnetic radiation constituting a color can be in one case grasped as an object of physical knowledge, and in another case "realized in immediate sentiency," given as an immediate quality or feeling. Similarly to contemporary identity theory[7], the same mixture of frequencies *is*, for Dewey, at once a functional property and a quality—only, *experienced* differently: in the former case as an object of scientific knowledge, in the latter case as an immediate feeling. As Dewey puts it, "qualities characteristic of sentiency are qualities of cosmic events," and "only because they are such, is it possible to establish a one to one correspondence which natural science does establish between series of numbers and spatial positions on one hand and the series and spectra of sensory qualities on the other" (LW1:204-205). There is nothing mysterious for Dewey in the fact that cosmic, physical events can be qualities, and there is nothing cognitive or mental when an organism undergoes a feeling. Instead of a metaphysical or epistemic gap, the difference between the knowledge of the functional and the immediacy of quality is just a difference of experiences.

With this Deweyan framework in mind, let's now turn to Chalmers's Naturalistic Dualism.

3. *Why Naturalistic Dualism Is Wrong*

Naturalistic Dualism (ND) is a form of property dualism.[8] Expanding on Thomas Nagel's understanding of qualia[9], Chalmers claims that while neurophysiological processes can be described in

---

7   Dewey's position is a form of *reductive* physicalism or identity theory *only* in the sense that according to him the natural processes studied by neurophysiology and the qualities of experience are metaphysically identical. Nevertheless, Dewey's proposal doesn't entail any form of *semantic reductionism* of the knowledge based on the qualities of experience to neurophysiological knowledge.

8   David J. Chalmers, *The Character of Consciousness* (Cambridge: Oxford University Press, 2010).

9   Thomas Nagel, "What Is It Like to Be a Bat?", *The Philosophical Review* 83 (4) (1974), 435-450 (p. 437).

functional, intentional, or computational terms, subjective experience cannot. Subjectivity is in fact purely qualitative, solely characterized by phenomenal or experiential properties. For this reason, qualities can be said to accompany physical episodes of information-processing, but not to be identical to them. They are the mostly regular "correlate" of episodes of physical information-processing to which one has access only from a first-person perspective.

So, Chalmers's philosophy of consciousness is committed to a strong dualism between functional-physical properties and phenomenal properties. Moreover, epistemic and metaphysical antiphysicalism go hand in hand: not only qualities are nonphysical properties, but also they lie beyond the explanatory power of the empirical sciences, at least if explanation is taken in the robust sense of saying *why* A causes B. At most, an empirical study of consciousness can show that there are more or less regular *correlations* among information-processing processes and qualities. But a science of correlations falls short of an explanatory science in the above sense.

In Chalmers's view, the "easy problems" of consciousness are easy because they are problems about the physical processes and are therefore treatable in terms of "functions" (2010: 6): the "mechanisms" that specify these functions are the explanation that we are expected to give to the easy problems. "Neurophysiological and cognitive modeling," as he says, are "perfect for the task":

> If we want a detailed, low-level explanation, we can specify the neural mechanism that is responsible for the function. If we want a more abstract explanation, we can specify a mechanism in computational terms. Either way, a full and satisfying explanation will result. Once we have specified the neural or computational mechanism that performs the function of verbal report, for example, the bulk of our work in explaining reportability is over. In a way, the point is trivial. It is a *conceptual* fact about these phenomena that their explanation involves only the explanation of various functions, as the phenomena are functionally definable." (Chalmers, *The Character of Consciousness*, p. 7)

Notice the shift in Chalmers's comment: he moves very quickly from the "conceptual" fact that physical properties are neurophysiologically *explainable* in functional terms to the other allegedly conceptual fact that they are *definable* along the same lines. Now, nobody would deny that physical properties can be treated in functional terms. But does this imply that physical properties can only be defined or identified with the object of knowledge of neurophysiological and cognitive modeling? Chalmers seems to answer affirmatively: this is in fact the way in which cognitive science understands physical properties and uses them to explain cognitive operations. The "hard problem" of consciousness *arises exactly because* the functional notions of physical properties do not seem to be able to account for subjective experience:

> What makes the hard problem hard and almost unique is that it goes *beyond* problems about the performance of functions. To see this, note that even when we have explained the performance of all cognitive and behavioral functions in the vicinity of experience—perceptual discrimination, categorization, internal access, verbal report—a further unanswered question may remain: *why is the performance of these functions accompanied by experience?* A simple explanation of the functions leaves this question open. . . . There is an explanatory gap (a term due to Levine 1983) between the functions and experience, and we need an explanatory bridge to cross it. (Chalmers, *The Character of Consciousness*, p. 8)

Given these reasons, a purely physicalist worldview would appear insufficient to accommodate the reality of subjective experience: "I suggest that a theory of consciousness should take experience as fundamental. We know that a theory of consciousness requires the addition of something fundamental to our ontology, as everything in physical theory is compatible with the absence of consciousness" (Chalmers, *The Character of Consciousness*, p. 17).

In Deweyan style, let's try to assess Chalmers's philosophy of consciousness by making its assumptions explicit. First, Chalmers assumes that the conditions of identification of a physical property are only given by a description of its neurophysiological functioning. But if this is so, ND's definition of the physical seems to be the result of what Dewey calls the mistake of considering "the object of knowledge as the reality *par excellence*" or as what is "eminently real" (LW1:202). This metaphysical mistake assumes one mode of experience as foundational or exclusive and turns what is given through that mode into a being that can only have the properties that have been thus found in it. In the case of ND, neurophysiological modeling is the privileged mode of singling out the physical. The physical is thus *identified with and reduced to* the *merely* functional. In this way, the physical is forever deprived of the possibility of being a qualitative phenomenon. But as I have tried to show in §2, Dewey reminds us that there is no reason to deny to the physical the capacity of being "had" in immediate sentiency as a quality. Rejecting this second possibility, as Chalmers does, is conducive to the typical problems of ND: What is the relationship of the physical, which is purely functional, to the conscious? How can we even hope to explain subjective experience given that physical systems are purely functional? *But a Deweyan redescription of experience shows that there is nothing that prevents us from believing that feelings and functional behaviors are the same piece of reality, the same physical process.* In other words, the "hard" problem of consciousness seems to be the consequence of the unjustified assumption that Dewey's approach helps to unmask. For the Deweyan philosopher, the "hard problem" of consciousness is a "conceptual fact" only in the sense that it is a *philosophical mistake*: the mistake of failing to see that the physical can be had as an episode of immediate sentiency.[10]

---

10   Some might worry that not having good reasons to *deny* that consciousness is physical falls short of *proving* that consciousness is, in fact, physical. This is generally true. Nevertheless, since the context of the discussion here is Chalmers's ND, the Deweyan point that we do not have good reasons to deny that consciousness is physical is sufficient to make a case for physicalism. In fact, Chalmers thinks that there are several good reasons to believe that consciousness is physical; nevertheless, he also thinks that there is one insurmountable problem with physicalism—the hard problem. Consequently, if we accept the naturalism of ND, dissolving the hard problem amounts to taking a decisive step toward physicalism. Thanks to an anonymous reviewer for allowing me to acknowledge this point.

Second, following Levine (1983), ND sees an explanatory gap between the functional and the qualitative. A functional explanation of the neurophysiological machinery *could never explain* the qualitative dimension of our psychic life. In fact, since qualities are not differential factors of computation, they remain beyond the explanatory power of any functional modeling. But here's how the Deweyan philosopher puts this epistemic worry to test. When I see red, my neurophysiological systems are modified. Such modification is a physical modification of my organism in interaction with the world. If I want to *explain why* I see red, I have various options: I can say 'I see red because I turn my eyes toward that sweatshirt' (non-specialized physical knowledge) or 'I see red because X, Y, and Z are in place' (where X, Y, and Z stand for any relevant specialized physical knowledge of what is going on). Is there a fundamental explanatory gap between the explanation of the functional and the qualitative? It doesn't seem so, unless we *dismiss the possibility that the physical might be itself the experience of seeing red*. And this is exactly what Chalmers does. In other words, it is perfectly fine to think that one can explain the experience of seeing red by describing its neurophysiology unless it is assumed that the conditions of identification of a physical process can only be functional.

Accordingly, the Deweyan philosopher of consciousness does not have to say that there is a mysterious *causal relation* between physical processes and nonphysical qualities of experience. Strictly speaking, the relation is one of *metaphysical identity*, not of causality. A science of consciousness will of course explain seeing red by speaking of causal connections among mathematically treated, nonqualitative physical processes and qualities of experiences, but this will only be a way to bridge two modes of experience through knowledge, not to articulate the causality between properties belonging to opposite metaphysical realms.[11] Thus, from a Deweyan perspective, explaining

---

11   Physical processes might be called "causes" of qualities in the sense of constitutive causes, as the parts of a tree are the "causes" of the tree. I would read in this way the passages in which Dewey says that the "objects of science" are the "existential causal conditions" of qualities and that these are the "consummatory manifestations of those conditions" (LW14:81).

consciousness implies only specific empirical problems—'What are the conditions X, Y, and X that amount to seeing red?'—and not an overarching epistemological problem such as the one envisioned by Levine's explanatory gap.

In short, a Deweyan rejoinder to ND would be something like the following:

> Change the metaphysical premise: restore, that is to say, immediate qualities to their rightful position as qualities of inclusive situations, and the problems in question cease to be epistemological problems. They become specifiable scientific problems: questions, that is to say, of how such and such an event having such and such qualities actually occurs. (LW1:203)

There is one last point to consider. Should we accept the qualities of experience as an ultimate fact? This seems to go against a scientific prescription of unrestricted questioning and inquiry, one that the pragmatist tradition has always cultivated. *Why* does a certain neurophysiological modification amount to a quality of experience? As Chalmers puts it, "For any physical process we specify there will be an unanswered question: why should this process give rise to experience?" (2010: 14). However, a Deweyan approach shows that Chalmers's worry would be legitimate only assuming that neurophysiological modifications and qualities of experience are metaphysically non-identical and that between the two there has to be something like a causal connection. But the distinction is exactly what must be proved, not what should be assumed. Accepting the qualitative nature of certain physical processes as an ultimate fact—*ultimate as to their quality, not to their neurophysiological functioning*—is not antiscientific simply because neurophysiological modifications and qualities of experience are *metaphysically identical*. Explaining the machinery is to explain the quality.[12]

---

12 Nevertheless, a Deweyan philosophy of consciousness is aware that explanation does not imply semantic reduction of knowledge based on qualities to functional knowledge, nor linguistic or conceptual equivalence of the two domains of discourse. By the same token, William G. Lycan, *Consciousness and Experience* (Cambridge: MIT Press, 1996), p. 175 rejects "linguistic physicalism" as incapable to account, for instance, for

As a consequence, it would be unfair to press a scientist asking why a physical process amounts to a quality of experience after a neurophysiological explanation has been given. More seriously, such question would manifest a confused opinion about the place of qualities in nature, a confusion that Dewey denounces with clarity: "The general fact that qualitative transition occurs . . . is something characterizing nature. It is something to be accepted rather than to be taken as posing a difficulty to be surmounted. There are problems of ascertaining the special conditions under which specific qualitative transitions take place, but not the problem of why the universe is as it is" (LW14:81). To the ear of the imaginative reader, Chalmers's 'Why?' question sounds almost like a Leibnizian metaphysical puzzlement—'Why is there something rather than nothing?' 'Why consciousness?' 'Why is a rose red?'—to which a poetical insight, once the scientist's work is done, seems to provide us with a better answer than ND: with the words of Gertrude Stein, "a rose is a rose is a rose"[13]—and seeing red is simply seeing red.

4. *How the Phenomenal Concept Strategy Could Be Better*

If ND is not a compelling account of consciousness, physicalism is not without its own difficulties.[14] One of the most interesting physicalist projects in the contemporary debate is the Phenomenal Concept Strategy (PCS). As I will show shortly, PCS, while denying

---

the monadicity and homogeneity of the perceptual field; see also Lycan, *Consciousness* (Cambridge: MIT Press, 1987), p. 53. David Papineau, *Philosophical Naturalism* (Cambridge and Oxford: Blackwell, 1993), pp. 93-95 distinguishes between "conceptual analysis" and "theoretical reduction," rejects the former but endorses the latter.

13 Gertrude Stein, "Sacred Emily."

14 The most widespread mistake is taking the already mentioned explanatory gap problem seriously, see e.g. Michael Tye, "Absent Qualia and the Mind-Body Problem", *The Philosophical Review* 115 (2) (2006), 139-168 (p. 164); Lycan, *Consciousness*, p. 53 and p. 79; John R. Searle, *The Mystery of Consciousness* (New York: A New York Review Book, 1997), p. 99; Sydney Shoemaker, "Qualia and Consciousness", *Mind* 100 (4) (1991), 507-524 (pp. 518-520).

the reality of nonphysical properties, maintains that there is an explanatory gap between the physical-functional and the qualitative aspects of sentiency. In order to cope with this gap, PCS introduces a special class of concepts called "phenomenal concepts" and proposes to consider them as "conceptually isolated" from any physical-functional concepts.[15]

What I want to suggest is that PCS's physicalist project would be better off if it realized that the explanatory gap is not a genuine

---

15   See Katalin Balog, "In Defense of the Phenomenal Concept Strategy", *Philosophy and Phenomenological Research* 1 (2012), 1-23; Ned J. Block, "Max Black's Objection to Mind-Body Identity", in *Phenomenal Concepts and Phenomenal Knowledge: New Essays on Consciousness and Physicalism*, ed. by T. Alter and S. Walter (Oxford: Oxford University Press, 2007), 249-306; Christopher S. Hill and Brian P. McLaughlin, "There Are Fewer Things in Reality Than Are Dreamt of in Chalmer's Philosophy", *Philosophy and Phenomenological Research* 59 (2) (1999), 445-454; Janet Levin, "What Is a Phenomenal Concept?", in *Phenomenal Concepts and Phenomenal Knowledge: New Essays on Consciousness and Physicalism*, ed. by T. Alter and S. Walter (Oxford: Oxford University Press, 2007), 87-111; B. McLaughlin, "In Defense of New Wave Materialism", in *Physicalism and Its Discontents*, ed. by C. Gillet and B. Loewer (New York: Cambridge University Press, 2001), 319-330; David Papineau, *Thinking about Consciousness* (Oxford: Clarendon Press, 2002); John Perry, *Knowledge, Possibility, and Consciousness* (Cambridge: MIT Press, 2001); Michael Tye, *Color, Consciousness, and Content* (Cambridge: MIT Press, 2000); Martine Nida-Rümelin, "What Mary Couldn't Know: Belief About Phenomenal States", in *Conscious Experience*, ed. by Thomas Metzinger (Paderborn: Schöningh, 1995); Brian Loar, "Phenomenal States", in *Philosophy of Mind: Classical and Contemporary Readings*, ed. by David J. Chalmers (New York: Oxford University Press, 2002), 295-311; Loar, "Qualia, Properties, Modality", *Philosophical Issues* 13 (2003), 113-129; Murat Ayede and Güven Guzeldere, "Cognitive Architecture, Concepts, and Introspection: An Information-Theoretic Solution to the Problem of Phenomenal Consciousness", *Noûs* 39 (2) (2005), 197-255; John H. Taylor, "Physicalism and Phenomenal Concepts: Brining Ontology and Philosophy of Mind Together", *Philosophia* 41 (2013), 1283-1297; Peter Carruthers and Benedicte Veillet, "The Phenomenal Concept Strategy", *Journal of Consciousness Studies* 14 (2007), 212-236; and Benedicte Veillet, "The Cognitive Significance of Phenomenal Knowledge", *Philosophical Studies* 172 (2015), 2955-2974 (p. 2955).

problem and that consequently there is no need for a class of concepts with peculiar logical properties. For this purpose, Dewey's framework is again one of the best philosophical resources we have. In other words, although PCS is not without merit, a Deweyan philosophy of consciousness is more apt. Let's take a brief look at the fundamental tenets of PCS. PCS is a way to account for the knowledge of 'what it's like to experience X.' So, "knowledge of what it's like to have perceptual experiences, e.g. of what it's like to see red or drink Turkish coffee, is phenomenal knowledge" (Veillet, "The Cognitive Significance", p. 2955). This idea of "phenomenal knowledge" is crucial because, as the rest of this section makes clear, most of the trouble with PCS results from a difficulty that advocates of PCS have in understanding the respective roles that sentiency and conceptuality play in what they call phenomenal knowledge. Phenomenal knowledge is so crucial that PCS deems it necessary to introduce special concepts, namely, phenomenal concepts, to account for it. Despite some differences,[16] all proponents of PCS ascribe to phenomenal concepts peculiar logical properties.

---

16   The most influential versions of PCS include: "phenomenal concept possession" and "concept acquisition" (Papineau, *Philosophical Naturalism*), "quotational view" (Papineau, *Thinking about Consciousness*), "concept application" (Scott Sturgeon, "The Epistemic Basis of Subjectivity", *Mind and Language* 20 (1994), 469-494), "conceptual faculties" (Hill and McLaughlin), "indexical" interpretation of phenomenal concepts (Perry; John O'Dea, "The Indexical Nature of Sensory Concepts", *Philosophical Papers* 31 (2) (2002), 169-181). An alternative classification is given by Balog, "In Defense of the Phenomenal Concept Strategy": "constitutional account" (Hill and McLaughlin; Block; Papineau; Katalin Balog, "Acquaintance and the Mind-Body Problem", in *The Mental, the Physical*, ed. by Christopher Hill and Simone Gozzano (New York: Cambridge University Press, 2011) and Balog, "In Defense of the Phenomenal Concept Strategy") and alternative views, including the "recognitional account" (Michael Tye, "A Theory of Phenomenal Concepts", in *Minds and Persons*, ed. by Anthony O'Hear (New York: Cambridge University Press, 2003), the "demonstrative account" (Levin, "What is a Phenomenal Concept?"; Perry), and the "information-theoretical account" (Ayede and Guzeldere).

First, phenomenal concepts are *non-descriptive concepts* capable of "capturing" phenomenal properties, the what it's like to experience X, and of doing so by some sort of first-person "direct access" to or "acquaintance" with these properties (Balog, "In Defense", p. 6). As Loar puts it, that "phenomenal concepts are not descriptive concepts" (Loar, "Qualia", p. 118) means that they relate *"directly"* to their referents.[17] They need to be thin enough not to be descriptive but also thick enough to allow for "re-identifying qualia of appropriate types" (Loar, "Qualia", p. 120). In Veillet's clear synthesis, "phenomenal concepts" are a kind of "type demonstrative/recognitional" concepts that "pick out (ultimately physical) properties of experience," and "what determines which properties of experience these concepts refer to are their users' dispositions to recognize, re-identify, or classify the properties in question" (Veillet, "The Cognitive Significance", p. 2958).

Second, phenomenal concepts are *conceptually isolated* from any physical-functional concepts. In other words, "no matter how much information we are given about conscious experience in physical, functional or intentional terms, that information won't really explain why our experiences should feel to us the way that they do" (Carruthers and Veillet 2007: 213).[18] The way experiences feel to us is conveyed by phenomenal concepts, which cannot be derived from any amount of physical knowledge and have therefore a totally different "cognitive value" compared to physical concepts.

The just-quoted passage by Carruthers and Veillet exemplifies why the Deweyan philosopher might have problems with PCS. It is important to stress again that phenomenal concepts are introduced by PCS to account for the seeming explanatory gap between two kinds of information, the functional information of physical knowledge and the phenomenal information that we acquire through experience. However, the Deweyan philosopher would remark that the notions of "information" and of "the way experiences feel like to

---

17   Loar, "Phenomenal States", p. 300 speaks of phenomenal concepts as "rigid designators."
18   A variant of the conceptual isolation thesis is the idea of "incommunicability," see Nida-Rümelin, pp. 237-238.

us" are used too loosely by PCS advocates. For example, the phrase "the way experience feels like" can be taken as a synonym for mere sentiency. Phenomenal information or knowledge would then be identical to mere sentiency. What Carruthers and Veillet write, in fact, is not that functional information-knowledge is incapable of explaining our information-knowledge about what our experiences feel like, but that it won't explain "why our experiences should feel to us the way they do"; namely, why a certain feeling is what it is. But under this interpretation of the *explanandum*, PCS makes the same error as Chalmers discussed at the end of the previous section, for it is an error to believe that there is something left to explain about colors when the machinery of color perceptions has been explained. In this case, the Deweyan philosopher of consciousness is in staunch opposition to PCS. However, PCS proponents and other interpreters of PCS might reject this interpretation and say that, despite some inevitable loose formulations, PCS's intention is to point out the explanatory gap between *conceptual* phenomenal information and functional knowledge. At this point, the Deweyan philosopher will ask: 'What can we *know about a feeling* through a phenomenal *concept* that is supposed to be non-descriptive, directly addressed to its phenomenal referent, and purely demonstrative-recognitional?' A likely answer would be, 'We do not know much, because such a concept is devoid of descriptive content, and nevertheless we know what a certain experience feels like because we can recognize it over and over again, and it is *this* knowledge of what an experience feels like that cannot be derived from any amount of functional knowledge.' At this level, PCS advocates and the Deweyan philosopher come closer, for Dewey also believes that the concept of what an experience feels like cannot be derived from any amount of physical knowledge. Nevertheless, the Deweyan philosopher would still point out some fundamental limitations of PCS, based on a very different understanding of the nature of concepts.

While the Deweyan philosopher *would agree* that the concept of what red looks like cannot be derived from any amount of functional knowledge, he *would never say* this is so because there are special concepts with *peculiar logical properties* which pose a *special problem to knowledge*. First, the Deweyan philosopher could never construe the idea of a concept of what an experience feels like in the way phenomenal concepts are construed. For him, in fact, knowledge is *always beyond* "pure denotation" (LW12:240-242) and purely demonstrative-recognitional concepts are simply a logical illusion. He would most likely suggest that the 'information' of what an experience feels like—information that according to the proponents of PCS depend upon descriptively empty phenomenal concepts—is actually the purely sensible information of an episode of sentiency. PCS advocates, in other words, deceive themselves in thinking that they are trying to account for a conceptual knowledge when they are actually trying to account for the mere quality of a feeling. Accordingly, the Deweyan philosopher would remark that positing one *kind* of concepts, constitutively linked to qualitative experience, and *logically different* from other concepts (isolated, non-descriptive, purely denotative-recognitional, etc.), sounds very much like repeating the empiricist error of supposing that empirical concepts have special logical features because they are 'closer to experience' than other concepts.[19] Second, he would observe that while it is true that the concept of what red feels like cannot be derived from any amount of functional knowledge, this is not because phenomenal concepts are isolated from functional ones, nor because there is an explanatory gap between the two. PCS, he would continue, rests on a *confusion in understanding the respective roles that sentiency and conceptual knowledge play in phenomenal knowledge.* Saying that any amount of functional knowledge about colors is insufficient to have the concept of what red feels like due to a logical isolation

---

19   Wilfrid Sellars, *Empiricism and the Philosophy of Mind* (Cambridge and London: Harvard University Press, 1997), p. 44 will repeat this Deweyan insight in his criticism of empiricism: "Now, it just won't do to reply that to have the concept of green, to know what it is for something to be green, it is sufficient to respond, when one is *in point of fact* in standard conditions, to green objects with the vocable 'This is green.' Not only must those conditions be of a sort that is appropriate for determining the color of an object by looking, the subject must *know* that conditions of these sort are appropriate," and this knowledge is always inferential. This implies rejecting the idea that "fundamental concepts pertaining to observable fact have that logical independence of one another which is characteristic of the empiricist tradition."

of the latter from the former, means *mistakenly invoking a problem of knowledge and concept-relation where the problem is first and foremost a 'phenomenal' one; that is, where the problem is the lack of physical exposure to the environmental stimuli capable of causing the feeling of red.* In other words, it is not necessary to draw the logical conclusion that there are special concepts; it is sufficient to point out that the development of knowledge *always* requires the exposure to the right facts. In short, the Deweyan philosopher does not maintain that PCS is meritless; rather, he claims that the facts for which PCS accounts could be explained better, and he shows *how* this can be done.

I will now elaborate on these points and explain why a Deweyan approach is a clearer and more economical construal of the same facts that PCS tries to interpret. PCS gives experience its due, and the Deweyan philosopher is certainly sympathetic with PCS's "experience thesis".[20] According to this thesis, "a thinker can possess phenomenal concepts only if she has had the right type of experience" (Veillet, "The Cognitive Significance", p. 2957; see also Tye, *Ten Problems*, p. 169; Lycan, "Perspectival Representation", p. 389), and this is supposed to be true both for the acquisition and application of phenomenal concepts. However, if we follow Dewey's insight, phenomenal knowledge doesn't seem to require *special* phenomenal concepts. Rather, certain concepts *might* be called 'phenomenal' *simply* because they are the way in which we discriminate and conceptually/linguistically classify certain feelings and qualities, usually in order to perform a certain task:

> Through language, sentience is taken up to into a system of signs, when for example a certain quality of the active relationship of organism and environment is named hunger, it is seen as an organic demand for an extra-organic object. . . . To name another quality "red" is to direct an interaction between an organism and a thing to some object which fulfills the demand or need of the situation. (LW1:199)

---

20 Daniel Stoljar, "Physicalism and Phenomenal Concepts", *Mind and Language* 20, 469-494.

Deweyan 'phenomenal' concepts would simply be concepts used to discriminate qualities, just like other concepts—say, the concept of a flower—allow us to pick out all the instances of flower-looking things. There is nothing special about concepts of qualities. In fact, the discrimination of red, if it is *conceptual* discrimination, must rely on *some* conceptual content, and in this is sense it is not different from the concept of flower. Such redescription seems to have further substantial advantages compared to PCS. Not only it avoids introducing a special class of concepts for accounting for phenomenal knowledge, but it also allows appreciating the difference between mere sentiency and knowledge proper in a less ambiguous way than PCS. The "direct access to" or "acquaintance with" phenomenal properties that seems to characterize phenomenal knowledge can be explained not as a peculiar form of knowledge, that of non-descriptive concepts having a direct epistemic access to phenomenal properties, but simply as the *lived having* of an organism-world transaction. Feelings are in themselves "anoetic," and become part of a cognitive "mental" activity only if used as signs for inferences (LW1:199). Thus, the directness characterizing phenomenal knowledge would not result from deploying special, non-descriptive concepts, but would be the fundamental feature of the feelings involved in phenomenal knowledge. Dewey explains that the qualitative dimension of our life is not dependent upon noetic activity:

> Complex and active animals *have* . . . feelings which vary abundantly in quality, corresponding to distinctive directions and phases— initiating, mediating, fulfilling or frustrating—of activities, bound up in distinctive connections with environmental affairs. They *have* them, but they do not know they have them. Activity is psycho-physical, but not "mental," that is, not aware of meanings. As life is a character of events in a peculiar condition of organization, and "feeling" is a quality of life-forms marked by complexly mobile and discriminating responses, so "mind" is an added property assumed by a feeling creature, when it reaches that organized interaction with other living creatures which is language. . . . (LW1:198)

What Dewey says here helps us explain why in order to account for the qualities of experience, there is no need to postulate a special class of concepts with unlikely logical properties such as lack of descriptive capacity and isolation. "Having" a feeling is a simple matter of *anoetic psychophysical processes.*

Keeping this framework in mind, let's assess PCS's most distinctive tenet, the *conceptual isolation thesis.* This thesis is important because according to PCS it is supposed to provide a solution to the knowledge argument and the explanatory gap without having to embrace metaphysical antiphysicalism. The knowledge argument is a famous antiphysicalist argument by Frank Jackson featuring Mary, a genius scientist specializing in color perception:

> Mary is a brilliant scientist who is . . . forced to investigate the world from a black and white room via a black and white television monitor. She specialises in the neurophysiology of vision and acquires, let us suppose, all the physical information there is to obtain about what goes on when we see ripe tomatoes, or the sky, and use terms like 'red', 'blue', and so on.... What will happen when Mary is released from her black and white room or is given a colour television monitor? Will she *learn* anything or not? It seems just obvious that she will learn something about the world and our visual experience of it. But then it is inescapable that her previous knowledge was incomplete. But she had *all* the physical information. *Ergo* there is more to have than that, and Physicalism is false. (1982: 130)[21]

While taking the problem posed by the knowledge argument seriously, PCS denies that giving up physicalism is the only available option. Rather, PCS maintains that it is because phenomenal concepts are *conceptually isolated* from all other concepts that one can explain why "deduction" of phenomenal knowledge is not available to Mary-in-the- cell: by relying on the conceptual isolation thesis, PCS "would explain, at the very least, why Mary is unable to deduce what it's like to see red from inside her room" (Veillet, "The Cognitive Significance", p. 2957). (Note again the same ambiguity discussed

---

21   Jackson believes now that his knowledge argument does not support anti-physicalism. See Fran Jackson, "Postscript on Qualia", in *Mind, Method, and Conditionals: Selected Essays* (London: Routledge, 1998), 76-79.

earlier: is Mary unable to "deduce" the sensible information of the episode of mere sentiency 'seeing red,' or is she incapable of deducing some conceptual, purely denotative information about the what-it's-like-ness of seeing red?[22]) Carruthers and Veillet explain the isolation thesis in the following way:

> To know what seeing red feels like requires deploying a phenomenal concept. It is just such concept that she learns upon leaving the room. And why couldn't she learn that concept before? Wasn't her extensive knowledge of color vision enough to enable her to learn that phenomenal concept? No. Since it is conceptually isolated, no physical (or functional, or representational) knowledge about color vision would have enabled her to learn the relevant phenomenal concept. So when she leaves her room, she does acquire the capacity to think some new thoughts (these are thoughts involving phenomenal concepts). Hence she also learns some new facts (in the sense of acquiring some new true thoughts). But for all that the argument shows, these new thoughts might just concern the very same physical facts that she already knew, only differently represented (not represented by means of phenomenal concepts) (Carruthers and Veillet, "The Phenomenal Concept Strategy", p. 215)

What I want to suggests is that if we handle Jackson's argument with Deweyan tools, the alleged difficulty presented by Mary's case dis- solves, and with it also the need for PCS's conceptual isolation thesis. The Deweyan philosopher of consciousness agrees with the two tenets expressed in this passage, namely, that Mary-outside-the-cell is likely to acquire "new thoughts" and "learn some new facts." However, this requires that Mary *learns how to use qualities as signs* for possible inferences. Dewey invites us to think about learning in

---

22   Quite rightly, Nida-Rümelin, pp. 232-233 points out that the knowledge argument does not distinguish between "having epistemic access to" (or "being acquainted with") a color (which is close to what is in a Deweyan perspective an episode of immediate sentiency) and "knowing" a color, i.e. having a concept of a color. Similarly, Ayede and Guzeldere, pp. 200-203 distinguish between "sense" and "perception". Nevertheless, they all maintain some version of the conceptual isolation thesis.

terms of acquiring 'if ... then' beliefs.[23] Mary can certainly learn the phenomenal fact that some roses are red, namely, that if she wants to locate a rose in the garden outside the cell, then she has to look for something that looks that specific way. She learns to use a quality as a sign for singling out an object. And it is clear that the knowledge of this fact implies more than the mere episode of immediate sentiency. It requires an acquired capacity to treat experience *inferentially*. It also seems clear that such capacity to use the quality of red as a sign within an inferential process could not have been acquired by Mary before she had *seen* red. Hence, Mary-in-the-cell *cannot derive* the concept of red consisting in the capacity to use the quality of red as a sign within an inferential process. But is this because the phenomenal concept of red is logically isolated from its functional concept? No, it is simply because the development of the capacity to use red as a sign is *dependent upon the prior possibility of seeing red things*.

On the other hand, if the fact that PCS wants to explain is sim- ply that Mary-outside-the-cell has access to colors while Mary-in-the-cell doesn't—in other words, if we have to understand "acquiring new thoughts" and "learning new facts" very loosely, merely as the sense information of what seeing red feels like—it seems implausible to believe that the best way to do so is by introducing a special class of concepts. The *anoetic lived having* of the relevant organism-world transaction seems to be just fine to account for the difference.[24] Either way, PCS's conceptual isolation thesis is hardly necessary to explain the facts.

---

23 For Dewey's discussion of "inquiry" as the context within which all the other logical terms should be understood, see LW12.

24 Under this interpretation, it would not be correct to claim, as some have done (David Lewis, "Should a Materialist Believe in Qualia?", *Australasian Journal of Philosophy* 73 (1) (1995), 140-144; Lewis, "Postscript to 'Mad Pain and Martian Pain'", in *Philosophical Papers*, vol. 1 (New York and Oxford: Oxford University Press, 1996), 130-132; Paul M. Churchland, "Reduction, Qualia, and the Direct Introspection of Brain States", *The Journal of Philosophy* 82 (1) (1985), 8-28), that Mary *knows* the same phenomenon in two different ways, e.g. by mathematical knowledge and by perceptual knowledge, or, in broader terms, by "knowledge-by-description" and "knowledge-by-acquaintance," and that

As for the difference in "cognitive value" that all the PCS advocates see between phenomenal concepts and functional-physical knowledge, the difference does not seem to amount to anything like an explanatory gap. It is ironic that PCS stresses the cognitive value of phenomenal concepts while at the same time thinking that these concepts are non-descriptive. On the contrary, the reidentification of a color, if it is enabled by *conceptual resources* and not simply by *sub-conceptual discriminatory systems*, has to rely on some kind of knowledge of an everyday variety and based on exemplars, for example 'Red is the way the old car looks like.' In this sense, not even concepts about qualities can be fully non-descriptive. As already mentioned, for Dewey knowledge is always beyond "pure denotation."[25] So, when I discriminate the color red from any other colors by relying on the (deeply habitual) knowledge of what a normally-sighted person would call 'red' (together with the habitual capacity to *re*produce—not produce!—a red patch in my imagination

---

these two kinds of knowledge imply different capacities (see also the distinction between "knowing-how" and "knowing-that," Lewis, "Postscript", pp. 142-143; cf. L. Nemirow, "So This Is What It's Like: A Defense of the Ability Hypothesis", in *Phenomenal Concepts and Phenomenal Knowledge: New Essays on Consciousness and Physicalism*, ed. by T. Alter and S. Walter (Oxford: Oxford University Press, 2007), 32-51 for a defense of the "ability hypothesis").

25   In this sense, "phenomenal concept" cannot be as "thin" as some contemporary philosophers think. According to Levin, p. 89, a "thin" and "non-ascriptive" understanding of phenomenal concepts implies that not only "the denotation of a phenomenal type-demonstrative will be the property— presumably physical—that's causally responsible for the application of that concept in the introspective recognition or reidentification of an experience," but also that the "reference" of such a "concept" is "determined solely ... by the fact" of being in "causal contact with a certain property." Erhan Demircioglu, "Physicalism and Phenomenal Concepts", *Philosophical Studies* 164 (2013), 257-277 (pp. 263-265) provides good reasons to be suspicious of the "thin" understanding of "phenomenal concepts." In other words, if the re-identification has to be "conceptual" and not simply based on psycho-physical discrimination, some "thickness" (i.e. some conceptual content working as a detector, so to speak) must be included in phenomenal concepts.

based on that knowledge), the same nontechnical knowledge that I am using is *explainable in terms of neurophysiological knowledge*. In fact, explaining why an object looks red to someone and clarifying the standards of what counts as normally-sighted are tasks that certainly fall within the scope and explanatory power of science. But this Deweyan stance is perfectly compatible with the tenet that the phenomenal concept of red and its physical explanation are different in cognitive value, and even more so, given that Dewey is not com- mitted to the idea that concepts of qualities are purely denotative. But their difference in cognitive value does not amount to an explanatory gap, but only to a *normal difference in content* of two different pieces of knowledge, the one nontechnical, the other specialized.

5. *In What Way A Priori Physicalism Goes Too Far*

I have shown how physicalism can be defended without having to accept the idea of an explanatory gap between functional concepts of physical properties and special phenomenal concepts. Now I want to conclude by highlighting the fact that if, on the one hand, we do not have to accept the explanatory gap, on the other hand, a full-fledged physicalist view of consciousness as Dewey's does not have to endorse A Priori Physicalism (APP).

The most radical thesis of APP is what I shall call physicalist deductionism, as it is maintained for instance by Daniel Dennett.[26] Physicalist deductionism maintains that a human being, from a sufficiently rich knowledge of his physical-functional status, would be able to derive not only the prediction of an episode of consciousness, but also *the episode of consciousness itself*. While PCS realizes correctly that the relation of derivability or deducibility can exist only among concepts but then wrongly concludes, in order to say that something is not derivable from Mary's physical knowledge, that phenomenal concepts are isolated from physical-functional

---

26 I speak of physicalist deductionism instead of a priori physicalism to bring the attention to the relation of deducibility.

concepts (explanatory gap), APP's physicalist deductionism rightly sees that, if physicalism is true (as both PCS and Dennett agree), then it is nonsensical to say that a certain conceptual content can resist the explanatory power of neurophysiology. But APP mistakenly concludes that *even the quality* of experience can be derived.

In "Quining Qualia" Dennett writes:

> Which idea of qualia am I trying to extirpate? Everything real has properties, and since I do not deny the reality of conscious experience, I grant that conscious experience has properties. I grant more- over that each person's states of consciousness have properties in virtue of which those states gave the experiential content that they do. That is to say, whenever someone experiences something as being one way rather than another, this is true in virtue of some property of something happening in them at that time, but these properties are so unlike properties traditionally imputed to consciousness that it would be grossly misleading to call any of them the long-sought qualia. Qualia are supposed to be *special* properties, in some hard-to- define way. My claim . . . is that conscious experience has no proper- ties that are special in any of the ways qualia have been supposed to be special. . . . I want to shift the burden of proof, so that anyone who wants to appeal to private, subjective properties has to prove first that in so doing they are *not* making a mistake.[27]

As it is clear, what Dennett denies is not that conscious experience is real and has therefore properties, as his eliminativist materialism is too often interpreted, but that one has to recur to qualia understood as "*special* properties" in order to account for consciousness. His eliminativism is polemically addressed against what Patricia Kitcher calls the "*mysterious features* of sentience," not against *sentience* itself.[28] On this, his view and Dewey's are simply identical.

Consider Dennett's appraisal of David Chalmers's ND:

> When he [Chalmers] confronts the vitalist parallel head-on, he simply declares that whereas vitalist skepticism was driven by doubts about

27   Daniel C. Dennett, "Quining Qualia", in *Mind and Cognition*, ed. by William G. Lycan (Oxford: Blackwell, 1988), p. 383.

28   Patricia Kitcher, "Phenomenal Qualities", *American Philosophical Quarterly* 16 (1979), 123-129 (p. 123).

whether physical mechanisms could "perform the many remarkable functions associated with life," it is otherwise with his skepticism: "With experience, on the other hand, physical explanation of the functions is not in question. The key is instead the conceptual point that the explanation of functions does not suffice for the explanation of experience." I submit that he is flatly mistaken in this claim. Whether people realize it or not, it is precisely the "remarkable functions associated with" consciousness that drive them to wonder about how consciousness could possibly reside in a brain. In fact, if you care- fully dissociate all these remarkable functions from consciousness—in your own, first-person case—there is nothing left for you to wonder about.[29]

This passage is a full-on rejection of the explanatory gap. Notice that what Dennett characterizes as "fatly mistaken" is Chalmers view that it is a "conceptual point" that "the *explanation* of functions does not suffice for the explanation of experience." The main idea behind Dennett's rebuttal is the following: all that in consciousness is *in need of explanation* can be explained in terms physical-functional properties; furthermore, there are no special concepts (phenomenal or otherwise) that cannot be bridged to and derived or deduced from any sufficiently exhaustive physical-functional knowledge (and thus explained by way of derivation or deduction). If the reconstruction of the previous sections is correct, this is not different from what also the Deweyan philosopher would argue against ND and PCS.

But Dennett's physicalist deductionism is much stronger than this and, I submit, it goes too far. In fact, APP entails not simply that physical-functional knowledge can produce (predictive or explanatory) knowledge of the qualities of experience, but also that it can produce the qualities themselves. This is due to the fact that Dennett tends to overlook the anoetic and purely psycophysical nature of feelings. Consider again a case like the following: 'If I underwent XYZ (where XYZ stand for physical conditions represented in physical knowledge), I would see (what normally sighted people call) red.' In order to endorse this statement, I do not have to have ever experienced red (this might in fact be one of

---

29   Daniel C. Dennett, "Facing Backwards on the Problem of Consciousness", *The Journal of Consciousness Studies* 3 (1) (1996), 4-6 (p. 5).

the standard ways in which Mary-in-the-cell thinks about colors).
Now, Dennett's point of view implies a further claim: 'If I *know*
everything there is to know about the physics of my organism, then I
can also *have access to* (by way of derivation or deduction, however
complex) what it feels to see red.'
    In "What RoboMary Knows," Dennett rehashes his example
of Mary dealing with the blue banana prank by clarifying that,
according to this example,

> Mary had figured out, using her vast knowledge of color science,
> exactly what it would be like for her to see something red, something
> yellow, something blue in advance of having those experiences. ... He
> repeats this point: "Mary puts all her scientific knowledge of color to
> use and *figures out* exactly what it is like to see red (and green and blue)
> and hence is not the least bit surprised when she sees her first rose" ...
> , But such extreme deductionism seems implausible.[30]

    Since according to APP every property of consciousness can be
in principle derived from physical-functional knowledge and thus
explained, also the quality of experiencing red *must* be deducible and
derivable. APP does not state that the *visual* experience of seeing red
can be deduced. Nevertheless, it is committed to the view that it is
possible to *derive an experientially equivalent information*, maybe
something like the "imagination" of red, or at least some equivalent
"color-system state" (p. 29). Imagining red is equivalent to seeing
red insofar as it gives Mary access to what red feels like: while seeing
red and imagining red are *two different feelings*, they are nevertheless
both feelings of red.[31] In other words, APP not only discards the idea
that qualities are nonphysical properties (ND) and that some special
concepts intrinsically related to qualities are isolated from any other
(PCS), but it also rejects the view that immediate sentiency of *feeling
has some autonomy compared to knowledge*.

---

30   Daniel C. Dennett, "What Robomary Knows", in *Phenomenal Concepts
      and Phenomenal Knowledge: New Essays on Consciousness and
      Physicalism*, ed. by T. Alter and S. Walter (Oxford: Oxford University
      Press, 2007), 15-31 (p. 16 and p. 25).
31   Dennett, "What RoboMary Knows", p. 23.

For APP, as with PCS, one of the major sources of error is perhaps the underlying idea of 'information,' which is understood as a too-loose umbrella term referring to too many things. For instance, Dennett writes: "Since she [Mary] already knows all the facts, has all the information needed to have anticipated all the noticeable, remarkable-upon properties of her debut experience in a colored world, she should not . . . be surprised".[32] Similarly, he defines experience as something "extremely rich in information" (p. 19). In this light, consciousness conveys some *information* (the what-it's-like-ness of seeing red) and scientific knowledge is *information at its best*, so believing that the former cannot be deduced from the latter seems ludicrous to Dennett. Is Mary "surprised" when she leaves the cell? Does she "learn" anything new? Since the notions of "surprise" and "learning" are parasitical upon the notion of information, it seems obvious to Dennett that the physically omniscient Mary would not be surprised and would not learn much upon leaving her cell. She would have already been able to deduce the experiential information of red. Hence, physical deductionism.

So, should a fully-fledged psychophysicalism of consciousness be committed to something like APP and physicalist deductionsim? It doesn't seem so, and Dewey's stance explains why: since the feeling of red is the quality of an organism-world transaction, it is impossible to deduce or derive something that is not knowledge, namely, *that quality*, from any amount of physical-functional knowledge, no matter how perfect. As Dewey puts it:

There is an issue closely related with the view that qualities ... are genuine natural existences. If scientific laws and objects are of the kind I have said they are [selections of correlations between changes], the connections which are involved in production of qualitative objects are necessary but not the qualities themselves. There is, then, room in nature for contingency and novelty. (LW14:82)

Mary-outside-the-cell would certainly experience the *novelty* of seeing red upon leaving the cell. So, the Deweyan philosopher, while remaining a wholehearted naturalist as Dennett's, does not need to commit himself to the extreme thesis that feeling itself is derivable.

---

32   Dennett, "What RoboMary Knows", p. 18.

From this point of view, APP fails to appreciate the variety of human experience, in particular the difference between knowledge and immediate sentiency, and tends to see experience as a fundamentally cognitive affair.

Moreover, Dennett's strategy is question-begging at times. As we have seen, Dennett writes that "Mary has figured out, using her vast knowledge of color science, exactly what it would be like for her to see something red ... in advance of having those experiences." If by "figuring out" Dennett means that Mary can *deduce* a new piece of (sensible) information from her vast functional knowledge of color vision, then his claim is original and quite radical, but hardly believable, for the reasons given above. However, if by "figuring out" he means that Mary *can put herself in the physical condition to have an experience equivalent* to the standard visual perception of red, then his claim is hardly a disavowal of the experience thesis, at least if we take 'experience' in a broad sense (as we should). Under this interpretation, Dennett's strategy becomes question-begging. In fact, if Dennett is saying that Mary can act on her scientific knowledge and intervene on her brain and visual system so to generate in her organism a state analogous to perceiving red—something like the "imagination" or the "phosphene" of red (22)—then his claim *implies* the experience thesis. In this case, Mary would not be deducing the sensible information about what-it's-like to see red. She would simply be putting herself in the physical condition of experiencing red, even though not a standard visual experience.[33]

Taking a different stance from Dennett's, Graham and Horgan write that Mary "will experience surprise and unanticipated delight, upon release from her monochromatic environment—which presumably

---

33   Dennett is admittedly unable to grasp the difference between the two alternatives just discussed: "Objection [to his view]: . . . What matters is whether Mary (or RoboMary) can *deduce* what it's like to see red from her complete physical knowledge, not whether one could use one's physical knowledge in some way or other to acquire knowledge of what it's like to see in color." Dennett's answer: "I just don't see that this is what matters. So far as I can see, this objection presupposes an improbable and extravagant distinction between (pure?) deduction and other varieties of knowledgeable self-enlightenment" (p. 29).

should lead her to repudiate the materialist theory she previously accepted".[34] However, the Deweyan philosophy of consciousness sketched in this chapter shows that while it is true, against Dennett, that Mary will experience surprise and delight when she sees a red object for the first time, simply because no episode of immediate sentiency is deducible from her prodigious physical knowledge, it is also true, against Graham and Horgan, that if Mary were led by her new experience of red to repudiate materialism, she would prove to be a bad philosopher despite her scientific genius. Since seeing red is the immediate having of certain physical processes, it is accountable for in purely physical-functional terms. And Mary's wrong philosophical conclusion—together with Graham's, Horgan's, Chalmers's, and many others—would be only another instance proving the critical need of something like a Deweyan philosophy of consciousness.

---

34   G. Graham and T. Horgan, "Mary Mary, Quite Contrary", *Philosophical Studies* 99 (2000), 59-87 (p. 74).

CHAPTER 4
DEWEY, SEMIOTICS, AND SUBSTANCES

The aim of the chapter is to introduce a semiotic reading of Dewey's theory of experience through the key notion of indexical existence. This approach can shed new light on Dewey's metaphysics. More specifically, the chapter shows that Dewey's theory of experience, once semiotically reconstructed, points in the direction of a semiotic metaphysics of substances.

1. Introduction

Although the Deweyan notion of experience has been largely developed by the pragmatist scholarship, it is surprising that its *semiotic structure* has been mainly overlooked.[1] The reasons for this

1   Richard J. Bernstein, "John Dewey's Metaphysics of Experience", *The Journal of Philosophy* 58(1) (1961), 5-14; Roberto Frega, *John Dewey et la philosophie comme épistémologie de la pratique* (Paris: L'Harmattan, 2006); Frega, *Pensée, expérience, pratique* (Paris: L'Harmattan, 2006); Warren G. Frisina, "Knowledge as Active, Aesthetic, and Hypothetical: An Examination of the relationship Between Dewey's Metaphysics and Epistemology", *Philosophy Today* 33(3) (1989), 245-263; Matthias Jung, "John Dewey and Action", in *The Cambridge Companion to John Dewey*, ed. by Cochran, Molly (Cambridge: Cambridge University Press, 2010), 145-165; Sholom J. Kahn, "Experience and Existence in Dewey's Naturalistic Metaphysics", *Philosophy and Phenomenological Research* 9(2) (1948), 316-321; Giovanni Maddalena, "The Limits of Experience: Dewey and Contemporary American Philosophy", *Quaestio* 4(4) (2004), 387-406; John J. Stuhr, *Experience as Activity: Dewey's Metaphysics.* Ph.D. Dissertation, Vanderbilt University (1976); Stuhr, "Dewey's Reconstruction of Metaphysics", *Transactions of the Charles S. Peirce Society* 28 (2) (1992), 161-176; E. J. Tiles, "Dewey's Realism: Applying

gap in the literature can be due to the fact that fact that 'semiotics' is usually associated with the work of Charles S. Peirce rather than Dewey, and that Dewey never developed a general theory of signs. The aim of this chapter is to introduce a *semiotic reading of Dewey's theory of experience* through the key notion of *indexical existence*. I believe that this reading can shed new light on Dewey's theory of experience as "interaction" or "transaction" (LW16:4-294) and on the metaphysics implied in it. In particular, if we take the problems of semantics and metaphysics as relevant for a Deweyan understanding of experience (against e.g. Rorty[2]), the notion of indexical existence proves to be not only heuristically fruitful, but also theoretically indispensable in order to make sense of a series of theses present in Dewey's work, including the non-fixism and pluralism of metaphysics, the continuity of inquiry, and the 'logical' nature of substances. Therefore, the reconstruction that I present here is an attempt to dig out the semiotic spirit already present in Dewey more than the introduction of external semiotic elements into Dewey's philosophy.

As evidenced by recent scholarship on Dewey, in order to grasp the meaning of Dewey's project, a new confrontation with the way pragmatism deals with realism and constructivism is necessary.[3]

---

the Term 'Mental' to a World without Withins", *Transactions of the Charles S. Peirce Society* 31(1) (1995), 137-166.

2   Richard Rorty, *Consequences of Pragmatism* (University of Minnesota Press, 1997), pp. 72-89.

3   For instance, *John Dewey between Pragmatism and Constructivism*, ed. by Larry A. Hickman, Stefan Neubert, and Kersten Reich (New York: Fordham University Press, 2009). Some scholars have dwelt more or less explicitly with the problem of constructivism in Dewey: Tom Burke, "Prospects for Mathematizing Dewey's Logical Theory", In *Dewey's Logical Theory. New Studies and Interpretations*, ed. by Tom Burke, Micah D. Hester, Robert B. Talisse (Nashville: Vanderbilt University Press, 2002), 121-159 (pp. 150-151); Gordon H. Clark, *Dewey* (Philadelphia: Presbyterian and Reformed Publishing Company, 1960), pp. 42-43; George Dicker, "John Dewey on the Object of Knowledge", *Transactions of the Charles S. Peirce Society* 8(3) (1972), 152-166 (pp. 152-153); David L. Hildebrand, *Beyond Realism and Anti-Realism: John Dewey and the Neopragmatists* (Vanderbilt University Press, 2003), p. 60; Douglas McDermid, *The Varieties of Pragmatism: Truth, Realism,*

Ideally, such confrontation would cast new light also on the way the pragmatist project as a whole should be interpreted. As it is known, the endeavor of American pragmatism is motivated since its very origin by a constant need for redefining its nature, its limits, and its goals. The aim of the present chapter is to contribute directly to the ongoing renewed attempt at understanding the specificity of Dewey's philosophy and, indirectly, at understanding pragmatism's overall metaphysical project. I will suggest that one of the best interpretative keys available to us is that of semiotics: Dewey's pragmatist metaphysics of experience is, at the bottom, a *genealogical and developmental metaphysics of signs.*[4] Thus, in this

---

and Knowledge from James to Rorty (London and New York: Continuum, 2006), p. 46 and pp. 82-83; Arthur E. Murphy, "Dewey's Epistemology and Metaphysics", in *The Philosophy of John Dewey*, ed. by Paul A. Schilpp (New York: Tudor Publishing Company, 1951), p. 205; Donald A. Piatt, "Dewey's Logical Theory", *The Philosophy of John Dewey*, ed. by Paul A. Schilpp (New York: Tudor Publishing Company, 1951), p. 126; Sandra B. Rosenthal, "The Pragmatic Reconstruction of Realism: A Pathway for the Future", In *Pragmatic Naturalism and Realism*, ed. by John R. Shook (Amherst NY: Prometheus Books, 2003), 43-53 (p. 46); John Ryder, "Reconciling Pragmatism and Naturalism", in *Pragmatic Naturalism and Realism*, ed. by John R. Shook (Amherst NY: Prometheus Books, 2003), 55-77 (p. 61); John R. Shook, "Dewey and Quine on the Logic of What There Is", In *Dewey's Logical Theory. New Studies and Interpretations*, ed. by Tom Burke, Micah D. Hester, Robert B. Talisse (Nashville: Vanderbilt University Press, 2002), 93-118 (p. 101); Beatrice Zedler, "Dewey's Theory of Knowledge", in *John Dewey: His Thought and Influence*, ed. by John Blewett (New York: Fordham University Press, 1960), p. 78.

4   This semiotic interpretative hypothesis would in particular bring Peirce's and Dewey's pragmatism closer. However, some qualifications are necessary. First, my interpretation does not claim that Dewey developed a general theory of semiotics, as Peirce did; only it maintains that a recovery of Dewey's metaphysics, sensitive to the realism-constructivism debate and to the general project of pragmatism, would benefit from a closer engagement with the semiotic notions *already present* in Dewey. Second, the semiotic interpretation does not aim at denying the profound differences between Peirce and Dewey, concerning especially the normative nature of logic and the nominalism-realism controversy in metaphysics.

chapter I try to fill in the gap in the literature about the role that semiotics plays in Dewey's metaphysics. While I believe that the present research has implications for understanding the project of pragmatism as a whole, I will not develop this 'semiotic portrait' of pragmatist metaphysics here. What I will do is providing a first step in the direction of a semiotic interpretation of *Dewey's* metaphysics of experience and inquiry.

Peter Godfrey-Smith[5] has argued that Dewey's pragmatism constitutes an alternative to the traditional forms of realism and constructivism because it attempts to articulate a metaphysics from the point of view of the "intelligent control" of events, which is neither mere representation nor pure invention. My interpretation attempts to push this line of thought further by showing that the intelligent control of experience is for Dewey always *an affair of signs*.

I proceed as follows. In §2 I build on Dewey's essay "Appearing and Appearance" and I introduce the notions of mere appearance, settled sign, and indexical existence. In §3 I present the related notion of indexical residuum, necessary to complete a reinterpretation of Dewey's theory of inquiry in semiotic terms. These two sections contain the groundwork for the entire semiotic reinterpretation of Dewey's metaphysics. The picture emerging from the analyses there contained is that Dewey's pragmatist metaphysics of experience is, as already mentioned, a genealogical and developmental metaphysics of signs. Finally, in §4 I draw some conclusions for a Deweyan semiotic metaphysics of substances.

2. *Appearances, Indexical Existence, and Semiotic Properties*

A possible justification for the use of the composed expression 'indexical existence' can be found in the forgotten essay "Appearing and Appearance" (LW3:55-72). In this essay, Dewey, in order to clarify the purport of his theory of experience, distinguishes and

---

5   Peter Godfrey-Smith, "Dewey and the Question of Realism", *Noûs* 50 (1) (2016), 73-89.

clarifies three different notions of "appearance." For this reason, this text is fundamental for an adequate understanding of his approach to semantics and metaphysics. The three notions of appearance analyzed by Dewey are the following:

(1) Appearance 1, a *mere physical existential interaction* between the perceptual apparatus of the human organism and environing conditions. Dewey calls this modality of appearance "appearing" or "coming into view" (LW3:56).

(2) Appearance 2, *a sign settled in its semiotic capacity*. Dewey calls this modality of appearance "manifestation," "exhibition," "revelation," "representation" (LW3:58), "display" or "expression" (LW3:70).

(3) Appearance 3, or *indexical existence*, that is, an existential interaction which is no more a mere physical existential interaction and not yet a sign settled in its specific semiotic function. Dewey refers to it as an "index" subject to inquiry (LW3: 62-63; 70).

The first meaning of the notion of appearance simply refers to the event of interaction between the organic perceptual structures of an agent and her environing conditions (LW3: 56-57). Let us call this first type of appearance 'mere appearance.' Mere appearance is a temporal event that has the form of an existential interaction between perceptual organic structures and extra-organic conditions due to which something becomes "emphatically realized" in the perceptive capacity of an organism. At this level, a purely physical description is suitable to account for the nature of the phenomenon. The first point to stress here is that this existential interaction does not have the nature of a "mental," "intentional," or "epistemic" relation between a subject and an object, taking "mental" and "epistemic" to mean, in a first approximation, something related to activities of inquiry and knowledge (LW3:57). With regard to this point, some scholars have addressed the problem of Dewey's consideration of realism and idealism.[6] What is important to stress here is that according

---

6   (Boisvert, *Dewey's Metaphysics*; Tiles, *Dewey*, pp. 130-153; Tiles, "Dewey's Realism"). Hildebrand (*Beyond Realism and Anti-Realism*) in

to Dewey, since the epistemological philosophies, including the forms of realism and idealism he criticizes, take appearance to be immediately dependent upon a "mind" or a "consciousness," appearance is uncritically interpreted as a mental state or as an external reality modified by the mind. On the contrary, Dewey points out that an appearance in the sense of mere appearance only refers to the actual existence of something in the external environment in relation to the perceptual apparatus of the human organism. This relation is "physical," not cognitive. As such, mere appearance is not an instance of knowledge (taking knowledge to mean both a present process of inquiry or the beliefs acquired through past inquiries) but only the *condition* for knowledge.

On Dewey's view, mere appearance is already a dimension of experience, although a primitive and undeveloped one. "Existences are immediately given in experience; that is what experience primarily is" (LW12:514). But mere appearance is right from the start "entering into more complex relationships" (LW3:57) than the relationships that constitute a phenomenon as a mere physical interaction. This means that mere appearance *tends to become* an object of intellectual interest and inquiry (LW3:60). As such, the existential interaction is susceptible of becoming "problematic" and can be intellectually "challenged" by the agent. When mere appearance becomes an object of such an intellectual interest, the existential interaction becomes a *potential sign*, the potential evidential basis for something else. In this sense, it is an *indexical existence* (LW3:70). It is neither a mere physical existential interaction anymore (mere appearance), nor a settled sign (what I have provisionally called appearance 2). At that moment, it is still something "*to be* known" (LW3:57) instead of something already known. The task of inquiry is turning "final" physical existences into "means" for grounded inferences, that is, into *settled signs*. Appearances 2 are settled signs.

Any mere appearance is as real as any other event in the world and stands on the same level as every other, since its ontological

---

particular deals with Dewey's "pragmatic realism," "naïve realism" (MW6:105 ff.; LW14:81), "technology" (LW15:88), and his mature rejection of New Realism, Critical Realism, and idealism.

nature is that of an interaction among physical conditions. Therefore, the problem is not establishing which one among different mere appearances is more "real," but distinguishing among them on the basis of the different semiotic and evidential functions they perform ("what is the *better sign* of ... ?", LW3:69-70). Thus, the opposition real/unreal is not the best conceptual tool to sort out the universe of our appearances; instead, we should appeal to the criterion of *semiotic fruitfulness*. The notion of reality is dependent upon that of semiotic fruitfulness. A certain mere appearance is a better sign for a certain inference, while a different mere appearance of the same existent can be a better sign for a different inference. *It is at this level of experience or in this intellectual context that the question of truth and falsity emerges as the problem of the right or wrong inferences that can be performed on the basis of X* (LW3:59-60).

However, the key to grasp Dewey's semiotic understanding of experience is what I have introduced as appearance 3, which corresponds to *indexical existence*. When a mere appearance becomes a problematic presence and is intellectually "challenged" by an inquirer, it becomes a potential sign, namely, it becomes a X or an indexical existence in experience. Such appearance is not a mere existence anymore, since it is now an object of intellectual attention and has the possibility of acquiring a determinate semiotic property by becoming the settled sign of something else. X, the indexical existence, is a *sign in the making*. Although it is not a settled sign yet, X has acquired nevertheless a property "additive" to the mere physical existence as a consequence of the "reflexive relationship" it now has to the inquirer (LW3:62). As such, X "sets a problem to be inquired to" (LW3:70) rather than an existent with a settled semiotic capacity. Dewey writes:

> The nub of the whole matter turns upon the nature of the reflexive relationship, the relation which an appearing object in its intrinsic qualities [appearance 1] bears to the properties that capacitate it to be a sign of something else. That the appearing object is *in* evidence is a truism; the statement is tautologous. But *of* what is it evidence? The latter question introduces a distinction *within* the thing used as a sign, a reflexive relation. That the relation to something else involved in being a sign of it is reflected into the appearing object itself is obvious from

the fact that we take things as signs when we do not know *of* what they
are signs. This happens in every inquiry, since inquiry implies first that
some appearing object is a sign, and secondly that we do not as yet
know of what it is a sign or evidence. This mode of taking would be
impossible unless there were a distinction and relation set up with the
appearing object between itself in its primary qualities and itself in its
signifying office. ... Relationships react into the thing used as symbol
to redetermine its *prior* estate. (LW3:62-63)

This shift in the function of the appearance, from mere physical
existential interaction in mere appearance to indexical existence in
the intermediate case of appearance, is expressed by the possibility
of *labeling X with an indexical term*, such as proper names and
demonstrative terms.[7] X is still an empty sign, a mere *"this* pointing
at ..." with a blank space. Nevertheless, for Dewey, pure denotative
terms and propositions with no descriptive content at all do not occur
in discourse.[8] Denotative terms always have a *minimum of descriptive
content*, even only as a consequence of a hypothetical and extremely
vague classification. The logical theories that claim that *"this"* can be
purely denotative assume a perspective that abstracts from specific
inquiries and that overlooks the fact that in a real inquiry the singular
referred to by the demonstrative is always the product of a "selective
discrimination" (see LW12:363-364). Although X is still a sign in
the making and does not allow for a highly specific classification, X,
as an actual object of inquiry, is at least classifiable as a possibility
of future highly specific classification. Continuity of experience
and inquiry make the presence of a mere denotative reference
impossible. At least in the sense of the possibility of classification
that eventually results from an inquiry, every denotative term has a
minimum of descriptive content.

The result of inquiry is "knowledge" in its honorific sense
(LW12:146), "belief," or "warranted assertibility" (see LW12:14-

---

7   In this sense, the idea of indexical existence as denoted by indices is close
     to Peirce's notions of "substance," "IT," or "present in general" in "On a
     New List of Categories."
8   It is Dewey's conviction that a purely denotative term does not occur in
     discourse (LW12:240-242), so that, using Peirce's jargon, rhematic
     indexical legisigns are not possible.

15) about X. These three expressions are synonyms for Dewey. The conclusion of an inquiry takes the form of a classification of X as a certain "kind," that is, the transformation of X as indexical existence into a settled sign (an appearance 2). Its semiotic function is settled, so that X has become a "sign of Z" and is classified more or less immediately as an object A. This classification of X is more or less circumscribed in its spatio-temporal conditions and more or less certain according to the level of justification of the conclusion.

At this point, Dewey's distinction between the logical notions of "quality," "characteristic" and "property" is fundamental (LW12:291-292). The same statement 'X is generous' can be interpreted in many different ways according to the different logical force it can have in different contexts of experience. Limiting our analysis to the case of the propositions produced within a process of inquiry, 'X is generous' can mean X is acting in a generous way here and now, or X acted in a generous way at some point in the past, or X will act in a generous way at some point in the future. In this case, the proposition is a *particular proposition* and the predicate is a *quality*, that is, the observation of a particular change of X as an isolated event. The predicate does not stand for a kind. However, the same statement can have a different logical force, on the basis not only of how we are using the proposition but also of our experience about X. X, as enabling "reasonably safe" inferences about certain consequences if certain conditions C occur, can be characterized as 'generous,' where 'generous' means now a kind. In this case, the proposition is a *singular proposition*: X is a specimen of a *kind* and the predicate stands for a general disposition or way of behaving instead of a simple punctual change. Further experience and knowledge about X provide the statement 'X is generous' with further logical force. The predicate 'generous' becomes a property when it is determined by implicit (but which can be made explicit) knowledge about both the positive and the negative conditions on which certain consequences would follow from X. In this case, the proposition is always singular but the predicate has a stronger logical force, since it stands for the possibility of better and more precise inferences about X. Only in this last case does the predicate denote a *universal* (LW12:351; see "abstraction" in LW1: 106; LW4:191).

Sometimes Dewey, in speaking about the content of a belief, refers to "objects" as distinct from "events" (LW1:132; 244-246; see also "things" and "characters" as distinct from mere "entities," MW3:83).[9] In this sense, an object is the reference of a settled sign, while an event is a mere appearance. It is necessary to remark upon the notion of object present in Dewey's later works because fundamental studies on this topic do not provide a sufficiently subtle account of the notion.[10] For instance, Gale writes that "the nature of objects is determined by what they are experienced as." It seems clear that, if left without qualification, this Deweyan statement could be easily read as a declaration of subjective idealism. The need for an interpretation of these statements based on the semiotic framework just provided is therefore clear. The semiotic reconstruction of Dewey's metaphysical theory of inquiry, in fact, shows how Dewey can strike a balance between realism and idealism precisely because his fundamental notions ("appearance," "property," "object," etc.) are *semiotic*. In other words, as *successful signs require both groundedness in pre-inquiry conditions and human creativity in inquiry*, a Deweyan account of the *genesis and development of signs in inquiry*, such as the one I am developing now, represents a privileged access to Dewey's metaphysics as a whole, which is neither realistic, nor idealistic.

According to Dewey, X has become an "object" insofar as X is a more or less settled sign established through past inquiries. As such, X has acquired a semiotic and semantic structure and has undergone therefore a *real* change. It is an X classified as this or that kind

---

9   For a different notion of "event," see LW12:222. The move from index to "object" is restated in Dewey's link between "objects" and "data" (LW4:79-80). For Dewey's account of the passage from an "event" to an "object," see LW1:244-245.

10   Raymond D. Boisvert, *Dewey's Metaphysics* (New York: Fordham University Press, 1988), p. 85; George Dicker, "Knowing and Coming-To-Know in John Dewey's Theory of Knowledge", *The Monist* 57(2) (1973), 191-219 (pp. 152-153; p. 158); Richard M. Gale, *John Dewey's Quest for Unity: The Journey of a Promethean Mystic* (Amherst NY: Prometheus Book, 2010), p. 127; Frank X. Ryan, "Primary Experience as Settled Meaning. Dewey's Conception of Experience", *Philosophy Today* 38 (1) (1994), 29-42.

when this classification is the content of a "grounded" judgment. The semiotic property of X "being a sign of Y" is a real property that "accrues" to X as any other property in consequence of certain events, in this case, a successful inquiry. Dewey's strategy, then, is to show that we should not resist including semiotic properties within our ontology. As *signs* are generated, developed, and settled through inquiry, so also (part of) *reality* is. No "*object* of knowledge" can be pre-existent to a successful inquiry (LW1:124-125). Again, such statement becomes crystal-clear if "object" is given a semiotic interpretation. What is "antecedent" to inquiry is not the object of knowledge, but the *conditions of the object of knowledge*, since inquiry necessarily "transforms" those antecedent conditions (LW14:62). The generic potentiality to become *a sign* inscribed in these conditions is what Dewey calls the "transition toward experience" (see "Reality as Experience"). What is pre-existent also has the potentiality of becoming *this* or *that* type of *sign*, a "sign of Y." When X is instituted as a sign with a specific referent, this new semiotic function becomes as real as any other artifact (e.g., LW1:108; 147). What is 'artificial' here, namely, what is dependent on human intervention, is not the given condition that X has the potentiality of becoming a "sign of Y" but the fact that X at a certain point actually becomes a "sign of Y" in the field of human practices and by virtue of human inquiry. An "object" is *always* a social object, a human institution, not because it is constructed as such but because its capacity of acquiring a semiotic property is only actualized through social practices of organization. The acquisition of this new semiotic property by X "marks a stage in the history of [the existential interaction X] ... owing to varied relations to other things" (LW3:57), in particular to the inquirer. It is now clear that for Dewey a semiotic function is a new property that really accrues to an existential interaction: it becomes part of the existential interaction's ontological constitution, and it is not something psychic or mentalistic.

This is the crux of what Dewey calls the "incorporation of the physical environment in the cultural" (LW12:48-49). When the inference is completed in the categorical assertion of an object, both the appearing (perceived) thing which has been employed as a sign and the inferred (intelligible) object lose the isolation they possess during the process of inquiry and delayed inference. They both become members of an interrelated inclusive whole, so that the category of "manifestation" becomes applicable (LW3:66-67). X is part of a "whole" not as a member is part of a class, but as an individual is an instance of a kind, a *"this"* which is a case or representative of a kind (LW12:292). In recognition, X is almost immediately classified as a kind, where immediately means that the classification is substantially a-problematic and does not require a process of inquiry.

3. *Inquiry, Acquaintance, and Indexical Residuum*

According to Dewey, the "problematic" character of a situation and the intellectual character of an experience are directly proportional to the "focal" role that an indexical existence has for the inquirer. Although Dewey scholars have dwelt have dwelt with the issue of inquiry in great depth[11], nobody has highlighted the

---

11   Thomas M. Alexander, "Dewey and the Metaphysical Imagination", *Transactions of the Charles S. Peirce Society* 28 (2) (1992), 203-215; Boisvert, *Dewey's Metaphysics*; Tom Burke, *Dewey's New Logic: A Reply to Russell* (Chicago: The University of Chicago Press, 1994); Burke, Hester, and Talisse, *Dewey's Logical Theory*; Frega, *John Dewey et la philosophie*; Frega, *Pensée, expérience, pratique*; Richard M. Gale, "The Problem of Ineffability in Dewey's Theory of Inquiry", *The Southern Journal of Philosophy* 44 (1) (2006), 75-90; Gale, *John Dewey's Quest*, pp. 29-42; pp. 61-87; Larry A. Hickman, "Contextualizing Knowledge: A Reply to "Dewey and the Theory of Knowledge", *Transactions of the Charles S. Peirce Society* 26 (4) (1990), 459-463; Hickman, *John Dewey's Pragmatic Technology* (Bllomington: Indiana University Press, 1990); Isaac Levi, "Dewey's Logic of Inquiry", in *The Cambridge Companion to John Dewey*, ed. by Molly Cochran (Cambridge: Cambridge University Press, 2010), 80-100; Henry C. Lu, "The Goal of Inquiry in Dewey's Philosophy", *Education Theory* 20 (1) (1970), 65-72; Joseph Margolis, "The Relevance of Dewey's Epistemology", in *New Studies in the Philosophy of John Dewey*, ed. by Steven M. Cahn (Hanover N.H.: The University of New England, 1977), 117-148; Scott L. Pratt, "Inquiry and Analysis: Dewey and Russell on Philosophy", *Studies in Philosophy and*

connection between problematic situation and focus on indexical existence. The crux of Dewey's theory of inquiry is expressed in the definition found in *Logic* and in many other texts. It reads: "Inquiry is the controlled or directed transformation of an indeterminate situation into one that is so determinate in its constituent distinctions and relations as to convert the elements of the original situation into a unified whole" (LW12:108). A likely objection addressed to this theory is that it reduces the process of thinking to a process deterministically or causally initiated by external environmental conditions. This criticism is sometimes parallel to criticisms of Peirce's theory regarding the origin of inquiry and the fixation of belief, as the "need" to remove the irritation of doubt expressed in "The Fixation" would prove. The usual response to this criticism is that, far from being hetero-determined, Dewey's concept of inquiry aims to highlight the fact that thinking is not intrinsically separated from non-linguistic and non-conceptual modalities of experience and behavior. Furthermore, the inquisitive process is not identifiable with psychical events but is essentially related to processes of concrete experimentation, manipulation and direction of the environing conditions, starting from organic perception (e.g. LW4, Ch.4; LW12:41). A "naturalistic" theory of thinking implies that no occult power of knowledge, in principle inaccessible to public consideration, can be admitted as a legitimate part of the theory (LW12:26). Accordingly, standard interpretations also stress the active and purposive role of the inquirer in this process. The stress of the purposive role of the inquirer goes together with Dewey's struggle to uproot the general picture of "epistemological" philosophies that the knower is a mirroring passive mind of a ready-made world. The importance of this point is that the purposive activity of the inquirer *can choose to focus on existential phenomena that have not been intellectually challenged yet, or aspects of the*

Education 17(2) (1998), 101-122; Melvin L. Rogers, "Action and Inquiry in Dewey's Philosophy", *Transactions of the Charles S. Peirce Society* 43 (1) (2007), 90-115; Ralph W. Sleeper, *The Necessity of Pragmatism: John Dewey's Conception of Philosophy* (New Haven: Yale University Press, 1986).

"objects" of experience that still have to be studied. This is a large part of the activity of scientific research. Dewey says:

> The remarkable difference between the attitude which accepts the objects of ordinary perception, use and enjoyment as final, as culmination of natural processes and that which takes them as starting points for reflection and investigation, is one which reaches far beyond the technicalities of science. It marks a revolution in the whole spirit of life, in the entire attitude taken toward whatever is found in existence. When the things which exist around us, which we touch, see, hear and taste are regarded as interrogations for which an answer must be sought (and must be sought by means of deliberate introduction of changes till they are reshaped into something different), nature as it already exists ceases to be something which must be accepted and submitted to, endured or enjoyed, just as it is. It is now something to be modified, to be intentionally controlled. It is material to act upon so as to transform it into new objects which better answer our needs. Nature as it exists at any particular time is a challenge, rather then a completion; it provides possible starting points and opportunities rather than final ends. (LW4:80-81)

What I want to suggest in the present section is that the nature of the Deweyan "problematic situation" can be better understood if seen in semiotic terms, especially through the notion of indexical existence and the related notion of *indexical residuum*. As I have indicated, indexical existence is a twofold notion: it carries within it both the pre-inquiry conditions and the constructive nature of reality, which represent well Dewey's alternative to both realism and idealism. Accordingly, I want to propose that a situation becomes problematic when indexical existence acquires an emphatic presence in experience. A problematic situation is a transactional moment in experience when *the possibility or the need (or both) for new signs becomes evident.* It is not always easy to see what philosophical resources Dewey has to justify the fact that, *given a world of settled objects*, there is always more and more to discover, new objects to think, new signs to develop. Does the construction of new objects cut the bridges with what was known before? If not, what allows inquiry to be truly continuous? I suggest that an answer to this problem is given by the presence of indexicals in experience. The continuity of experience and inquiry, then, finds in the semiotic idea of indexicality its pivotal point – or at least this is what I am going to claim.

The "problem" which originates within a situation and around which inquiry develops is always constituted by the *presence in experience of an indexical existence*. The condition of this presence is not sometimes there and sometimes not. As the quotation on scientific activity and the many passages on purposive experimentation in *The Quest for Certainty* show, reality can always become an object of study, inquiry and discovery, so that it can always become problematic. It is true that there are dimensions of experience (or different *individual* experiences) where the overarching quality is not determining a full inquiry. However, this fact only shows that there is a gradation in experience that ranges from contexts in which the focus is entirely about inquiry and contexts in which inquiry or intellectual activity are extremely limited and only functional to practical and volitional uses. *When the focus is on the indexical existence X as such, then we have a genuine problematic situation, whereas when the focus on indexical aspects of what "appears" in experience (in the sense of appearance 2) is overlooked for the most part, the intellectual aspect of activity becomes secondary and subordinated.* The purposive mediation of the inquirer does not rule out the fact that in a certain sense the "problem" characterizing a situation is given in an individual quality and that it regulates the development of inquiry teleologically. On the contrary, it only means that reflection is always a matter of "selective emphasis" (LW1:31).

There are modalities of experience different from those of inquiry in a strict sense. These are:

(1) "Recognition" (LW1:154-155; 247) or "apprehension" (LW12:146-147) or "identification" or educated perception of X (LW1:144).
(2) Practical and volitional use of X.
(3) Affective focal experience of X.
(4) Esthetic fruition of a meaning (theoretical contemplation).[12]

---

12   E.g. LW1:102; 249 ff.; LW12:64.

These modalities of experience are usually taken to be cases of "immediate knowledge" (LW1:35; LW12:142-143; 154, LW14:12). On the contrary, according to Dewey, these are all "non-cognitive" modalities of experience, resulting from past successful experiences and inquiries. It is important to stress that the term "non-cognitive" in Dewey's vocabulary does not have the same meaning it has assumed in contemporary metaethical debates, in which cognitive and non-cognitive ethics are distinguished according to the epistemic status of moral judgments and the ontological status of moral values. It does not even refer to Quine's understanding of non-physical languages as non-cognitive. For Dewey, a modality of experience is non-cognitive insofar as it is different from "inquiry," "reflection" and "intelligence" properly taken. In semiotic terms, this means that a modality of experience is non-cognitive *when it does not promote the birth of new signs.* (1), (2), (3) and (4) are all forms of "acquaintances" with the objects of the world and not stages in experience in which the overarching quality is asking for or directing the solution of a problem (LW1:154; 248-249). In general, acquaintance means "knowing *how* to make appropriate active responses to an event" (LW15:31). It means "intimate connection with emotion and ability to act" (LW12:154). Therefore, the property "… is non-cognitive" refers to a modality of experience in which the focus is not at all or is only minimally about an indexical existent. These types of experiences and their objects, "immediate empirical things," are always the "endings of natural histories" (LW1:110). In the case of a mere appearances, these histories are only physical and physiological events that eventually become indexes when they are intellectually challenged. In the case of settled signs, or "objects," which are the result of past experiences, the histories involved are not only conditioned by physical events, but they are also already histories of past successful inquiries, judgments and semantic syntheses. In the former case, we have something like a pure indexical existence, while in the latter case we have structured objects characterized by what we might call *indexical residuum.* As some scholars have pointed out[13],

---

13   Gregory F. Pappas, *John Dewey's Ethics: Democracy as Experience*
      (Bloomington: Indiana University Press, 2008), p. 35; Hildebrand,

the main difference between Deweyan pragmatism and contemporary neopragmatism is the fact that for Dewey experience is not linguistic all the way through and that no matter how the organism is developed in its habits and functions in grasping "objects," there is always more in experience than our classification and semantic skills, linguistic or not. This becomes philosophically poignant when this experiential phenomenon is traced back to the ontological and semiotic nature of the indexical existence in experience, either in the form of a pure indexicality or in that of an indexical residuum. *While not wholly linguistic, Deweyan experience is semiotic through and through.*

The reality of an indexical residuum is shown in Dewey's understanding of the "intension" of a demonstrative term (or a proper name and in general an indexical expression). Dewey claims that proper names, pronouns, demonstrative and indexical terms in general are "inexhaustible in their meaning in intension." (LW 12:364) I have already shown that according to Dewey a pure demonstrative term is impossible, since in the continuity of experience and inquiry a demonstrative term always has a minimum of descriptive content. In dealing with the intension of a demonstrative, Dewey writes:

> What is demonstratively denoted by a proper name is inexhaustible in its meaning in intension, instead of being lacking in all such meaning. Take London, England, for example, as a conventional mark enabling a singular object to be the subject of discourse and inquiry. Its meaning in intension is first of all topographical, but it extends far beyond physical location and area. Its meaning in intension is historic, political, cultural; it includes a past, a present and potentialities not yet realized. What is true of its intension is that it cannot be completely circumscribed at any given time by any set of descriptive qualifications; i.e., its meaning in intension is inexhaustible. The same statement holds in principle of any singular term, for such a term denotes a spatio-temporal career. (LW 12:364)

Beyond Realism and Anti-Realism; Richard Shusterman, "Dewey on Experience: Foundation or Reconstruction?", in *Dewey Reconfigured: Essays on Deweyan Pragmatism*, ed. by Casey Haskins and David I. Seiple (Albany: State University of New York Press, 1999), 193-219.

The notion of intension can only be understood in relation to the notions of extension and comprehension, insofar as intension refers to the property of a term in denoting a singular or an individual, while extension and comprehension denote or designate kinds (LW12:357-360; 364). The "extension" of a term is the property of a term that refers to kinds instead of singulars and designates all the kinds that are included or might be included in that term. In the case of the term "ship," "the extension is simply and strictly the *kinds* of ship that exist or have existed or will exist." The comprehension of a term is the necessary conceptual content of an "abstract universal" once it becomes more determinate, so that it coincides with the "definition" of that term. In the case of the term triangle, its comprehension is e.g. "right-angled," "scalene" and "isosceles." The notion of intension instead refers to the property of a term as denoting a singular or individual indexical existent *in all its possible meanings*, classifications or kinds, already developed or yet to be developed. In this sense, a proper name, a pronoun, a demonstrative and in general all the other indices (like "here" and "now") in denoting a singular or individual existential indexical are "inexhaustible in their meaning in intension." This means that the same X not only is susceptible at present of different classifications, but also that it can always be developed into new classifications on the basis of new inquiries. In other words, the same X can support different "kinds," "objects" and semiotic properties. We can appreciate here how also Dewey's *pluralism* in metaphysics can be ultimately grounded in his semiotic theory of inquiry. The classification of an X through a "kind" and reference to it through a demonstrative term can be both delimiting and widening in different respects (LW12:292). Insofar as the potential meaningfulness of X is at stake, the intension of a demonstrative term is the "full qualitative existence," namely, X in all its potentiality as an object or a sign, so that *its intension is more ample than any actual classification as this or that kind*. In this respect, intension represents widening while classification represents limitation. However, as a mere indexical existent, X is not an object or a sign yet. In this sense, its semiotic and logical force or functionality is only potential and ineffective. The "determination of a singular as one of a kind involves a limitation of *this*," but at the same time establishes the effective power of drawing from X certain inferences. In this respect, intension represents limitation while classification represents widening.

If it is true that a demonstrative reference is inexhaustible in its meaning in intension (although it is not such in its extension and in its comprehension), it follows that every modality of experience, including (1), (2), (3) and (4), *always includes an indexical residuum which can demand a certain amount of intellectual activity*, although minimum. "A singular as a mere *this*," says Dewey, "always sets a problem" (LW12:249).

In *Experience and Nature* (LW1:233; 261) Dewey addresses the issue of intellectual activity in establishing a connection between reflection and "redirection of meanings." The points in experience in which a redirection of meanings is required are different instances of focal "conscious" activity. "Consciousness, an idea, is that phase of a system of meanings which at a given time is undergoing re-direction, transitive transformation" (LW1:233). "Consciousness" is taken here as a logical notion rather than a mere psychological or physiological notion. Although the moment of maximum focal consciousness is represented by an inquiry, it is true that (1), (2), (3) and (4) represent instances of conscious activity in their own right, distributed along a scale or gradation. This is to say, conscious activity in "acquaintance" ranges from (a) focal consciousness as educated perception of "objects" (minimum of intellectual activity, intellectual properties (like explicit signification, LW1:237) and problems), (b) through all the other different non-cognitive modalities of experience (see LW1:240), to (c) focal consciousness in inquiry (maximum of intellectual activity, intellectual properties and problems).[14] The point is that all these forms of experience, (1), (2), (3) and (4), are forms of *contextual inferences* and *new semantic syntheses*, although these operations are not comparable to implication and rational discourse (LW1:250) and have more the nature of a contextual application (LW12:375) of old regulative semantic commitments rather than of the judgment that brings a new problem to a new conclusion. What characterizes the first three cases

---

14 See LW1:230 ff.

of acquaintance is a minimum of intellectual or cognitive activity. In these cases, intellectual activity is given by the need for application of different regulative semantic commitments to Xs, in which case a minimum of semantic synthesis, or "redirection of meaning," is needed. This dynamic is well expressed in the following passage:

> "This," whatever *this* may be, always implies a system of meanings focused at a point of stress, uncertainty, and need of regulation. It sums up history, and at the same time opens a new page; it is record and promise in one; a fulfillment and an opportunity. It is a fruition of what has happened and a transitive agency of what is to happen. It is a comment written by natural events on their own direction and tendency, and a surmise of whither they are leading. Every perception or awareness, marks a "this," and every "this" being a consummation involves retention, and hence contains the capacity of remembering. Every "this" is transitive, momentarily becoming a "that." In its movement it is, therefore, conditioning of what is to come; it presents the potentiality of foresight and prediction. (LW1:264-265)

However, case (4), "contemplation" (LW1:249 ff.; 262) seems to have a different status. It seems that it is the form in which intellectual activity is almost absent. This is because in theoretical contemplation the role of the indexical is completely isolated, or excluded, while in the first three cases of acquaintance its function, although mostly latent and not prominent, is nevertheless not completely absent. In the case of contemplation, semantic synthesis is the mere repetition of past meanings and associations, while no indexical element is allowed into the process. It is an intellectual and repetitive manipulation of "self-sufficient objects" (LW1:118). In the context of a theoretical contemplation as such, no genuine intellectual "problem" can arise. This possibility is on the contrary present in the first three cases of acquaintance.

According to Dewey, an existence cannot be reduced to a singular or to a finite multitude of objects. "The same existential events are capable of an infinite number of meanings" (LW1:240). Pluralism is a necessary corollary of Dewey's theory of inquiry because his theory of inquiry has a semiotic nature. In the metaphysical constitution of reality, the indexical, given residuum implicit in every object and the constructive nature of every object are the two wings of the same *pragmatic semiotic realism* that are overlooked by both idealism and presentative realism (LW1:234-235; 241-242; 245). In particular, on the one hand, some of Dewey's arguments against idealism rely on his rejection of the thesis that an event is ultimately a bundle of meanings which lacks indexical residuum. In this sense, Dewey is much closer to Peirce's reclamation of the role of 2ndness in experience against an orthodox Hegelian understanding of it, in which the presence of 3rdess becomes overwhelming. On the other hand, Dewey's refusal of presentative realism consists in rejecting the thesis that perception is intrinsically and immediately cognition of "objects," which would have therefore an "antecedent" reality previous to any form of inquiry.

While there is continuity among the different modalities of experience, there is no sharp distinction or dichotomy between dimensions of experience that play different functions. This is well exemplified in the Deweyan distinction between "primary" and "reflective" experience (e.g., LW1:15-16). All Dewey scholars have virtually dealt with this distinction in Dewey's theory of experience, although only a few in my opinion have grasped its functional import.[15] "Primary" understood in a functional sense refers, first, to the dimension of experience that might result in an inquiry and that is prior to an inquiry, and, second, to the dimension of experience that constitutes the background of an inquiry. As such, it is "had" (LW1:111; 113). What is important here is that something can be "had" as a mere physical interaction (appearance 1), as an indexical existence (appearance 3), or as a semantic structure or "object" (appearance 2). In the third case, "immediately had" means one of the non-cognitive modalities of experience (see 1, 2, 3 and 4) in which the indexical existence or indexical residuum X does not constitute the focus and is at most the focus of operations of application and tends to disappear in (4). In the case of (1), (2), (3), the imperfect reference of regulative semantic commitments to the indexical existence X (appearance 3) is relevant, so that, on the

---

15   Douglas Browning has done this, see his "Dewey and Ortega" 71-72 in
      particular.

one side, they represent borderline cases of intellectual, conscious activity and, on the other side, they can perform the function of "primary" experience and be the starting point of a new process of inquiry, in which intellectual and conscious activity is furthered and becomes maximal (LW1:264-265). In describing his theory of primary and reflective experience, Dewey also characterizes (1), (2), and (3) respectively in relation to their "objects" (LW1:15-16). While primary experience is characterized by a "gross, macroscopic, crude subject-matter," reflective experience is characterized by "refined, derived objects of reflection." Again, these two functional dimensions of experience have to be taken prospectively and can be better understood in relation to the notion of indexical residuum. As a matter of fact, the same "object" can be considered as a case of a gross, macroscopic subject-matter G, or as a refined, derived object R. As an R, the object is the result of past, successful inquiries; as a G, it is the starting point of new inquiries. However, even as a G, the object is *not necessarily absolutely "gross,"* except for the borderline case of a mere appearance. This means that the object of primary experience G is a refined object (settled sign) in the function of becoming the subject-matter of an inquiry because of its indexical residuum. Although G is already an object with a semantic structure, it can be considered "gross" because of its indexical residuum and in relation to the further inquiries which will reflectively shape G into more refined objects (LW1:262).

Therefore, indexicality plays different functions in experience between primary and reflective phases of it: (i) a mere physical event is the potentiality of an indexical existence and of signs (a mere appearance as a potentiality of a settled sign and an indexical existence); (ii) an indexical existent is the possibility of different developed signs (a mere appearance as the potentiality of different settled signs); (iii) a sign is the possibility of further signs because of its indexical residuum (a settled sign is the potentiality of new and different settled signs because of its indexical residuum).

4. Substance, Existential Conditions, and Predication of Kinds

It is now time to move to Dewey's notion of "substance." Some scholars have dwelt with Dewey's theory of substance providing insightful and historically informed analysis of this concept.[16] However, these reconstructions are not conducted in a *semiotic spirit*. Therefore, a new consideration of Dewey's claims on substance is needed, not only to put to test the semiotic-metaphysical framework of the previous sections, but also to prove its fruitfulness. The advantage of a semiotic interpretation of substance is that the notion of substance, *understood as a cluster of settled signs indexically open to new reconstructions*, shows the advantages of both realism and constructivism without including their shortcomings.

One of the most explicit series of statements on substance is in *Logic* (LW12:130-133). The fundamental claim to be unpacked is that "substance" is first and foremost a *logical* notion and not an ontological one. ""Substance" represents ... a logical, not an ontological, determination" (LW12:131). "Logical" refers in this context to the semiotic properties acquired by an X when it is settled as this or that sign or set of signs, and represents therefore a semiotic function. "Substance" is therefore a synonym of "object." "The condition – and the sole condition that has to be satisfied in order that there may be substantiality, is that certain qualifications hang together as dependable signs that certain consequences will follow when certain interactions take place. This is what is meant when it is said that substantiality is a logical, not a primary

---

16   Boisvert, *Dewey's Metaphysics*; Dicker, "John Dewey on the Object"; Burke, *Dewey's New Logic*, p. 59, pp. 81-82, pp. 246-247; Burke, "Prospects for Mathematizing", p. 147; Thomas Gardner, "The Subject Matter of Dewey's Metaphysics", *Transactions of the Charles S. Peirce Society* 36 (3) (2000), 393-405; James W. Garrison, "Dewey on Metaphysics, Meaning and Maps", *Transactions of the Charles S. Peirce Society* 41 (4) (2005), 818-844 (p. 826); Hildebrand, *Beyond Realism and Anti-Realism*, pp. 81-82; John H. Randall Jr., *Nature and Historical Experience* (New York: Columbia University Press, 1958), p. 223, pp. 231-235; Randall, "Substance as Process", *The Review of Metaphysics* 10 (4) (1957), 580-601.

ontological determination" (LW12:131-133). A Deweyan definition
of "substance" would then read:

> Substance: a set of existential factors *used as a warranted sign*
> for sets of stable inferences, predicaments and operations in general;
> similarly, a set of existential factors that would produce certain
> consequences if certain conditions occurred.

In what follows I explain the different components of this definition
in detail. The claim that a substance is first and foremost a semiotic
and semantic structure, a consequence of past experiences and
inquiries, does not deny that this semiotic structure is "warranted"
by the existent conditions that have made inquiries possible and
successful. The birth certificate of a substance is the construction
of a judgment and its conclusive function in inquiry. As an abstract
substance, its locus is the "assertion" ("subject-matter which has
been prepared to be final," LW12:123), while as an actual substance,
it coincides with the "affirmation" or final judgment (LW12:123-
125). In this sense, substances are not original but are a "happy
outcome of a complex history" (LW1:135; see also LW1:143).
In talking about the structure of the judgment, Dewey introduces
the notion of logical substance as the "coherent whole" structured
through inquiry and judgment in a final assertion:

> The subject is existential, either a singular this, or a set of singulars.
> But there are conditions of inquiry which must be satisfied by anything
> taken to be a subject. (1) It must delimit and describe the problem in
> such a way as to indicate a possible solution. (2) It must be such that new
> data, instituted by observational operations directed by the provisional
> predicate (representing a possible solution), will unite with its subject-
> matter to form a coherent whole; and it is capable of incorporating into
> itself other predicated qualifications until it becomes, as such, a unity of
> inter-connected distinctions, or "properties." (LW12:130-131)

The *same* indexical existent X, here taken in the form of the
existential conditions to which the demonstrative refers, is something
that becomes in the course of different completed experiences and
inquiries the *evidential basis* for different inferential predicaments.

The experience of different existential consequences following different manipulations with X shows that X *allows* for different inferences. The "properties" that are taken to reside, cohere, inhere, or be instantiated in an object are in reality the content of conclusions of different warranted inferences drawn on X, of different signs built around X. When I say that the same X is sweet, white, granular etc., I am committing myself to the provisional statement that the same X, when experienced in certain conditions C, will produce the feeling that is called "sweet"; in other conditions C1, it will produce a certain "quality" commonly labeled as "white", etc. Once established as "unified whole," X is treated as an object, "sugar"; it is used and enjoyed as such in daily practices of life and symbolically represented in language and communication. The more complex the interactions in which an X enters and is experienced, the more properties the correspondent substance will contain.

There are at least four reasons why Dewey claims that a substance is first and foremost a logical and not an ontological notion. First, every substance is *selective* of what an X is. As it is clear from the study of Dewey's theory of inquiry, the "data," or the manipulation of the subject-matter of an inquiry, are never "given," but more appropriately "taken" (actualized or "produced" through operations and selected for their contextual logical functional force, LW12:127) on the basis of the needs of the situation and the tasks of inquiries. The "selective emphasis" implied in the process of construction of a substance refers to the "specified functional way" in which an X is settled as consequence of operations of inquiry (LW12:132; see also LW1:31; LW4:191). Selection is due to different reasons such as human structural organic conditions and interests. What X is warranted to be when it is classified as a "substance" or an "object" is always in a certain sense semantically poorer than what X *is* also outside our organizing practices and furthermore of what X *could* be as a sign. Dewey claims that "essence is never existence, and yet it is the essence, the distilled import, of existence" (LW1:143). As I have shown, according to Dewey, the singular denoted by a demonstrative term is inexhaustible in its meaning in intension, so that every classification cannot help but be a semantic demarcation. At the same time, however, a substance instituted as a semiotic structure actualizes some of the potentialities that were unexpressed and latent in X, namely the potentialities of performing this or that semiotic function. Once an event becomes a substance it enters a new phase of its career and gains a "double life" (LW1:132), in such a way that it can be object of "ideal experimentation" beyond the "interaction with crude and raw events" which it has as a mere existent.

The fact that substance has a selective dimension based on the organizing practices performed by human beings does not mean that the existent conditions have no structure in themselves apart from their semiotic life. On the contrary, Dewey denies that

> ... there is or can be any such thing as mere existence – phenomenon unqualified as respects organization and force, whether such phenomenon may be psychic or cosmic. (MW2:333; cf. Sleeper, *The Necessity of Pragmatism*)

Reflection and institution of semiotic properties in X are like the "organic growth" of an experience which is "already organized" and which keeps sustaining the sign-significance relationships among parts of reality. The fact that the existent conditions are already organized, at least as a set of potentialities, and that every singular is inexhaustible in meaning in intension further clarifies the reasons why Dewey stresses his theory of the primary logical purport of the notion of substance. What he wants to claim in saying that the import of substance is not immediately ontological but primarily logical is the fact that, as some other naturalists have made clear (mainly, Randall Jr. and Woodbridge), what an X is as an event and *can* be as a semiotic structure is never reducible to what X *is* presently taken to be as this or that substance.

Second, the status of substantiality is not dependent upon long existential duration in time (LW4:103). A fast event such as lightening has the same substantial character as a mountain. In this sense, Dewey says that a substance has first and foremost "*logical* solidity and endurance" (LW12:133) and not metaphysical endurance in the sense of existential duration in time. A substance is not a durable set of existential conditions, but is the stable relation, fixed through inquiry, between a set of existential factors and given conditions whenever they occur and for the time they occur, and the consequences that follow. When a "transitory event" becomes "subject of scientific judgment," that is, when it becomes a target of warranted predication, enters the condition of substantiality. This is because a substance has primarily a "functional nature." In other words, it refers to the inferential possibility of taking existential conditions as dependable evidential signs of certain consequences, independently from the extension of their temporal endurance. Dewey also claims that in this sense substances can be taken to be "eternal" (LW1:119), although only as dialectical and non-existential objects. Although this claim might bring Dewey close to a nominalist position, the first implication of such a claim is again that substance has first and foremost a logical import and not a direct ontological one. The almost immediate existential transitivity of certain existential conditions is not an objection to the possibility of attributing to them a comprehensive substantial status, which is first and foremost inferential. The substantive character of existential conditions is quite independent from their duration, so that, if an event has a brief existential permanence (e.g., a lightening), this "property" of having a brief duration becomes part of the series of classifications in which the substantiality of X can be expressed.

Third, the existential conditions and the "substances" *really* grow through development of experience and knowledge, in the sense that the semiotic properties instituted in X are *real* properties. *The signs built around X what X has become.* They are real actualization and institutionalization in X of semiotic functions that were only *potential* before. Dewey's tenet is that what grows is not only the agent's set of beliefs and habits about X, but *X itself*, which, as appearance 3, is already the growth of appearance 1 and which in turn can be institutionalized as this or that substance, that is, an appearance 2. In their temporal "career," existential conditions acquire new properties, among which are also semiotic properties. This is because the knowing-relation, understood as inquiry, implies phases of interaction-experimentation on existential conditions. It not only produces new phenomena and actualities, but it also brings about as its conclusion a final reorganization of these existential conditions into new wholes. "Any predications," says Dewey, "is a requalification, or operational means of instituting a requalification, and so involves a change" (LW12: 239-240). The *symbolic predication marks already in itself the emergence of a new property in X as an actualization of its semiotic potentialities.* The new organization produced in the judgment, once verified in the overt action, is not merely "mental" or "psychic," but is the constructive production of a new real artifact at its fundamental level in the form of an institutionalized sign or cluster of signs, that is, a substance. Semiotic properties are at the same time "ideal" (dependent on the constitutive or constructivist agency of man's intelligent behavior) and "real" (they become new real properties of X and are grounded in the potentialities of X of acquiring these new semiotic properties). Semantics is the first step in the human contribution to the real development of the universe.[17] In this sense, Gale's idea that Dewey's "naturalism is at bottom a "humanism" acquires a new specification by the interpretation of substances as clusters of signs. The new substance that emerges from X at *t2* is not entirely new, since the inferential consequences which were previously operable on X at *t1* are still possible. However, the substance at *t2* is not the same substance as that of *t1*, although they are both new phases and developmental stages in the career of X.

Thus, Dewey's opposition to presentative realism and idealism relies on the following considerations. According to Dewey, "knowing is something that happens to things in the natural course of their career, not the sudden introduction of a "unique" non-natural type of relation – that to mind or consciousness" (MW6:121). In the "natural continuity" between *existents* and *knowns*, "things in becoming known undergo a specific and detectable qualitative change" (MW6:121). Accordingly, Dewey denies (1) that the knowing-relation is only a presentative relation of transparency and not a relation of construction and selection (VS. presentative realism); (2) that the semiotic properties fixed in a substance are not the product of a real change undergone by X on the basis of its potentialities and

---

17 On Dewey's evolutionary naturalism as "humanism," see Richard M. Gale, "The Naturalism of John Dewey", in *The Cambridge Companion to John Dewey*, ed. by Molly Cochran (Cambridge: Cambridge University Press, 2010), 55-79.

of real operations of inquiry, but are pre-existent and actual in X and only manifested by inquiry (VS. presentative realism); (3) that reality is ultimately reducible to "objects" and "substances," with no further existential residuum (VS. idealism). In *Logic* (LW12:137), Dewey makes clear that inquiry and judgment produce a temporal reconstruction of their subject-matter. The temporality of inquiry and judgment does not refer to the trivial fact that the act of inquiry and judgment takes time, but that at the beginning *t1* of the process of inquiry, X does not have certain semiotic properties that it has at the successful conclusion of the process of inquiry *t2*.

It is in the light of these considerations that some interpretations of Dewey's constructive side regarding to the notion of substance prove to be inadequate.[18] According to these interpretations, Dewey's notion of "object" has to be understood only in an epistemological and not in an ontological sense. The simplification of these interpretations does not stem from the fact that a "substance" is the semantic structure relative to X, which is the result of a successful inquiry (or series of inquiries) on X, but in the assumption that the acquired semantic structure, that is, the genesis and development of signs, is not something real that has become part of the temporal reality, or "career," of X.[19]

In conclusion, a "substance," explained in its semiotic structure, proves to be a set of existential occurrences which are taken as the sign of the occurrence of other eventual existents on the basis of a constant relation between the first set of occurrences and the second set. All the factors implied in this definition are *something real*, including the semiotic relation, the property of functioning (actually or potentially) as a sign.

---

18   Boisvert, *Dewey's Metaphysics* 87-88; 171; Dicker, "John Dewey on the Object".

19   My position is close to Piatt's reading. It is worth noting that Sleeper, *The Necessity of Pragmatism*, pp. 6-7 sees in Dewey both an Aristotelian and a Kantian legacy.

CHAPTER 5
CAN THOMISM AND PRAGMATISM
COOPERATE?

This chapter explores the possibility of the philosophical cooperation between Thomism and American pragmatism by resurrecting an unjustly forgotten debate between Wilmon Henry Sheldon and Jacques Maritain. The discussion focuses primarily on two topics, the compatibility between a substance and a pragmatist-evolutionary ontology, and the compatibility between the Scholastic and the pragmatist theory of truth. The chapter claims that, if we bring Peirce's version of pragmatism into the picture, the cooperation is not only possible, but also highly desirable.

0. *Introduction*

In 1944, *The Modern Schoolman* published a series of articles in which Wilmon Henry Sheldon and Jacques Maritain discuss to what extent Thomism and American pragmatism can cooperate.[1] Maritain's contribution was later published in his 1952 [1948] *The Range of Reason*.[2] Despite its intricacies, the kernel of the debate could be summarized in the following way: on the one hand, Sheldon claims that the two tradition s are compatible if correctly understood; he also suggests that they ought to cooperate in order to

---

1   Wilmon H. Sheldon, "Can Philosophers Co-Operate?", *The Modern Schoolman* 21 (1944), 71-82; "Can Philosophers Co-Operate?", *The Modern Schoolman* 22 (1944), 131-142; "Professor Maritain on Philosophical Co-Operation", *The Modern Schoolman* 22 (2) (1944), 88-97; Jacques Maritain, "Philosophical Co-Operation and Intellectual Justice", *The Modern Schoolman* 22 (1) (1944), 1-15.
2   Jacques Maritain, *The Range of Reason* (New York: Charles Scribner's Son, 1952), pp. 30-50.

learn from each other; on the other hand, Maritain is more hesitant about endorsing the doctrines of pragmatism and seems to stress the fact that what is good in pragmatism is already contained *in nuce* in the Aristotelian-Thomistic tradition.

Both Sheldon and Maritain take pragmatism to mean roughly the "naturalistic" philosophy of John Dewey. As it clearly appears in Maritain's general remarks about pragmatism, what pragmatism means for him is a form of reductive naturalism, not too different from logical positivism in its insistence on experiments, verification, and scientific-mathematical approach to phenomena. Sheldon agrees with Maritain on the "naturalism" of the tradition of classical pragmatism culminating with Dewey, but he wishes for a new phase in which pragmatism could free itself from its historical boundaries and could finally cooperate with Thomism. In this sense, no matter how "enriched,"[3] both our authors think that classical pragmatism is nothing more than a form of naturalism. There is certainly some truth in this reading. For one, Dewey went as far as giving his philosophical proposal the name of "technology",[4] henceforth strengthening those interpretations that saw in his pragmatism a kind of philosophy completely dependent on the contents and methods of the empirical sciences and their practical applications.

One of the aims of this chapter is to challenge this reading of pragmatism. In fact, ever since Arthur O. Lovejoy pointed out that "pragmatism" is a constellation of meanings (the same could be said of "naturalism"),[5] we know that pragmatism encompasses very

---

3   Cf. Peter Hare, "The American Philosophical Tradition as Progressively Enriched Naturalism", in *Pragmatism with Purpose: Selected Writings of Peter Hare*, ed. by Joseph Palencik, Douglas R. Anderson, and Steven A. Miller (New York: Fordham University Press, 2015), pp. 117-121. On how "closed" Dewey's naturalism is, see Robert J. Roth, "How 'Closed' Is John Dewey's Naturalism", *International Philosophical Quarterly* 3 (1) (1963), 106-120.

4   All references to Dewey are from The Later Works of John Dewey, 1925-1953, 17 vol. (= LW #, #), ed. J.A. Boydston (Carbondale and Edwardsville: Southern Illinois University Press, 1981-1990). The label "technology" is in LW15, p. 88.

5   Arthur O. Lovejoy, "The Thirteen Pragmatisms. I", *The Journal of Philosophy, Psychology, and Scientific Methods* 5 (1) (1908), 5-12; "The

different views and has been subject to significant changes since its founder, Charles S. Peirce, introduced the "pragmatic maxim" in 1878 as a tool "to make our ideas clear."[6] Dewey's pragmatism carries within itself both metaphysical aspirations, chiefly anticipated by Peirce, and nominalist tendencies, whose immediate products were George H. Mead's philosophy of the act[7] and Percy W. Bridgman's operationalist conception of science.[8] For this reason, it is hard to assess the debate between Sheldon and Maritain without putting Dewey's pragmatism into perspective. The aim of the present chapter is to review the Sheldon-Maritain debate in light of the broader context of the pragmatist tradition, integrating Dewey's proposal with the philosophies of William James and especially Charles S. Peirce, and to bring up once again the question, Can Thomism and Pragmatism cooperate?

After a brief contextualization and methodological introduction to the debate, I will focus mainly on two problems: the metaphysics of substance and process (or being and becoming, as Maritain says in the passage below), and the relationship between Thomistic truth and pragmatist verification. Maritain himself stresses that these are the two fundamental problems with which we have to come to grips if we want to try to answer Sheldon's question, 'Can Thomism and Pragmatism Cooperate?'; Sheldon seems to agree.[9] Maritain writes:

Thirteen Pragmatisms. II", *The Journal of Philosophy, Psychology, and Scientific Methods* 5 (2) (1908), 29-39.

6   See Charles S. Peirce, "How to Make Our Ideas Clear," in *The Essential Peirce: Selected Philosophical Writings, vol. 1: 1867-1893* (= EP1, #), ed. by Nathan Houser and Christian Kloesel (Bloomington and Indianapolis: Indiana University Press), pp. 124-141. References to Peirce are also taken from *The Essential Peirce: Selected Philosophical Writings, eds. vol. 2: 1893-1913*, ed. by The Peirce Edition Project (Indianapolis: Indiana University Press) (= EP2, #) and *The Collected Papers of Charles S. Peirce, 8 vols.*, eds. C. Hartshorne, P. Weiss, and A.W. Burks (Cambridge: Harvard University Press, 1931-1958) (= CP #.#).

7   Cf. George H. Mead, *The Philosophy of the Act* (Chicago: The University of Chicago Press, 1938).

8   Cf. Percy W. Bridgman, *The Logic of Modern Physics* (New York: Macmillan, 1927).

9   Cf. Sheldon, "Professor Maritain", pp. 94-95.

In the last analysis we are confronted with a metaphysical opposition which is more basic and more comprehensive than any partial agreement. At the root of Thomistic philosophy lies the affirmation of the primacy of being over becoming. At the root of Pragmatist philosophy ... lies the affirmation of the primacy of becoming over being. We could express this opposition in another way, by stating that the crucial place which is occupied in Thomism by truth is occupied in Pragmatism by *verification*.[10]

The goal of the following pages is to review and extend, although not to settle, the Sheldon-Maritain debate. In the more positive part of the chapter, I will suggest that the mutual enrichment that Sheldon envisages between Thomism and pragmatism is not only possible, but also desirable, especially if we bring into the picture Peirce's metaphysics and concept of truth. Sheldon claims prudently that "the project of harmony between philosophies," Thomism and pragmatism in this case, "is more or less a millennial one."[11] Less prudently, I shall suggest that the cooperation is already possible if Peirce's philosophy is brought into the picture.

1. Contextualizing the Debate: Mutual Interpretations and Common Methodologies

The exchange between Sheldon and Maritain is striking for many reasons. I will mention only three. First, it is striking that both Maritain and Sheldon treat each other's philosophies not only with acute understanding, but also with charity and originality. On the one hand, in *The Range of Reason*, Maritain acknowledges to the pragmatist the merit of describing in a new and interesting way the socially and historically concrete dimension of human experience and the role that our intelligence plays in it.[12] Even more interestingly, Maritain characterizes pragmatism as the project to turn moral philosophy into first philosophy – a sort of titanic yet

---

10   Maritain, *The Range of Reason*, pp. 38-39.
11   Sheldon, "Professor Maritain", p. 89.
12   Maritain, *The Range of Reason*, 42.

tragic attempt to reduce metaphysics and philosophy of nature to the categories of ethics.[13] As I will show in a moment, this interpretation of pragmatism, which was not new among Catholic philosophers and theologians in France,[14] was of course a big source of worry for Maritain. On the other hand, Sheldon characterizes Thomism as one of the most important synthetic systems that Western philosophy has ever produced, and in a certain sense, the most important one,[15] due to its refinement and balance. This positive assessment of Thomism is, to my knowledge, an isolated case among pragmatist philosophers working in the 40s, and this makes it even more remarkable. Unlike Maritain's preoccupation with pragmatism, Sheldon's reflection on Thomism is constant and systematic. As exemplified in works such as 1918 *Strife of Systems and Productive Duality*[16] and 1942 *America's Progressive Philosophy*,[17] Sheldon's philosophical method blends together a reflection on the history of philosophy and

---

13 Maritain, *The Range of Reason*, p. 41.

14 Cf. for instance Garrigou-Lagrange's criticisms of the pragmatic theory of truth (with reference to William James, Édouard Le Roy, and Maurice Blondel) as subverting the "eternal notion of truth" understood as conformity of thought and reality, in *Reality: A Synthesis of Thomistic Thought* (St. Louis: Herder, 1958), Ch. 57. For a broader discussion of the reception of pragmatism in France, see *The Reception of Pragmatism in France and the Rise of Roman Catholic Modernism, 1890-1914*, ed. by David G. Schultenover (Washington DC: The Catholic University of America Press, 2011). For the broader reception of pragmatism in France (with particular reference to Peirce), see Mathias Girel, "Peirce's Reception in France", *European Journal of Pragmatism and American Philosophy* 6 (1) (2014), 15-23.

15 According to Andrew J. Reck, *Speculative Philosophy: A Study of Its Nature, Types, and Uses* (Albuquerque: University of New Mexico Press, 1972), pp. 44 ff.

16 Wilmon H. Sheldon, *Strife of Systems and Productive Duality: An Essay in Philosophy* (Cambridge: Harvard University Press, 1918). A book by a similar title was published by Nicholas Rescher in 1985, *The Strife of Systems: An Essay on the Grounds and Implications of Philosophical Diversity* (Pittsburgh: University of Pittsburgh Press, 1985). Rescher's involvement in this debate is not accidental. I briefly discuss Rescher's problematic relationship to pragmatism in the following two sections.

17 Wilmon H. Sheldon, *America's Progressive Philosophy* (London and New Haven: Yale University Press, 1942).

a more frankly speculative approach. More specifically, his method consists in individuating in the development of Western metaphysics those moments in which human thought reaches forms of definite maturation and systematization, which he calls "polarities." He tries to see how these polarities can enter a mutually fruitful dialogue without being reduced to each other.[18] His interest in Thomism and pragmatism lies exactly in the fact that he recognizes in these two schools two fundamental polarities waiting to be brought together in cooperation.[19] According to Sheldon, the overarching merit of Thomism is not only that of having avoided both idealism and materialism,[20] but also that of having put what he calls "common sense" at the center of its philosophical outlook.[21] Interestingly, Sheldon's interpretation of the Thomistic common sense is eminently practical[22] – a reading that is therefore very different from the more 'objectivist' interpretation of common sense given for instance by Réginald Garrigou-Lagrange,[23] and maybe also by Maritain. He calls Thomism "the practical synthesis."[24] According to him, Thomism assigns to "human life," i.e., the lived human experience seen through

---

18   According to many witnesses, Sheldon always adopted a truly 'Catholic' approach in his philosophical work. See the entry in *The Dictionary of Modern American Philosophers*, ed. by John R. Shook and Richard T. Hull (Bristol: Bloomsbury, 2005), pp. 2205-2208.

19   Sheldon, "Professor Maritain", p. 95: "I feel that polarity will be an ingredient in the final metaphysics (a category, by the way, which permeates the Thomist system)."

20   Sheldon, *America's Progressive Philosophy*, pp. 32-33.

21   Sheldon, *Strife of Systems*, pp. 346 ff.

22   In his discussion of Aquinas's "common sense" philosophy, G.K. Chesterton writes: "The Pragmatist sets out to be practical, but his practicality turns out to be entirely theoretical. The Thomist begins by being theoretical, but his theory turns out to be entirely practical. That is why a great part of the world is returning to it today." G.K. Chesterton, *St. Thomas Aquinas* (New York: Image Books, 1956).

23   For Garrigou-Lagrange, common sense means roughly the knowledge human beings have of certain truths based on the objective evidence of being.

24   Sheldon's reading of Thomism from the standpoint of practical philosophy squares with Maritain's diagnosis that pragmatism is an exemplification of a radical practical turn in philosophy.

the lenses of its natural desire for God and practical aspirations, full epistemic authority to reveal something about the fundamental nature of reality. Through the lenses of his natural desire for God and through the practical dynamism that emerges thereof, says Sheldon in his interpretation of Thomism, the human being is given the resources for believing in the reasonableness of the hypothesis of an infinite God and in the content of Christian revelation.[25] But Sheldon is also extremely appreciative of pragmatism. In his view, the truth of pragmatism consists in its rediscovery of activity and growth as fundamental dimensions of reality, and in seeing concrete experience as the telos of intelligence.

Sheldon is much more optimistic than Maritain concerning the possibility of a deep and long-lasting cooperation between pragmatism and Thomism. Nevertheless, it is worth stressing that both philosophers share a similar methodological approach. They agree on what cooperation looks like and what it should accomplish ideally. Two quotations, one from Maritain and one from Sheldon, are sufficient to prove this point. For Maritain, cooperation is accomplished as long as "each system succeeds (1) in recognizing for the other, its own specific life and principles to a higher degree of achievement and extension."[26] Similarly, Sheldon writes that "It is no lasting solution of a deep-seated opposition between sincere and intelligent thinkers for either party to say to the other, 'You are right in the main but I have already included your view; mine is the fundamental and total, yours the derivative and partial, mine the absolute, yours the relative truth.' The only real solution is one which gives to each party an indispensable and ultimate truth which indeed the other party can consistently admit, and might naturally suggest, but which is not necessarily *implied* by its principles, and nevertheless adds a new significance to them. ... Peace, to be enduring, means working together, co-operation; and co-operation is mutual contribution, not dictation by one to the other."[27]

---

25 Sheldon, *Strife of Systems*, pp. 362-365.
26 Maritain, *The Range of Reason*, p. 31.
27 Sheldon, "Can Philosophers Co-Operate?", pp. 73-74.

The debate between Sheldon and Maritain could be pursued along multiple lines. One interesting way to reassess the debate would be to explore the relation between the Thomist doctrine of the common sense and what Peirce calls "critical common sensism," which is for him an integral part of pragmaticism.[28] Despite its importance, the doctrine of common sense is not the focus of the exchange I am examining, and for this reason I will not pursue it here.

Now that the methodological background of the debate is clear, I can turn to the discussion of the central problem of ontology – in other words, whether a Thomistic and a pragmatist ontology can cooperate in the sense just explained.

2. *Substance and Pragmatist Ontology*

In spite of the fact that part of the exchange between Sheldon and Maritain takes the shape of an assessment of evolution, both agree that the key point is more fundamental than evolution. In fact, Thomists have shown that a substance ontology is not at all incompatible with evolution.[29] Similarly, Sheldon points out that a substance ontology has within itself the resources to allow for a form of becoming in nature that is not mere change, but actual growth and novelty.[30] The topic of growth is of course very dear to the pragmatist, according to whom the differentiation of forms, the increase of complexity, and the emergence of new structures are the most fundamental traits of nature – the most fundamental because they show what nature truly is, namely, generativity. For his part, Maritain has no difficulty pointing out that growth, if correctly understood with reference to potentiality and actuality, is easily accommodated by a hylomorphic substance ontology. After all, the "eduction" of new, actual, emergent forms from the potentiality intrinsic to prior forms

---

28   Cf. Charles S. Peirce, "Issues of Pragmaticism", EP2, pp. 346 ff.
29   See for instance Jacques Maritain, "Toward a Thomistic Idea of Evolution", in Jacques Maritain, *Untrammeled Approaches* (Notre Dame, Indiana: University of Notre Dame Press, 1997), pp. 85-131.
30   Sheldon, "Can Philosophers Co-Operate?", pp. 138-139.

is nothing else than a way to speak of growth.[31] At this level of the discussion, then, the cooperation is fruitful: through pragmatism, Thomism can realize that its own doctrine of the eduction of the forms points in the direction of a view of nature understood as a generative matrix of novelties; and through Thomism, pragmatism is put in the condition to acknowledge that its own doctrine of growth in nature is not incompatible with, but actually requires, substantial, formal distinctions in nature, and that this should go together with a stronger appreciation of the principle of potentiality.

The productive cooperation exemplified by Sheldon and Maritain is even more interesting given that too often pragmatism has been interpreted as a process philosophy incompatible with a substance ontology. Hence, authors such as Charles Hartshorne,[32] Douglas Browning,[33] Nicholas Rescher,[34] and Sandra Rosenthal,[35] who read pragmatism through the lens of the metaphysics of Whitehead, think that a pragmatist ontology and a substance ontology can only be two diametrically opposite views of the world. However, at least at the level just discussed, Sheldon and Maritain seem to say that this is not the case: pragmatism is not necessarily a process philosophy which annihilates substantiality within becoming, and Thomism is not by any means opposed to growth and novelty in nature.[36]

---

31 Maritain, *The Range of Reason*, pp. 36-37. Recently, James F. Ross has pointed out the need for a more systematic study of the dynamics and logic of "eduction" in nature, see his "The Fate of the Analysis: Aristotle's Revenge", *Proceedings of the American Catholic Philosophical Association* 64 (1990), 51-74.

32 See for instance *Existence and Actuality: Conversations with Charles Hartshorne*, ed. by John B. Cobb and Franklin I. Gamwell (Chicago: University of Chicago Press, 1984).

33 Cf. *Philosophers of Process*, ed. by Douglas Browning (New York: Random House, 1965).

34 See Nicholas Rescher, *Process Philosophy: A Survey of Basic Issues* (Pittsburgh: University of Pittsburgh Press, 2000).

35 See Sandra B. Rosenthal, *Speculative Pragmatism* (Amherst: The University of Massachusetts Press, 1986); see also Maria Regina Brioschi, "The Dismissal of 'Substance' and 'Being' in Peirce's Regenerated Logic", *Logic and Logical Philosophy* (2002), 1-26.

36 As Rosenthal recognizes (*Speculative Pragmatism*, p. 113), Peirce never uses the category of process.

Before considering a couple of points on which the cooperation seems to our authors harder, if not impossible, I would like to pause for a second to point out how some convergence between an Aristotelian and a pragmatist ontology was already known to and believed to be of critical importance by the classical pragmatists between the end of the 19th and the beginning of the 20th. There are cases of later thinkers, either pragmatists or heavily influenced by pragmatism, who also acknowledged the importance of Aristotle and substance in order to build a convincing ontology, and Sheldon is certainly one of them.[37] However, the classical pragmatists were already aware that Aristotle had made an immortal contribution to ontology. James writes that while the positivist "thinks that there is no nature in things," the pragmatists "say that things behave so and so because of their nature"; while "nihilism denies continuity," common sense, pragmatism, and, we might add, Aristotelianism, are right in holding a thing "to exist potentially or in substance"; insofar as being continuous "is what people mean when they affirm a substance, substance must be held to exist."[38] Peirce declares, "I should call myself an Aristotelian of the scholastic wing ... but going much further in the direction of scholastic realism" (EP2: 180) and in the explanation of his pragmaticism he articulates the fundamentals of a hylomorphic view of nature by reinterpreting the Aristotelian categories of potentiality and actuality and matter and form in dialectical and emergentist terms, namely, as having at their center the idea of growth (EP2: 373-374).[39] And this is

---

37   See for instance Frederick J.E. Woodbridge, John Herman Randall Jr., Andrew J. Reck, Paul Weiss, Vincent Potter, John E. Smith, John Deely, Manley Thompson, Vincent M. Colapietro, and Kory Sorrell. Also Max Fisch and Joseph Ransdell are essential for an Aristotelian reading of Peirce. Cf. Vincent Colapietro, "Review of *Pragmatism, Kant, and Transcendental Philosophy*, ed. by Gabriele Gava and Robert Stern", *Notre Dame Philosophical Reviews*.

38   William James, "Against Nihilism", in *The Thought and Character of William James*, vol. 1, ed. Ralph Barton Perry (Boston: Little, Brown, and Co., 1935), pp. 525-526. Cf. Hare, p. 86.

39   On this interpretation, potentiality is thesis, actuality is antithesis, and emerging form is synthesis, the "third" irreducible to any prior element, and arguably, the thesis of new dialectical moves. Actuality is interpreted

not an isolated case for Peirce, since Peirce's ontology relies in a revision of Aristotelian notions, such as final causes (EP2: 120), entelechy (EP2: 324), and real natural kinds (EP2: 125-126). He also makes explicit the use of the notion of "substance" understood as a "bundle of habits" (CP 1.4141). Among the pragmatists, Dewey was probably the most reluctant to openly declare his agreement with an Aristotelian ontology, and partly because he certainly was, together with Mead, the pragmatist with the strongest nominalist tendencies.[40] Nevertheless, not even Dewey was immune to the fascination with the philosophy of Aristotle, probably through the influence of Woodbridge and Randall Jr.[41] It is in fact possible to find in his work a critical appropriation of a theory of substance, heavily mediated by his theory of inquiry and by his nominalism: Dewey synthesizes traditional ontology and pragmatist philosophy in what he calls "technology," which is a semantic and inquiry-based theory of objects in evolution.[42]

---

as the fundamental moment of opposition, necessary for the form to emerge.

40   See, however, Raymond D. Boisvert, *Dewey's Metaphysics* (New York: Fordham University Press, 1988). John Deely points out Dewey's nominalism in *Four Ages of Understanding* (Buffalo, Toronto: University of Toronto Press, 2001), pp. 615-615 and p. 779.

41   Cf. Frederick J.E. Woodbridge, *Aristotle's Vision of Nature* (New York: Columbia University Press, 1965); John Herman Randall Jr., *Aristotle* (New York: Columbia University Press, 1960).

42   Dewey, LW15, p. 88. Cf. Sheldon, "Professor Maritain", p. 94: "Professor Maritain's doubts about the pragmatist accepting substance and finality I share; for the pragmatist does tend to interpret the behavior of things in terms of sense-perception only." Sheldon's claim is either a misrepresentation of James's and Peirce's philosophy, or an unjustified reduction of pragmatism to the most nominalist tendencies present in Dewey's metaphysics. Moreover, teleology is absolutely central in Peirce, to the point that it is impossible to understand his metaphysics without it. On this, see Vincent Colapietro, "C.S. Peirce's Reclamation of Teleology", in *Nature in American Philosophy*, ed. by Jean De Groot (Washington, D.C.: Catholic University of America Press, 2004), pp. 88-108; Menno Hulswit, "Peirce's Teleological Approach to Natural Classes", *Transactions of the Charles S. Peirce Society* 33 (2) (1997), pp. 722-772.

However, it would be a mistake to believe that Sheldon and Maritain agree on the possibility of an unlimited and unproblematic cooperation between Thomism and pragmatism. Maritain raises in fact at least two points that seem to shut down the possibility of any further productive exchange between the two approaches. After illustrating the two points of contention, I will assess them conjointly, and I will suggest that, if we adopted a broadly Peircean ontology – a version of pragmatism that was unfortunately unknown in its complexity to Maritain – Sheldon's suggestion could be given a solution that also the Thomist could accept, and maybe even appreciate and endorse.

The first problem of contention concerns the problem of change. Sheldon, in his extremely liberal appropriation of Thomism, goes as far as to advance the hypothesis that growth should not simply be taken in the sense of the accidental growth of given substances or of eduction of new forms from prior forms, but also in the sense of what he calls "essential growth."[43] On this point, Maritain strongly dissents.[44] Sheldon exemplifies his point that also essences "grow" through the analogy of a spiral. A spiral is "a curve that starts small enough, the tiniest of coils, yet grows greater and greater indefinitely." While indefinitely growing, a spiral has a fixed equation, which is, says Sheldon, "the analogous of the substantial form."[45] Essences could grow in the same way. To this, Maritain answers by stressing again the distinction between substantial and accidental change: substances certainly grow, but there is no intermediate category between transformation and merely accidental modification: what Sheldon is after might be simply understood as a form of accidental change.[46]

---

43   Sheldon, "Can Philosophers Co-Operate?", p. 139.
44   Maritain, *The Range of Reason*, pp. 35-38.
45   Sheldon, "Can Philosophers Co-Operate?", pp. 138-139.
46   Nothing similar to the idea of essential change is discussed in "Toward a Thomistic Idea of Evolution." Maritain ventures into speaking of an "expansive movement at the very core of the human species" (p. 100), but he does not give this notion the same systematic treatment that Sheldon hopes for.

The second issue is the difference between being and becoming and the priority of the former over the latter. Maritain claims that any view that does not admit of a fundamental distinction between becoming/behavior and being is not capable of grasping the deep nature of things, what he calls here the "intelligible behavior" of things.[47] It seems safe to say that Sheldon would disagree. As Sheldon puts it, a substance is, after all, a way of behaving in a certain general way. Is there a way to make the two positions cooperate also at the level of the distinction between being and behavior? Moreover, is there a solution that can accommodate not only this opposition, but also Sheldon's reasons for pushing for essential growth and Maritain's reasons to resist it?

I would like to suggest that, among the pragmatists, Peirce's ontology has the resources to bring the alleged incompatible desiderata of Sheldon and Maritain into a unitary framework. The reason is that, among the pragmatists, Peirce is the philosopher with the most robust ontology, especially the ontology of real modalities (henceforth, real modalism). Peirce speaks of the modalities in a variety of ways – as possibilities, actualities, and necessities; as qualities, occasions, and laws; as might-bes, existents, and would-bes; as Firstnesses, Secondnesses, and Thirdnesses. It is also important to note for our discussion that Peirce declares his real modalism to be a corollary of his pragmaticism:

> Another doctrine which is involved in Pragmaticism as an essential consequence of it ... it the scholastic doctrine of realism. This is usually defined as the opinion that there are real objects that are general [laws, necessity], among the number being the modes of determination of existent singulars [actuality], if, indeed, these be not the only such objects. But the belief in this can hardly escape being accompanied by the acknowledgment that there are, besides, ... real *possibilities*. (EP2: 354)

The importance of this claim is, again, that it proves that pragmatism is neither exclusively nor primarily a form of reductive naturalism or nominalism. On the contrary, Peirce's pragmatism has

---

47   Maritain, *The Range of Reason*, p. 35.

at its center a realist interpretation of the modalities.[48] *Real* modalism means not only that the modes of possibility and necessity are not extensionally reducible, but also that they are "objective" – in other words, not all possibilities and necessities depend upon a knowing subject (e.g., "if a person does not know that a proposition is false, he calls it *possible*", EP2: 354) because some of them constitute the very structure of being (e.g., "I *can* go to the seashore if I like", EP2: 355).

Now let's go back to our specific concern. How can a modal ontology make us understand better the relationship between being and behavior? Here's my proposal: if by behavior we mean the *actual behavior* of a thing, as Maritain remarks, then a thing's being cannot be identical or reduced to its behavior. However, what if we speak of a thing's possible behavior? What if we include in the conception of this thing *all the possible behaviors* that a thing *would* manifest if put to work even in the most unlikely conditions? What if we included in it also those "hidden necessities," as Ross calls them, that nobody will ever know and that will never be actually manifested, but that could be known and would be manifested given the right triggering conditions? In short, what if our ontology looked at substances as bundles of stable dispositions of possible behaviors? This is what Peirce is after when he characterizes substances as

---

48 Peirce's approach to modal semantics avoids any kind of extensionalism or reductionism of modality and provides the framework for an extremely broad realistic view of the modalities. Peirce's real modalism would be beneficial to some recent modal developments in Aristotelian ontology, for instance James F. Ross's neo-Aristotelian ontology in *Thought and World: The Hidden Necessities* (Notre Dame, Indiana: University of Notre Dame, 2008), and David S. Oderberg's real essentialism in *Real Essentialism* (New York and London: Routledge, 2007). Ross and Oderberg, while sympathetic with a realistic grounding of the modalities in "real natures" and "real essences," still have a hard time making peace with the contemporary analytic discourse on modality, so centered on an unpalatable possible worlds semantics. Peirce's real modalism would provide them with a different, realist framework for bringing together semantics and metaphysics, while at the same time articulating the meaning of the modalities not through a possible worlds semantics but through a pragmatic clarification.

"bundles of habits" (CP 1.414). I suggest, then, that the solution to the problem of the distinction between being and behavior lies in understanding the old Scholastic maxim for which *agere sequitur esse*, the thing behaves as it is, *in modal terms*. In other words, there is no distinction between *agere* and *esse* if not in terms of *modality*. *Esse* in this maxim stands for the possibility of general-dispositional modes of behavior of a thing, while *agere* stands for its actual determinations.[49] Consequently, as long as we understand behavior modally and counterfactually, there is no harm in likening being to behaving – on the contrary, this can be seen as a sound version of Aristotelian ontology.

A frankly modal approach to substances and essences would reveal that being and behavior are in truth overlapping, coextensive categories. Given his familiarity with the pragmatism of Dewey, who develops a less systematic view of modality, and given Sheldon's silence on the issue, Maritain is right in lamenting that pragmatism cannot account for the distinction between being and behavior. He is also right in reminding us that the Thomistic distinction is of the essence. Nevertheless, as I have suggested, if we appreciate Peirce's real modalism, we get a different picture of what pragmatism means by likening a thing's being and behavior. This seems to me a viable direction for continuing the cooperation between the Thomist and the pragmatist.

As for the other issue, namely, whether is it possible or desirable to speak of an essential growth, Peirce's real modalism seems again a very important resource. What Sheldon has in mind is that we should find a way to account for the possibility that an essence can remain the same essence while changing radically the habitual nature that is standardly associated with it in the individuals that instantiate it. This strikes me as an idea very close to intraspecific evolution, which already St. Augustine considered as a likely doctrine.[50] Now, I do not think there is anything that in principle prevents a Thomist from accounting for such phenomenon. Maritain

---

49   The translation of the Scholastic maxim into pragmatist categories is of course not limited to the sketch I provide here.

50   Cf. *De Genesi ad litteram*, book V, ch. 7, parr. 20-22; ch. 20 par. 41.

seems to respond to Sheldon simply by saying that either a change is a case of substantial change, or it is a case of accidental change in a substance – *tertium non datur*. Nevertheless, I think that Sheldon has a point in making the case for essential growth, understood as a middle case between substantial change and mere accidental change. Again, I think that also a Thomist has a story to tell in accounting for this phenomenon, and maybe Maritain, worried to rescue the substantial/accidental change distinction from the blurring effects of Sheldon's proposal, simply did not address the issue properly. More specifically, I think that Peirce's real modalism has the resources to indicate what the cooperation on this point could look like. In fact, one of the essential aspects of Peirce's real modalism is its *evolutionary* dimension. In other words, according to Peirce, the modalities constituting a substance *grow* over time. "In growth … we find that the three Universes [possibility, necessity, and actuality] conspire" (EP2: 439). Peirce sees a direct Aristotelian legacy in his evolutionary account of modality: "of all these achievements [in ontology], the greatest in the eye of reason, that of brining to light the supremacy of the element of *Growth*, was, after all, nothing but a special application of Aristotle's pure vision" (EP2: 373). And it is striking to see that for him Aquinas is in the same evolutionary tradition: "Today, the idea uppermost in most minds is Evolution. … Whatever in the philosophies of our day … is not Ockhamism is evolutionism of one kind or another; and every evolutionism must in its evolution eventually restore that rejected idea of law as a reasonableness energizing in the world (no matter through what mechanism of natural selection or otherwise) which belonged to the essentially evolutionary metaphysics of Aristotle, as well as the scholastic modifications of it by Aquinas" (EP2: 72). Thus, I propose to spell out Peirce's idea of evolution as reasonableness progressively energizing the world through his real modalism. For Peirce, each kind of thing or substance is first of all a real possibility (Firstness), which generates specific ways of behaving, or habits (Thirdness) and therefore corresponding actual properties (Secondnesses). In the encounter we have with them, substances tend to reveal stable specific habits. Nevertheless, inferring that substances have always had the same defining habits, i.e., the habits that we usually define as 'standard' for those substances, would be a mistake according to Peirce. In fact, the real possibility constituting a substance is, according to Peirce, first and foremost a *possibility of being realized through different and evolving habits*. If this is the case, then, we can see intraspecific evolution through the lens of a very elegant pragmatist ontological framework: different things, which are always things of a certain kind, undergo substantial and accidental changes, but in addition to that, the kinds or essences to which these things belong, through time, undergo a growth, in the sense of a diversification and specialization of their proper habits, which is neither a substantial change, nor simply an accidental change of the things in which the essence's growth happens.

In discussing Scholastic realism, Peirce often stresses the essential connection between kinds, generals, or habits, and their possible realizations, and he points out their irreducibility to what is already actualized: "the idea of a general involves the idea of possible variations which no multitude of existents things could exhaust" (EP2: 183). Each actual being transcends itself in virtue of its general constitution and of the possible growth of the essence to which it belongs. If we take "essence" to mean the real possibility defining a certain kind of substance, we can then interpret the process of diversification and specialization of its habits as a form of essential growth. In fact, if we assume an evolutionist perspective on ontology, we have to admit that the habits "flowing from" an "essence"[51] have not always been the same. The intraspecific growth of a substance occurring through the diversification-specialization (growth) of the habits flowing from the substance's essence corresponds to Sheldon's idea of essential change, and this idea fits perfectly with the evolutionary dimension of Peirce's real modalism: one and the same real possibility diversifies itself *as a real bundle of habits*, while remaining the same *as real possibility*, by developing different habits and laws of behavior (real necessities) and therefore manifesting different concrete traits (real actualities).

In short, the product of the cooperation between the Thomist and the pragmatist on this topic would be the following. Pragmatism

---

51   ST I, q. 77, a. 6 c.

learns from Thomism that the dynamic nature of being does not imply constant flux or transformation. Dynamism is at the very heart of the ontology of act of being: the dimension for which a substance, though subject to change, does not undergo substantial change, is nevertheless always active in the sense of being the ultimate source of the actual manifestations of that being. In turn, Thomism learns from pragmatism that the Aristotelian categories are not the only categories, nor necessarily the most fundamental categories, to unpack the features of the hylomorphic structure of substances. Might-bes, actualities, and would-bes, in their complex transitional relation, can describe the inner modal life of hylomorphism at a deeper level of analysis.

3. *Truth, Transcendentals, and Pragmatism*

Let us now turn to the problem of truth, which both Sheldon and Maritain recognize as the second most pressing issue at stake. Here, according to Maritain, the disagreement between the two orientations is complete.[52] Sheldon calls it "the root-opposition."[53] Before entering the details of the discussion, it is important to stress again the popular interpretation of the pragmatic theory of truth that

---

52 Similarly, Étienne Gilson characterizes (James's and Dewey's) pragmatism as a form of skepticism about truth, obviously incompatible with Thomism. Cf. *Being and Some Philosophers* (Toronto: Pontifical Institute of Medieval Studies, 1952), pp. viii-ix: "The only dogmatic tenet still held as valid in such [pragmatist] philosophical circles is that, if a philosopher feels reasonably sure of being right, then it is a sure thing that he is wrong, because it is of the very essence of philosophical knowledge merely to express 'a certain attitude, purpose, or temper of conjoined intellect and will.' The man whose will uses every effort to let his own intellect see things just as they are, is then bound to appear as a self-satisfied fellow, a living insult to those who don't happen to see reality as he does. He is a man to steer clear of; in short, he is a fanatic."

53 Sheldon, "Professor Maritain", p. 94. However, he concludes: "If for the pragmatist truth is one with verification, is not the truth for him that which is verified? You can't separate verification from what is verified, can you? And if not, surely then each is 'one with' the other. My contention throughout has been that the mutual exclusions are *needless*."

was circulating in the 40s and later, and which to some extent is still discussed today, including within neo-Aristotelian circles.[54] On the one hand, pragmatic truth was taken to mean something like practical satisfaction: a belief is true if and when it satisfies the goals that a subject pursues by acting upon that belief.[55] On the other hand, the pragmatic approach to truth was reduced to crass sense-experience verificationism, a theory similar to that of the logical positivists.[56] Thus, the popular depiction of the pragmatic truth as what "works" (for the believer, for a community of believers, etc.) underlies the two elements just mentioned, that of practical satisfaction and that of verification. Reasons to believe that this was in fact the pragmatist theory of truth can be found in different degrees in all the classical pragmatists. However, as I will point out soon, these reasons are ultimately partial and they are to some extent the result of a misinterpretation of the pragmatist project. To this brief sketch, we can add a third element, which is usually associated with Dewey's theory of inquiry and which is probably what both Sheldon and Maritain had in mind as another fundamental aspect of the pragmatic theory of truth, namely, the idea of truth as "warranted assertibility" (LW12: 15). The troubling aspect of this chiefly Deweyan characterization of truth is its extremely limited applicability and its impossibly tight dependence on actually successful inquiry: if truth is what we can justifiably believe and assert because our responsible inquiries have convinced us that we can do so, it follows that only what *has been successfully tested* can properly be said to be true. For many, this position is unpalatable, and rightly so, because it leaves out too much – most importantly, what is *un*verified and what is properly *un*verifiable.

---

54   For instance, see Ross, *Thought and World*, pp. 80-82.
55   This version has been given new life, through Wittgenstein, by J.T. Whyte's "success semantics," see his "Success Semantics", *Analysis* 50 (3) (1990), 149-157. Robert Brandom, one of the Pittsburgh pragmatists, has criticized this view in his "Unsuccessful Semantics", *Analysis* 54 (3) (1994), 175-178.
56   Cf. the classical neopositivist reading of pragmatism by Alfred J. Ayer, *The Origins of Pragmatism* (San Francisco: Freeman, Cooper, 1968).

Since G.E. Moore and Bertrand Russell ridiculed the pragmatic theory of truth,[57] by relying primarily on their knowledge of James, Dewey, and Schiller, the pragmatists have painstakingly attempted to point out the many misrepresentations of their approach to truth, unfortunately without success. The incommunicability between Sheldon and Maritain about truth seems the aftermath of this sad story of mutual misunderstandings. There would be much to say in defense of the pragmatic idea of truth, and I will not go into the details here. However, I will give a taste of the overall issue by mentioning James. James was extremely vocal in clarifying that the "satisfaction" that is at the center of the pragmatic theory of truth is not the irrational and whimsical fulfilment of the subject's desires, but the idea that something (a belief, an expectation, a proposition, an idea, a concept, etc.) is true when it is successful in "linking satisfactorily" different parts of our experience.[58] James's pragmatism was never meant to deny the fundamental intuition that truth is the correspondence between mind and reality; only, its aim was to develop this notion by moving from a rationalistic description of correspondence as a "static relation" to a description of it as a "rich and active commerce" between our thoughts and the great universe.[59] All James ever wanted to maintain was that

The truth of an idea is not a stagnant property inherent in it. Truth *happens* to an idea. It becomes true, is *made* true by events. Its verity is

---

57   G.E. Moore, "William James's 'Pragmatism'", in *William James: Pragmatism in Focus*, ed. by Doris Olin (London and New York: Routledge, 1992), pp. 161-195; Bertrand Russell, "William James's Conception of Truth", in *William James: Pragmatism in Focus*, pp. 196-211. For a Deweyan response to Russell's criticisms of the pragmatist theory of truth, cf. Tom Burke, *Dewey's New Logic: A Reply to Russell* (Chicago and London: The University of Chicago Press, 1994).

58   *The Writings of William James: A Comprehensive Edition*, ed. by John J. McDermott (New York: The Modern Library, 1968), p. 382.

59   *The Writings of William James*, p. 386. John E. Smith calls Peirce's and James's approach a "dynamic correspondence" theory of truth, see his *Purpose and Thought: The Meaning of Pragmatism* (New Haven: Yale University Press, 1978), p. 58.

in fact an event, a process: the process namely of its verifying itself, its very-*fication*. Its validity is the process of its valid-*ation*.[60]

The main point of James's view, then, is that what makes a belief true is the process through which a state of affairs veri-fies (or does not falsify) that belief. A belief is true only if it *can* be made true by a truthmaker, and a truthmaker is a truthmaker *primarily in the process* of truthmaking a belief. As Brian Embry has shown, a very similar way of treating truth was developed by some 17th-century Scholastics.[61] The word used then was *verificativum*, namely, that which makes a belief true. If we dynamize the Scholastic notion of *verificativum*, what we obtain is veri-fication – exactly the term used by James. The way pragmatism and some Scholastic authors think about truth is very similar indeed.

Let us go back now to the exchange between Sheldon and Maritain. Sheldon points out that the pragmatist's stress on verification in experience – for instance, the verification of the belief in the existence of God derived from the Thomistic *viae* – should be welcomed as a suitable extension of the Thomist's belief in the capacity of reason to grasp truth, including the truth of conclusions produced by demonstrations and proofs. He points out a limitation, a historical limitation but not a structural limitation, of the pragmatist, namely, his refusal to take the Thomistic *viae* seriously, and by

---

60   *The Writings of William James*, p. 430. Cf. how Anton C. Pegis characterizes the special nature of human intellect according to Aquinas, "St. Thomas and the Unity of Man", in *Progress in Philosophy*, ed. by James A. McWilliams, S.J. (Milwaukee: The Bruce Publishing Company, 1967), 170-171: "Intellect, senses, and bodily organs together constitute in man a complete intellect. Why is not the human intellect by itself adequate as an intellect? Because by itself it cannot do the work of an intellect. Why not? Because it falls short of *verifying* [my emphasis] within itself of all the conditions necessary to its work. ... To know not only man but also John Smith; indeed, to know man as John Smith and John Smith himself as a man, the human intellect must work with the senses, so that the co-operative while of intellect and the senses knows the individual John Smith adequately."

61   See Brian Embry, "Truth and Truthmaking in 17th-Century Scholasticism," Dissertation, University of Toronto (2015).

extension any purely abstract argument which is not grounded in empirical verifiability.[62] For his part, Maritain sympathizes with the pragmatist interest in the concreteness of human experience, but he laments at the same time a fundamental deficiency in the pragmatist approach to reason and truth – a metaphysical deficiency. In Maritain's view, the pragmatist reduces the work of reason and the resource of truth to what is *empirically tested* and therefore *verified* and denies to reason the "metaphysical intuition" and speculative contemplation of being. In one passage Maritain connects this issue with the problem of being and becoming:

> In the eyes of the Thomist, verification is only a way and a means of grasping the truth. And when the intellect has made itself true, the truth thus attained possesses objective consistency because it is the vital conformity of the intellect with what exists (actually or possibly) independently of the mind; and, however humble it may be, this truth is an end in which the intellect comes to fruition and has its perfection, rest, and joy. ... To enjoy the truth ... is the very life of the intellect *qua* intellect, and the aim of science *qua* science as well as that of metaphysical wisdom. Whereas the Thomist emphasizes in this way the contemplative import of knowledge, the Pragmatist distrusts it as a 'static' illusion, opposed to the reality of the intellectual life which is only becoming and laboring. The quarrel better Being and Becoming, and between Truth and Verification, reveals a deep-seated antagonism that the best efforts cannot overcome.[63]

This passage shows with great clarity the troublesome consequences of certain popular Deweyan rhetorical attacks against the static and unprogressive nature of traditional (allegedly Platonic and Aristotelian) ontology, which includes the idea of contemplation, allegedly responsible for discrediting the world of practice as inferior and irrelevant to cognition.[64] If this were all that pragmatism had to

---

62 Sheldon is not quite bold enough, however, in defending the pragmatist idea if truth appropriately. See his discussion of confirmation, "Can Philosophers Co-Operate?", pp. 75-76.

63 Maritain, *The Range of Reason*, p. 39.

64 Cf. Dewey's 1929 *The Quest for Certainty*, LW4. Dewey's work contains many valuable ideas, which are too often criticized because they are not understood properly. Unfortunately, his work is often filled with an

offer to a philosophical understanding of truth, it would be indeed a poor contribution, certainly incapable of inviting the cooperation of the Thomist.

Despite the limitations of Dewey's philosophy, I would like to suggest that the conflict between Thomism and pragmatism is not necessary if we go to the roots of pragmatism, that is, if we bring again Peirce into the picture. If we look at the issue from the point of view of Peirce's pragmatic understanding of truth, the cooperation between the Thomist and the pragmatist becomes not only possible, but mutually illuminating. When I speak of truth here, I mainly refer to the Scholastic tradition of the transcendentals.[65] The *locus classicus* for appreciating the Aquinas's understanding of truth as transcendental is probably *De Veritate* q. 1 a. 1, where Aquinas explains that truth is the way in which the notion of reality is declined when it us thought in relation to the human mind, a mind which is, as Aristotle already taught, capable in principle of being everything. The conformity in which truth consists, then, is not primarily the correspondence or agreement of a particular intellectual judgment with a particular state of affairs, but more deeply, the original connaturality of thought and being. Maritain himself stresses this dimension when pushed to say what is according to him the "central intuition" of Thomistic philosophy: "It is the intuition of the basic intelligible reality of being, as analogically permeating everything knowable."[66]

My proposal can be illuminated through the following question: What would happen to our understanding of truth if we connected the transcendental meaning of truth and the judgment-dependent meaning of truth? Following Alice M. Ramos, who has written about

---

antitraditional bias such that also his best metaphysical insights are sometimes weakened by his overall rhetoric.

65 For a historical and theoretical overview of the topic, see Jan A. Aertsen, *Medieval Philosophy as Transcendental Thought: From Philip the Chancellor (ca. 1225) to Francisco Suárez* (Leiden and Boston: Brill, 2012).

66 Maritain, *The Range of Reason*, p. 43.

the need to think the Thomistic transcendentals "dynamically,"[67] my question can be formulated in the following way: What would happen if the dynamic nature of the transcendental idea of truth were seen in light of its consequences, that is, in light of *all its conceivable consequences*, for the human mind? Or, even better, for all rational minds? If being is intelligible, and if all human minds are open to the entirety of being as such (transcendental idea of truth), then it is plausible to say that true judgments and habits of representations *are* what these minds *would achieve in the long run*, and that the interaction among these minds *would tend to converge* in the long run toward an agreement, toward a common liberation from falsity. Wouldn't this be a beautiful way to look at the dynamic nature of truth without losing its metaphysical rootedness in the intelligibility of being?

This is, I submit, Peirce's own view of truth, which I will call the eschatological agreement theory of truth.[68] In 1907 "Pragmatism," Peirce writes that

> ... the objectivity of truth really consists in the fact that, in the end, every sincere inquirer will be led to embrace it; – and if he be not sincere, the irresistible effect of inquiry in the light of experience will be to make him so. This doctrine appears to me, after one subtraction, to be the corollary of pragmatism. I set it in a strong light in my original presentation of the method. ... I hold that truth's independence of individual opinions is due (so far as there is any 'truth') to its being the predestined result to which sufficient inquiry *would* ultimately lead. (EP2: 419)

The predestined result of inquiry is the final belief toward which all rational minds irresistibly tend, and about which they would agree if sufficient experience, time, and freedom from perverting factors

---

67 Alice M. Ramos, *Dynamic Transcendentals: Truth, Goodness, and Beauty from a Thomistic Perspective* (Washington, D.C.: Catholic University of America Press, 2012).

68 Cf. Cheryl J. Misak, *Truth and the End of Inquiry: A Peircean Account of Truth* (New York and Oxford: Clarendon Press, 2004); Catherine Legg, "Charles Peirce's Limit Concept of Truth", *Philosophy Compass* 9 (3) (2014), 204-213.

were given to inquirers (EP1: 88-89). We all aspire to the revelation of reality in its full meaning because this revelation is the vocation, the *Bestimmung*, conjointly, of rationality, reality, and the beliefs (more or less true) that we already entertain. But why is it so? Why is this eschatological agreement the essential explication of the idea of truth? Only because truth is grounded in reality, in the sense that reality is intrinsically intelligible and that the mind is structurally open to knowing it. As Peirce stresses since his first writings, "Over against any cognition, there is an unknown but knowable reality; but over against all possible cognition, there is only the self-contradictory. In short, *cognizability* (in its wider sense) and *being* are not merely metaphysically the same, but are synonymous terms" (EP1: 25). *Ens et verum convertuntur.*[69] Truth is the "entelechy of reality" (EP2: 324) the orientation of reality to be represented as it ought to be represented, to become faithful cognition.[70] The human mind, in turn, has an affinity with and an "instinct" for truth (EP2: 444-445): the mind is the "seed of knowledge," the "field of consciousness" within which the intelligibility of being can become true representation (EP2: 374). It is the "Seme of Truth."[71] Put bluntly, Peirce's eschatological agreement theory of truth is the pragmatic explication of the traditional transcendental idea of

---

69 Peirce's take on the convertibility of the transcendentals being and true (cognizable) is very strong as it implies not only metaphysical identity but also synonymy; not only extensional identity, but also intensional coincidence. To my knowledge, no Scholastic theory of the transcendentals goes this far.

70 Cf. André De Tienne, "Peirce's Logic of Information," Seminario del Grupo de Estudios Peirceanos, Universidad de Navarra, 28 Sep. 2006, Online: "If everything is cognizable for Peirce, it is not only because nothing can escape representation, but even more strongly because everything 'wants' to be cognized: not the will of an efficient cause, but the telic will of a final conditional cause." According to the telic will of the final conditional cause, reality 'actively tries' to find strategies for being correctly represented. It is in this sense that reality is at the bottom (not only, but at the bottom) an "idea" (a general), more precisely a "living" idea (a telic will seeking strategies for being represented properly).

71 Charles S. Peirce, "Prolegomena to an Apology for Pragmaticism", *The Monist* 16 (4) (1906), p. 523.

truth. The pragmatic and dynamic clarification of the transcendental idea of truth brings to light many before-hidden ramifications of the Scholastic idea, revealing once more the opportunity of a cooperation between Thomism and pragmatism.[72]

Peirce's theory of truth has been given perverted interpretations and has been harshly criticized. For instance, it is sometimes held that Peirce's understanding of truth *replaces* the traditional idea of truth as correspondence with the idea of "ideal agreement" at the end of inquiry. (It doesn't seem to matter to those who advance this interpretation that the agreement is supposed by Peirce to be final, intersubjective, and destined.[73]) This mistaken interpretation has both defenders and detractors. For Nicholas Rescher, for instance, Peirce's "consensus theory of truth," just like that of its followers Juergen Habermas and Karl O. Apel, is not capable of accounting for the obvious difference between intersubjective agreement and truth, as it is proved by the fact that agreement is possible also about

---

72 Nobody so far has attempted such project. Robert J. Roth, *Radical Pragmatism: An Alternative* (New York: Fordham University Press, 1998), pp. 69-71, compares Lonergan's notion of transcendental with Peirce's idea of man-nature attunement, but his comparison is hardly more than a side note. An interpretation compatible with the one I am sketching is Demetra Sfendoni-Mentzou, "Toward a Potential-Pragmatic Account of Peirce's Theory of Truth", *Transactions of the Charles S. Peirce Society* 27 (1) (1991), 27-77. Reading Peirce's eschatological agreement theory of truth in light of the transcendental philosophy of the Scholastics shows why it is wrong to oppose Peirce's allegedly "epistemic" view and a realist view of truth, as William P. Alston does in his *A Realist Conception of Truth* (Ithaca: Cornell University Press, 1996), pp. 188 ff.

73 Interestingly, among contemporary Thomists, James Ross has developed a quasi-Peircean model of truth for the faith in the eschatological promises of Christ (Second Coming, resurrection, final judgment, heaven and hell), according to which the truthmaker of faith is the "cognitive consonance between belief *in via* and cognition in the end," or "how the last things will be experienced" by all the saved at the end of times. The "being true" of a belief *in via* is its final "fulfilment" in the knowledge of the Communion of Saints at the second coming. See his "Eschatological Pragmatism," in *Philosophy and the Christian Faith*, ed. by Thomas V. Morris (Notre Dame, Indiana: University of Notre Dame Press, 1988), pp. 279-300.

falsity.[74] On the opposite side of the spectrum, Richard Rorty claims that the pragmatic idea of truth understood as agreement must be welcomed because it finally allows us to subtract truth from the field of epistemology and metaphysics and to turn it into a much more powerful tool of social emancipation; for him, inquiry is aimed at truth not in the sense that it aims at getting things right or the way things are, but only in the sense that what we actually do in our scientific and democratic practices is try to convince other people to agree with us.[75]

Both Rescher's criticisms and Rorty's approval rely on a wrong understanding of Peirce's idea of truth. One of the ways to counteract this misleading version of pragmatism is to show, as I am trying to do here, that Peirce's eschatological-agreement theory of truth is best understood as the pragmatic clarification of the transcendental idea of truth proposed by Aquinas. If my suggestion has some value, then, we must conclude that also at this level the cooperation of the Thomist and the pragmatist can be extremely productive and mutually enriching. I have already explained in what way the Thomist could benefit from a pragmatist approach to truth. What could the pragmatist learn from the Thomist? He could learn a great deal. In particular, he could learn that transcendental philosophy did not begin with Kant, and that the Kantian version of the transcendental (the role of which for Peirce the pragmatists still debate fiercely[76]) is a late and corrupted articulation of an older,

---

74 Nicholas Rescher, *Pluralism: Against the Demand for Consensus* (Oxford: Clarendon Press, 1993), pp. 57-62. Cf. Misak, *Truth and the End of Inquiry*, for the idea that Peirce's eschatological view of truth does not compromise the objectivity of truth.

75 Richard Rorty, "Truth without Correspondence to Reality", in *Philosophy and Social Hope* (London and New York: Penguin Books, 1999), pp. 23-46.

76 See again Colapietro's review of Gava and Stern; Giovanni Maddalena, "Review of Gava, *Peirce's Account of Purposefulness: A Kantian Perspective*", *Transactions of the Charles S. Peirce Society* 53 (3) (2017), 503-509. Kant was aware that his sense of "transcendental" was new compared to the Scholastic tradition, see Aertsen, *Medieval Philosophy*, p. 14: "In the second edition of his *Critique of Pure Reason* (1787), he [Kant] added a section, in which he points to the 'Transcendental

glorious idea. Pragmatists, old and new, even when they do not have any antipathy for metaphysics (Peirceans generally don't), certainly have a resistance to the idea of the transcendental because they see in it the mark of the *categorical a priori*. For most pragmatists it is as if the question, 'Does the transcendental play any role in Peirce's philosophy?,' could be given only a Kantian interpretation. This is not without reason, given that Peirce's introduction to philosophy was certainly through Kant. Nevertheless, Peirce's philosophical maturation was not in the line of Kant, but in that of Scholastic realism and Medieval logic. This is why Thomism can bring the transcendental spirit of Peirce's philosophy to a greater level of self-awareness. More specifically, Thomism can show the pragmatist that the real *a priori* is the fundamental sympathy between mind and reality, which is neither an innate idea, nor an *a priori* categorical schema, but is, again, an onto-logical transcendental.

Philosophy of the Ancients' and quotes the proposition, 'so famous among the Schoolmen': '*quodlibet ens est unum, verum, bonum.*' At the same time the section added manifests Kant's 'Copernican Revolution.' While the Scholastics believed transcendentals to be the most general predicates of *things*, they are in fact 'nothing but logical requirements and criteria of all *knowledge* of things' (Kant's italics). Kant emphasized the fundamental discontinuity with Scholastic thought, but the fact remains that it is an opposition to a 'transcendental philosophy.' It is historically and philosophically appropriate to consider the medieval doctrine as a distinctive form within the tradition of transcendental thought; it is in fact the origin of transcendental philosophy."

BIBLIOGRAPHY

Agler, David W, "Peirce's Direct, Non-Reductive Contextual Theory of Names", *Transactions of the Charles S. Peirce Society* 46(4) (2010), 611-640.

Aertsen, Jan A., *Medieval Philosophy as Transcendental Thought: From Philip the Chancellor (ca. 1225) to Francisco Suárez* (Leiden and Boston: Brill, 2012).

Alexander, Thomas M., "Dewey and the Metaphysical Imagination", *Transactions of the Charles S. Peirce Society* 28 (2) (1992), 203-215.

Almeder, Robert F., "Charles Peirce and the Existence of the External World", *Transactions of the Charles S. Peirce Society* 4(2) (1969), 63-79.

Almeder, Robert F., "Peirce's Theory of Perception", *Transactions of the Charles S. Peirce Society* 6(2) (1970), 99-110.

Alston, William P., *A Realist Conception of Truth* (Ithaca: Cornell University Press, 1996).

Andreatta, Moreno, Nicolas, François, and Alunni, Charles, *A la lumière des mathématiques et à l'ombre de la philosophie. Dix ans de séminaire* mamuphi *'Mathematiques, musique et philosophie* (Paris: Delatour-IRCAM, 2012).

Annoni, Marco and Maddalena, Giovanni (eds.), *Alle origini del pragmatism: corrispondenza tra C. Peirce e W. James* (Torino: Aragno, 2011).

Anscombe, G. E. M., "The First Person", in *Mind and Language*, ed. by Samuel Guttenplan (Oxford: Clarendon Press, 1975), 45-65.

Apel, Karl O., *Charles S. Peirce: From Pragmatism to Pragmaticism* (Amherst: University of Massachusetts Press, 1981).

Apel, Karl O., "Transcendental Semiotic and Hypothetical Metaphysics of Evolution: A Peircean or Quasi-Peircean Answer to a Recurrent Problem of Post-Kantian Philosophy", in *Peirce and Contemporary Thought*, ed. by Kenneth L. Ketner (New York: Fordham University Press, 1995), 366-397.

Ayede, Murat and Güzeldere, Güven, "Cognitive Architecture, Concepts, and Introspection: An Information-Theoretic Solution to the Problem of Phenomenal Consciousness", *Noûs* 39 (2) (2005), 197–255.

Ayer, Alfred J., *The Origins of Pragmatism: Studies in the Philosophy of Charles Sanders Peirce and William James* (San Francisco: Freeman, Cooper, 1968).

Baggio, Guido, *La mente bio-sociale. Filosofia e psicologia in G. H. Mead* (ETS: Pisa, 2015).

Balog, Katalin, "Acquaintance and the Mind-Body Problem", in *The Mental, the Physical*, ed. by Christopher Hill and Simone Gozzano (Cambridge: Cambridge University Press, 2011).

Balog, Katalin, "In Defense of the Phenomenal Concept Strategy", *Philosophy and Phenomenological Research* (1) (2012), 1–23.

Barnham, Chris, *The Natural History of the Sign: Peirce, Vygotsky and the Hegelian Model of Concept Formation* (Mouton, Amsterdam: De Gruyter, 2022).

Bella, Michela, *Ontology after Philosophical Psychology. The Continuity of Consciousness in William James's Philosophy of Mind* (Lanham: Lexington Books, 2019).

Bellucci, Francesco, *Peirce's Speculative Grammar: Logic as Semiotics* (New York and London: Routledge, 2018).

Bernstein, Richard J., "Action, Conduct, and Self-Control", in *Perspectives on Peirce: Critical Essays on Charles Sanders Peirce*, ed. by Richard J. Bernstein (New Haven: Yale University Press, 1965), 66-91.

Bernstein, Richard J., "John Dewey's Metaphysics of Experience", *The Journal of Philosophy* 58(1) (1961), 5-14.

Bernstein, Richard J., "Peirce's Theory of Perception", in *Studies in the Philosophy of Charles Sanders Peirce. Second Series*, ed. by Edward C. Moore and Richard S. Robin (Amherst: The University of Massachusetts Press, 1964), 165-189.

Bernstein, Richard J., *The Pragmatic Turn* (Cambridge MA: Polity, 2010).

Block, Ned J., "Max Black's Objection to Mind-Body Identity", In *Phenomenal Concepts and Phenomenal Knowledge: New Essays on Consciousness and Physicalism*, ed. by T. Alter and S. Walter (Oxford: Oxford University Press, 2007), 249–306.

Boersema, David, "Peirce on Proper Names and Reference", *Transactions of the Charles S. Peirce Society* 38(3) (2002), 351-362.

Boisvert, Raymond D., *Dewey's Metaphysics* (New York: Fordham University Press, 1988)

Boler, John F., *Charles Peirce and Scholastic Realism: A Study of Peirce's Relation to John Duns Scotus* (Seattle: University of Washington Press, 1963).

Bonfantini, Massimo, Fabbrichesi, Rossella, and Zingale, Salvatore (eds.), *Su Peirce. Interpretazioni, ricerche, prospettive* (Milano: Bompiani, 2015).

Brandom, Robert, *Perspectives on Pragmatism: Classical, Recent, and Contemporary* (Cambridge, MA.: Harvard University Press, 2009).

Brandom, Robert, "Unsuccessful Semantics", *Analysis* 54 (3) (1994), 175-178.

Bridgman, Percy W., *The Logic of Modern Physics* (New York: Macmillan, 1927).

Brioschi, Maria Regina, "The Dismissal of 'Substance' and 'Being' in Peirce's Regenerated Logic", *Logic and Logical Philosophy* (2002), 1-26.

Browning, Douglas, *Act and Agent: An Essay in Philosophical Anthropology* (Coral Gables: University of Miami Press, 1964).

Browning, Douglas, "Dewey and Ortega on the Starting Point", *Transactions of the Charles S. Peirce Society* 34 (1) (1998), 69-92.

Browning, Douglas (ed.), *Philosophers of Process* (New York: Random House, 1965).

Brunning, Jacqueline and Paul Forster (eds.), *The Rule of Reason. The Philosophy of Charles Sanders Peirce* (Toronto-Buffalo-London: University of Toronto Press, 1997).

Burke, Tom, *Dewey's New Logic: A Reply to Russell* (Chicago: The University of Chicago Press, 1994).

Burke, Tom, "Prospects for Mathematizing Dewey's Logical Theory", in *Dewey's Logical Theory. New Studies and Interpretations*, ed. by Burke, Tom, Micah D. Hester, and Robert B. Talisse (Nashville: Vanderbilt University Press, 2002), 121-159.

Burke, Tom, Micah D. Hester, and Robert B. Talisse (eds.), *Dewey's Logical Theory. New Studies and Interpretations* (Nashville: Vanderbilt University Press, 2002).

Calcaterra, Rosa Maria, *Contingency and Normativity. The Challenges of Richard Rorty* (Lanham: Brill-Rodopi, 2019).

Calcaterra, Rosa Maria, "Varieties of Synechism. Peirce and James on Mind-World Continuity", *Journal of Speculative Philosophy* 25 (4) (2011), 412-424.

Calcaterra, Rosa M., Maddalena, Giovanni, and Marchetti, Giancarlo (eds.), *Il pragmatismo. Dalle origini agli sviluppi contemporanei* (Roma: Carocci, 2015)

Campbell, John, "On the Thesis that "I" Is not a Referring Term", in *Immunity to Error through Misidentification*, ed. by Simon Prosser and François Recanati (Cambridge: Cambridge University Press, 2012), 1-21.

Carruthers, Peter and Benedicte Veillet, "The Phenomenal Concept Strategy", *Journal of Consciousness Studies* 14 (2007), 212–236.

Cassam, Quassim (ed.), *Self-Knowledge* (Oxford: Oxford University Press, 1994).

Castañeda, Hector-Neri. "'He': A Study in the Logic of Self-Consciousness", in *Self-Reference and Self-Awareness*, ed. by Andrew Brook and Richard C. DeVidi (Amsterdam and Philadelphia: John Benjamins Publishing Company, 2001), 51-79.

Chalmers, David, "Facing Up to the Problem of Consciousness", *Journal of Consciousness Studies* 2(3) (1995), 200-219.

Chalmers, David J., *The Character of Consciousness* (Cambridge: Oxford University Press, 2010).

Chesterton, Gilbert K., *St. Thomas Aquinas* (New York: Image Books, 1956).

Chisholm, Roderick, "On the Observability of the Self", *Philosophy and Phenomenological Research* 30 (1969), 7-21.

Churchland, Paul M., "Reduction, Qualia, and the Direct Introspection of Brain States", *The Journal of Philosophy* 82 (1) (1985), 8–28.

Clark, Gordon H., *Dewey* (Philadelphia: Presbyterian and Reformed Publishing Company, 1960).

Cobb, John B. and Franklin I. Gamwell, *Existence and Actuality: Conversations with Charles Hartshorne* (Chicago: University of Chicago Press, 1984).

Colapietro, Vincent M., "C.S. Peirce's Reclamation of Teleology", in *Nature in American Philosophy*, ed. by Jean De Groot (Washington, D.C.: Catholic University of America Press, 2004), 88-108.

Colapietro, Vincent M., "Inwardness and Autonomy: A Neglected Aspect of Peirce's Approach to Mind", *Transactions of the Charles S. Peirce Society* 21(4) (1985), 485-512.

Colapietro, Vincent M., *Peirce's Approach to the Self: A Semiotic Perspective on Human Subjectivity* (Albany: State University of New York Press, 1989).

Colapietro, Vincent M., "Peirce's Guess at the Riddle of Rationality: Deliberative Imagination as the Personal Locus of Human Practice", in *Classical American Pragmatism: Its Contemporary Vitality*, ed. by Sandra Rosenthal, Carl R. Hausman, and Douglas R. Anderson (Chicago: University of Illinois Press, 1999), 15-30.

Colapietro, Vincent, "Portrait of an historicist: an alternative reading of Peircean semiotic", *Semiotiche*, 2 (2004), 49-68.

Colapietro, Vincent M., "The Proof of the Pudding: An Essay in Honor of Richard S. Robin", *Transactions of the Charles S. Peirce Society* 48(3) (2012), 285-309.

Conway, Charles G., "The Normative Sciences at Work and Play", *Transactions of the Charles S. Peirce Society* 44(2) (2008), 288-311.

Colapietro, Vincent M., "Toward a Pragmatic Conception of Practical Identity", *Transactions of the Charles S. Peirce Society* 42(2) (2006), 173-205.

Corrington, Robert S., *An Introduction to C.S. Peirce: Philosopher, Semiotician, and Ecstatic Naturalist* (Lanham: Rowman and Littlefield, 1993).

Dalton, Thomas C., *Becoming John Dewey: Dilemmas of a Philosopher and Naturalist* (Bloomington and Indianapolis: Indiana University Press, 2002).

Demircioglu, Erhan, "Physicalism and Phenomenal Concepts", *Philosophical Studies* 165 (2013), 257–277.

De Tienne, André, "Peirce on the Symbolical Person", in *Semiotica e fenomenologia del sé*, ed. by Rosa M. Calcaterra (Torino: Aragno, 2006), 91-109.

De Tienne, André, "Peirce's Logic of Information", Seminario del Grupo de Estudios Peirceanos, Universidad de Navarra, 28 Sep. 2006, Online.

De Tienne, André, "Peirce's Revolution: Semiotic VS. Transcendental Unity", in *Semiotics Around the World: Synthesis and Diversity. Vol. 1*, ed. by Irmengard Rauch and Gerald F. Carr (Berlin: Mouton de Gruyter, 1996).

De Waal, Cornelis, *Peirce: A Guide for the Perplexed* (London: Bloomsbury, 2013).

De Waal, Cornelis, "Science Beyond the Self: Remarks on Charles S. Peirce's Social Epistemology", *Cognitio* 7(1) (2006), 149-163.

Deely, John, *Four Ages of Understanding* (Buffalo, Toronto: University of Toronto Press, 2001).

Delaney, Cornelius F., "Peirce's Account of Mental Activity", *Synthese* 41(1) (1979), 25-36.

Delaney, Cornelius F., "Peirce's Critique of Foundationalism", *The Monist* 57(2) (1973), 240-251.

Delaney, Cornelius F., *Science, Knowledge, and Mind: A Study in the Philosophy of Charles S. Peirce* (Notre Dame and London: Notre Dame University Press, 1993).

Dennett, Daniel C., "Facing Backwards on the Problem of Consciousness", *The Journal of Consciousness Studies* 3 (1) (1996), 4–6.

Dennett, Daniel C., "Quining Qualia", in *Mind and Cognition*, ed. by William G. Lycan (Oxford: Blackwell, 1988).

Dennett, Daniel C., "The Path Not Taken", *Behavioral and Brain Sciences* 18 (1995), 252–253.

Dennett, Daniel C., "What RoboMary Knows", in T. Alter and S. Walter (2007), 15–31.

Dewey, John, *Logica sperimentale. Teoria naturalistica della conoscenza e del pensiero*, ed. by Roberto Frega (Macerata, Quodlibet, 2008).

Dewey, John, *The Early Works of John Dewey, 1882-1898*, 5 vols., ed. by J. A. Boydston (Carbondale and Edwardsville: Southern Illinois University Press, 1969-1972).

Dewey, John, *The Middle Work of John Dewey, 1899-1924*, 15 vols., ed. by J. A. Boydston (Carbondale and Edwardsville: Southern Illinois University Press, 1976-1983).

Dewey, John, *The Later Works of John Dewey, 1925-1953*. 17 vols., ed by J. A. Boydston (Carbondale and Edwardsville: Southern Illinois University Press, 1981-1990).

Dicker, George, "John Dewey on the Object of Knowledge", *Transactions of the Charles S. Peirce Society* 8(3) (1972), 152-166.

Dicker, George, "Knowing and Coming-To-Know in John Dewey's Theory of Knowledge", *The Monist* 57(2) (1973), 191-219.

DiLeo, Jeffrey R., "Charles Peirce's Theory of Proper Names", in *Studies in the Logic of Charles Sanders Peirce*, ed. by Nathan Houser, Don D. Roberts, and James Van Evra (Bloomington and Indianapolis: Indiana University Press, 1997), 574-594.

DiLeo, Jeffrey R., "Peirce's Haecceitism", *Transactions of the Charles S. Peirce Society* 27(1) (1991), 79-109.

Dreon, Roberta, *Human Landscapes: Contributions to a Pragmatist Anthropology* (Albany: State University of New York Press, 2022).

Dretske, Fred, "Introspection", *Proceeding of the Aristotelian Society* 94 (1993), 263-278.

Embry, Brian, "Truth and Truthmaking in 17th-Century Scholasticism" (Dissertation, University of Toronto, 2015).

Evans, Gareth, *The Varieties of Reference* (Oxford: Oxford University Press, 1982).

Fabbrichesi, Rossella, "From Gestures to Habits: A Link Between Semiotics and Pragmatism," in *The Bloomsbury Companion to Contemporary Peircean Semiotics*, ed. by Tony Jappy (London: Bloomsbury, 2020).

Fabbrichesi, Rossella, *Sulle tracce del segno. Semiotica, faneroscopia e cosmologia nel pensiero di C.S.Peirce* (Firenze: La Nuova Italia, 1986).

Fernandez, Jordi, "Priviledged Access Naturalized", *The Philosophical Quarterly* 53 (2003), 352-372.

Fish, Max H., *Peirce, Semeiotic, and Pragmatism*, ed. by Kenneth L. Ketner and Christian Kloesel (Bloomington: Indiana University Press, 1986).

Fitzgerald, John J., *Peirce's Theory of Signs as Foundation for Pragmatism* (The Hague: Mouton, 1966).

Forster, Paul, *Peirce and the Threat of Nominalism* (New York: Cambridge University Press, 2011).

Frega, Roberto, *John Dewey et la philosophie comme épistémologie de la pratique* (Paris: L'Harmattan, 2006).

Frega, Roberto, *Pensée, expérience*, pratique (Paris: L'Harmattan, 2006).

Frisina, Warren G., "Knowledge as Active, Aesthetic, and Hypothetical: An Examination of the relationship Between Dewey's Metaphysics and Epistemology", *Philosophy Today* 33(3) (1989), 245-263.

Fumerton, Richard A., *Metaepistemology and Skepticism* (Lanham: Rowman and Littlefield, 1996).

Gale, Richard M., *John Dewey's Quest for Unity: The Journey of a Promethean Mystic* (Amherst NY: Prometheus Book, 2010).

Gale, Richard M., "The Naturalism of John Dewey", in *The Cambridge Companion to John Dewey*, ed. by Molly Cochran (Cambridge: Cambridge University Press, 2010), 55-79.

Gale, Richard M., "The Problem of Ineffability in Dewey's Theory of Inquiry", *The Southern Journal of Philosophy* 44(1) (2006), 75-90.

Gardner, Thomas, "The Subject Matter of Dewey's Metaphysics", *Transactions of the Charles S. Peirce Society* 36(3) (2000), 393-405.

Garrigou-Lagrange, Reginald, O.P., *Reality: A Synthesis of Thomistic Thought* (St. Louis: Herder, 1958).

Garrison, James W., "Dewey on Metaphysics, Meaning and Maps", *Transactions of the Charles S. Peirce Society* 41(4) (2005), 818-844.

Gartenberg, Zachary M., "Intelligibility and Subjectivity in Peirce: A Reading of his 'New List of Categories'", *Journal of the History of Philosophy* 50(4) (2012), 581-610.

Gertler, Brie, "Self-Knowledge", *Stanford Encyclopedia of Philosophy* (2008).

Gilson, Étienne, *Being and Some Philosophers* (Toronto: Pontifical Institute of Medieval Studies, 1952).

Girel, Mathias, *L'esprit en acte. Psychologie, mythologies et pratique chez les pragmatistes*. (Paris: Vrin, 2021).

Girel, Mathias, "Peirce's Reception in France", *European Journal of Pragmatism and American Philosophy* 6 (1) (2014), 15-23.

Godfrey-Smith, Peter, "Dewey and the Question of Realism", *Noûs* 50 (1) (2016), 73-89.

Godfrey-Smith, Peter, "John Dewey's *Experience and Nature*", *Topoi* 33 (1) (2014), 285–291.

Goudge, Thomas A., "Peirce's Index", *Transactions of the Charles S. Peirce Society* 1(2) (1965), 52-70.

Graham, G. and T. Horgan, "Mary Mary, Quite Contrary", *Philosophical Studies* 99 (2000), 59–87.

Haack, Susan, *Evidence and Inquiry* (Cambridge: Blackwell Publishers, 1993).

Hare, Peter, "The American Philosophical Tradition as Progressively Enriched Naturalism", in *Pragmatism with Purpose: Selected Writings of Peter Hare*, ed. by Joseph Palencik, Douglas R. Anderson, and Steven A. Miller (New York: Fordham University Press, 2015), 117-121.

Harrison, Stanley M., "Peirce on Persons", in *Proceeding of the C.S. Peirce Bicentennial International Congress*, ed. by Kenneth L. Ketner (Lubbock: Texas Technical University Press, 1981), 217-221.

Hickman, Larry A., "Contextualizing Knowledge: A Reply to "Dewey and the Theory of Knowledge", *Transactions of the Charles S. Peirce Society* 26(4) (1990), 459-463.

Hickman, Larry A., *John Dewey's Pragmatic Technology* (Bloomington: Indiana University Press, 1990).

Hickman, Larry A., Stefan Neubert, and Kersten Reich (eds.), *John Dewey between Pragmatism and Constructivism* (New York: Fordham University Press, 2009).

Hildebrand, David L., *Beyond Realism and Anti-Realism: John Dewey and the Neopragmatists* (Nashville: Vanderbilt University Press, 2003).

Hill, Christopher S. and Brian P. McLaughlin, "There Are Fewer Things in Reality Than Are Dreamt of in Chalmers's Philosophy", *Philosophy and Phenomenological Research* 59(2) (1999), 445–454.

Hilpinen, Risto, "Peirce on Language and Reference", in *Peirce and Contemporary Thought: Philosophical Inquiries*, ed. by Kenneth L. Ketner (New York: Fordham University Press, 1995), 272-303.

Holmes, Larry, "Prolegomena to Peirce's Philosophy of Mind", in *Studies in the Philosophy of Charles Sanders Peirce. Second Series*, ed. by Edward C. Moore and Richard S. Robin (Amherst: The University of Massachusetts Press, 1964), 359-381.

Hookway, Christopher, *Peirce* (London: Routledge, 1985).

Hookway, Christopher, *Truth, Rationality and Pragmatism. Themes from Peirce* (New York: Oxford University Press, 2002).

Hookway, Christopher, *The Pragmatic Maxim: Essays on Peirce and Pragmatism* (Oxford: Oxford University Press, 2012).

Horkheimer, Max, *Eclipse of Reason* (New York: Continuum, 2004).

Hulswit, Menno, "A Guess at the Riddle of Semiotic Causation", *Transactions of the Charles S. Peirce Society* 34(3) (1998), 641-688.

Hulswit, Menno, "Peirce's Teleological Approach to Natural Classes", *Transactions of the Charles S. Peirce Society* 33 (2) (1997), 722-772.

Ishida, Masato, *A Philosophical Commentary on C. S. Peirce's "On a New List of Categories": Exhibiting Logical Structure and Abiding Relevance* (Doctoral Dissertation, Pennsylvania State University, State College PA, 2009).

Jackson, Frank, "Epiphenomenal Qualia", *Philosophical Quarterly* 32 (1982), 127–136.

Jackson, Frank, "Postscript on Qualia", in Frank Jackson, *Mind, Method, and Conditionals: Selected Essays* (London: Routledge, 1998), 76–79.

James, William, "Against Nihilism", in *The Thought and Character of William James*, vol. 1, ed. Ralph Barton Perry (Boston: Little, Brown, and Co., 1935), 525-526.

Jung, Matthias, "John Dewey and Action", in *The Cambridge Companion to John Dewey*, ed. by Molly Cochran (Cambridge: Cambridge University Press, 2010), 145-165.

Kahn, Sholom J., "Experience and Existence in Dewey's Naturalistic Metaphysics", *Philosophy and Phenomenological Research* 9(2) (1948), 316-321.

Kemp-Pritchard, Ilona, "Peirce on Individuation", *Transactions of the Charles S. Peirce Society* 14(2) (1978), 83-100.

Kitcher, Patricia, "Phenomenal Qualities", *American Philosophical Quarterly* 16 (1979), 123–129.

Koopman, Colin, *Pragmatism as transition. Historicity and Hope in James, Dewey, and Rorty* (New York: Columbia University Press, 2009).

Krolikowski, W. P., "The Peircean *Vir*", in *Studies in the Philosophy of Charles Sanders Peirce. Second Series*, ed. by Edward C. Moore and Richard S. Robin (Amherst: The University of Massachusetts Press, 1964), 257-270.

Lane, Robert, *Peirce on Realism and Idealism* (Cambridge: Cambridge University Press, 2018).

Lane, Robert, "Peirce's Modal Shift: From Set Theory to Pragmaticism", *Journal of the History of Philosophy* 45(4) (2007), 551-576.

Lane, Robert, "Persons, Signs, Animals: A Peircean Account of Personhood", *Transactions of the Charles S. Peirce Society* 45(1) (2009), 1-26.

Legg, Catherine, "Charles Peirce's Limit Concept of Truth", *Philosophy Compass* 9 (3) (2014), 204-213.

Levi, Isaac, "Dewey's Logic of Inquiry", in *The Cambridge Companion to John Dewey*, ed. by Molly Cochran (Cambridge: Cambridge University Press, 2010), pp. 80-100.

Levin, Janet, "What Is a Phenomenal Concept?", in T. Alter and S. Walter (2007), 87–111.

Levine, Joseph, "Materialism and Qualia: The Explanatory Gap", *Pacific Philosophical Quarterly* 64 (1983), 354–361.

Lewis, David, "Postscript to "Mad Pain and Martian Pain"", in *Philosophical Papers vol. 1* (New York and Oxford: Oxford University Press, 1996), 130–132.

Lewis, David, "Should a Materialist Believe in Qualia?", *Australasian Journal of Philosophy* 73(1) (1995), 140–144.

Liszka, James J., *A General Introduction to the Semeiotic of Charles Sanders Peirce* (Bloomington and Indianapolis: Indiana University Press, 1996).

Lizzadri, Antonio, *Dal realismo scientifico al realismo interno. Putnam verso il pragmatismo* (Sesto San Giovanni: Mimesis International, 2022).

Loar, Brian, "Phenomenal States", in *Philosophy of Mind: Classical and Contemporary Readings*, ed. by David J. Chalmers (New York: Oxford University Press, 2002), 295–311.

Loar, Brian, "Qualia, Properties, Modality", *Philosophical Issues* 13 (2003), Philosophy of Mind, 113–129.

Longo, Giuseppe, "Le conseguenze della filosofia", in *A Plea for Balance in Philosophy*, ed. by Roberta Lanfredini e Alberto Peruzzi (ETS: Pisa, 2015), 17-44.

Lovejoy, Arthur O., "The Thirteen Pragmatisms. I", *The Journal of Philosophy, Psychology, and Scientific Methods* 5 (1) (1908), 5-12; "The Thirteen Pragmatisms. II", *The Journal of Philosophy, Psychology, and Scientific Methods* 5 (2) (1908), 29-39.

Lu, Henry C., "The Goal of Inquiry in Dewey's Philosophy", *Education Theory* 20 (1) (1970), 65-72.

Lycan, William G., *Consciousness* (Cambridge Mass: MIT Press, 1987).

Lycan, William G., *Consciousness and Experience* (Cambridge Mass: MIT Press, 1996).

Lycan, William G., "Perspectival Representation and the Knowledge Argument", In *Consciousness: New Philosophical Essays*, ed. by Q. Smith and A. Jokie (Oxford: Oxford University Press, 2003).

Maddalena, Giovanni, "Esperienza e soggettività. Un confronto tra Peirce e Dewey", in *Semiotica e fenomenologia del sé*, ed. by Rosa M. Calcaterra (Torino: Nino Aragno Editore, 2006), 111-122.

Maddalena, Giovanni, *Metafisica per assurdo. Peirce e i problemi dell'epistemologia contemporanea* (Soveria Mannelli: Rubbettino, 2009).

Maddalena, Giovanni, "Peirce's Incomplete Synthetic Turn", *The Review of Metaphysics* 65(3) (2012), 613-640.

Maddalena, Giovanni, "Peirce's Theory of Assent", in *Ideas in Action*, ed. by M. Bergman, A.V. Pietarinen, H. Rydenfelt, and S. Paavola (Helsinki: Nordic Studies in Pragmatism, 2010), 211-223.

Maddalena, Giovanni, "Review of Gava, *Peirce's Account of Purposefulness: A Kantian Perspective*", *Transactions of the Charles S. Peirce Society* 53 (3) (2017), 503-509.

Maddalena, Giovanni, "The Limits of Experience: Dewey and Contemporary American Philosophy", *Quaestio* 4(4) (2004), 387-406.

Maddalena, Giovanni, *The Philosophy of Gesture: Completing Pragmatists' Incomplete Revolution* (Montreal & Kingston – London – Chicago: McGill-Queen's University Press, 2015).

Magada-Ward, Mary, "'As Parts of One Esthetic Total': Inference, Imagery, and Self-Knowledge in the Later Peirce", *The Journal of Speculative Philosophy* 17(3) (2003), 216-223.

Marchetti, Giancarlo (ed.), *The Ethics, Epistemology, and Politics of Richard Rorty* (London, Routledge, 2021).

Margolis, Joseph, "The Relevance of Dewey's Epistemology", In *New Studies in the Philosophy of John Dewey*, ed. by Steven M. Cahn (Hanover, N.H.: The University of New England, 1977), 117-148.

Maritain, Jacques, "Philosophical Co-Operation and Intellectual Justice", *The Modern Schoolman* 22 (1) (1944), 1-15.

Maritain, Jacques, *The Range of Reason* (New York: Charles Scribner's Son, 1952).

Maritain, Jacques, "Toward a Thomistic Idea of Evolution", in Jacques Maritain, *Untrammeled Approaches* (Notre Dame, Indiana: University of Notre Dame Press, 1997), 85-131.

McDermid, Douglas, *The Varieties of Pragmatism: Truth, Realism, and Knowledge from James to Rorty* (London and New York: Continuum, 2006).

McDermott, John J. (ed.), *The Writings of William James: A Comprehensive Edition* (New York: The Modern Library, 1968).

McLaughlin, B., "In Defense of New Wave Materialism", in *Physicalism and Its Discontents*, ed. by C. Gillet and B. Loewer (New York: Cambridge University Press, 2001), 319–330.

Mead, George H., *The Philosophy of the Act* (Chicago: The University of Chicago Press, 1938).

Menand, Louis, *The Metaphysical Club: A story of ideas in America* (New York, Farrar, Straus and Giroux, 2001).

Menary, Richard, "Our Glassy Essence: Pragmatist Approaches to the Self", in *The Oxford Handbook of the Self*, ed. by Shaun Gallagher (Oxford: Oxford University Press, 2011), 609-632.

Michael, Emily, "Peirce on Individuals", *Transactions of the Charles S. Peirce Society* 12(4) (1976), 321-329.

Misak, Cheryl J., "A Peircean Account of Moral Judgment", in *Peirce and the Value Theory: On Peircean Esthetics and Ethics*, ed. by Herman Parret (Philadelphia: John Benjamins Publishing Company, 1994), 39-48.

Misak, Cheryl J., "C.S. Peirce on Vital Matters", in *The Cambridge Companion to Peirce*, ed. by Cheryl J. Misak (New York and Cambridge: Cambridge University Press, 2004), 150-174.

Misak, Cheryl J., *The American Pragmatists* (Oxford: Oxford University Press, 2013).

Misak, Cheryl J., *The Cambridge Companion to Peirce* (New York and Cambridge: Cambridge University Press, 2004).

Misak, Cheryl J., *Truth and the End of Inquiry: A Peircean Account of Truth* (Oxford: Clarendon Press, 2004).

Misak, Cheryl, *Verificationism: Its History and Prospects* (London and New York: Routledge, 1995).

Moore, G.E., "William James's 'Pragmatism'", in *William James: Pragmatism in Focus*, ed. by Doris Olin (London and New York: Routledge, 1992), 161-195.

Moore, Harold, "Ayer and the Pragmatic Maxim", *Transactions of the Charles S. Peirce Society* 7(3) (1971), 168-175.

Moran, Richard, *Authority and Estrangement: An Essay on Self-Knowledge* (Princeton: Princeton University Press, 2001).

Murphy, Arthur E., "Dewey's Epistemology and Metaphysics", in *The Philosophy of John Dewey*, ed. by Paul A. Schilpp (New York: Tudor Publishing Company, 1951).

Muoio, Patricia A., "Peirce on the Person", *Transactions of the Charles S. Peirce Society* 20(2) (1984), 169-181.

Myers, Gerald E., "Knowing One's Own Mind", in *Charles S. Peirce and the Philosophy of Science: Papers From the Harvard Sesquicentennial Congress*, ed. by Edward C. Moore (Tuscaloosa and London: The University of Alabama Press, 1993), 300-308.

Nagel, Thomas, "What Is It Like to Be a Bat?", *The Philosophical Review* 83(4) (1974), 435–450.

Nemirow, L., "So This Is What It's Like: A Defense of the Ability Hypothesis", in T. Alter and S. Walter (2007), 32–51.

Nida-Rümelin, Martine, "What Mary Couldn't Know: Belief About Phenomenal States", in *Conscious Experience*, ed. by Thomas Metzinger (Paderborn: Schöningh, 1995), 219–241.

Noë, Alva, *Out of Our Heads* (New York: Hill and Wang, 2009).

O'Dea, John, "The Indexical Nature of Sensory Concepts", *Philosophical Papers* 31(2) (2002), 169–181.

Oderberg, David S., *Real Essentialism* (New York and London: Routledge, 2007).

Olshewsky, Thomas M., "Realism and Semiosis", in *Proceedings of the C. S. Peirce Bicentennial International Congress*, ed. by Kenneth L. Ketner (Lubbock: Graduate School, Texas Technical University Press, 1981), 87-92.

Pape, Helmut, "A Peircean Theory of Indexical Signs and Individuation", *Semiotica* 31(3/4) (1980), 215-243.

Papineau, David, *Philosophical Naturalism* (Cambridge Mass and Oxford: Blackwell, 1993).

Papineau, David, *Thinking about Consciousness* (Oxford: Clarendon Press, 2002).

Pappas, Gregory F., *John Dewey's Ethics: Democracy as Experience* (Bloomington: Indiana University Press, 2008).

Parker, Kelly, *The Continuity of Peirce's Thought* (Nashville and London: Vanderbilt University Press, 1998).

Pearce, Trevor, *Pragmatism's Evolution: Organism and Environment in American Philosophy* (Chicago: University of Chicago Press, 2020).

Pegis, Anton C., "St. Thomas and the Unity of Man", in *Progress in Philosophy*, ed. by James A. McWilliams, S.J. (Milwaukee: The Bruce Publishing Company, 1967), 170-171.

Peirce, Charles S., Manuscripts in the Houghton Library of Harvard University, as catalogued in Richard Robin, *Annotated Catalogue of the Papers of Charles S. Peirce* (Amherst: University of Massachusetts Press, 1967).

Peirce, Charles S., *The Collected Papers of Charles Sanders Peirce*, ed. by Charles Hartshorne and Paul Weiss (vols. 1-6) and Arthur Burks (vols. 7-8) (Cambridge: Cambridge University Press, 1931-58).

Peirce, Charles S., *The Essential Peirce: Selected Philosophical Writings*, ed. by Nathan Houser and Christian Kloesel (vol. 1) and the Peirce Edition Project (vol. 2) (Bloomington and Indianapolis: Indiana University Press, 1992-98).

Peirce, Charles S., *Writings of Charles S. Peirce: A Chronological Edition*, ed. by the Peirce Edition Project (vols. 1-6, 8) (Bloomington and Indianapolis: Indiana University Press, 1982-2009).

Perry, John, *Knowledge, Possibility, and Consciousness* (Cambridge: MIT Press, 2001).

Piatt, Donald A., "Dewey's Logical Theory", in *The Philosophy of John Dewey*, ed. by Paul A. Schilpp (New York: Tudor Publishing Company, 1951).

Pietarinen, Ahti-Veikko, "Peirce's Pragmatic Theory of Proper Names", *Transactions of the Charles S. Peirce Society* 46(3) (2010), 341-363.

Potter, Vincent G., S. J., *Charles S. Peirce on Norms and Ideals* (Amherst: The University of Massachusetts Press, 1967).

Potter, Vincent G., S. J., "Normative Science and the Pragmatic Maxim", *Transactions of the Charles S. Peirce Society* 5(1) (1967), 41-53.

Pratt, Scott L., "Inquiry and Analysis: Dewey and Russell on Philosophy", *Studies in Philosophy and Education* 17(2) (1998), 101-122.

Prosser, Simon and François Recanati (eds.), *Immunity to Error through Misidentification* (Cambridge: Cambridge University Press, 2012).

Quine, Willard V. O., *From a Logical Point of View* (Cambridge: Harvard University Press, 1961).

Ramos, Alice M., *Dynamic Transcendentals: Truth, Goodness, and Beauty from a Thomistic Perspective* (Washington, D.C.: Catholic University of America Press, 2012).

Randall, John H., *Aristotle* (New York: Columbia University Press, 1960).

Randall, John H. Jr., *Nature and Historical Experience* (New York: Columbia University Press, 1958).

Randall, John H. Jr., "Substance as Process", *The Review of Metaphysics* 10 (4) (1957), 580-601.

Recanati, François, "Immunity to Error Through Misidentification: What It Is and Where It Comes From", in *Immunity to Error through Misidentification*, ed. by Simon Prosser and François Recanati (Cambridge: Cambridge University Press, 2012), 180-201.

Reck, Andrew J., *Speculative Philosophy: A Study of Its Nature, Types, and Uses* (Albuquerque: University of New Mexico Press, 1972).

Rescher, Nicholas, *Pluralism: Against the Demand for Consensus* (Oxford: Clarendon Press, 1993).

Rescher, Nicholas, *Process Philosophy: A Survey of Basic Issues* (Pittsburgh: University of Pittsburgh Press, 2000).

Rescher, Nicholas, *The Strife of Systems: An Essay on the Grounds and Implications of Philosophical Diversity* (Pittsburgh: University of Pittsburgh Press, 1985).

Riley, Gresham, "Peirce's Theory of the Individuals", *Transactions of the Charles S. Peirce Society* 10(3) (1974), 135-165.

Robin, Richard S., "Classical Pragmatism and Pragmatism's Proof", in Brunning and Forster 1997, 139-152.

Robinson, Andrew, *God and the World of Signs: Trinity, Evolution, and the Metaphysical Semiotics of C.S. Peirce* (Leiden and Boston: Brill, 2010).

Rockwell, Teed, *Neither Brain Nor Ghost: A Nondualist Alternative to the Mind-Brain Identity Theory* (Cambridge: MIT Press, 2005).

Rogers, Melvin L., "Action and Inquiry in Dewey's Philosophy", *Transactions of the Charles S. Peirce Society* 43(1) (2007), 90-115.

Rorty, Richard, *Consequences of Pragmatism* (Minneapolis: University of Minnesota Press, 1997).

Rorty, Richard, *Philosophy and Social Hope* (New York: Penguin Books, 1999).

Rorty, Richard, *Philosophy and the Mirror of Nature* (Princeton: Princeton University Press, 1979).

Rorty, Richard, "Pragmatism, Categories, and Language", *The Philosophical Review* 70 (2) (1961), 197-223.

Rosenthal, Sandra, "Peirce's Pragmatic Account of Perception: Issues and Implications", in *The Cambridge Companion to Peirce*, ed. by Cheryl J. Misak (New York and Cambridge: Cambridge University Press, 2004), 193-213.

Rosenthal, Sandra, "Peirce's Theory of the Perceptual Judgment: An Ambiguity", *Journal of the History of Philosophy* 7(3) (1969), 303-314.

Rosenthal, Sandra B., "The Pragmatic Reconstruction of Realism: A Pathway for the Future", in *Pragmatic Naturalism and Realism*, ed. by John R. Shook (Amherst NY: Prometheus Books, 2003), pp. 43-53.

Rosenthal, Sandra B., *Speculative Pragmatism* (Amherst: The University of Massachusetts Press, 1986).

Ross, James F., "Eschatological Pragmatism", in *Philosophy and the Christian Faith*, ed. by Thomas V. Morris (Notre Dame, Indiana: University of Notre Dame Press, 1988), 279-300.

Ross, James F., "The Fate of the Analysis: Aristotle's Revenge", *Proceedings of the American Catholic Philosophical Association* 64 (1990), 51-74.

Ross, James F., *Thought and World: The Hidden Necessities* (Notre Dame, Indiana: University of Notre Dame, 2008).

Roth, Robert J., "Did Peirce Answer Hume on Necessary Connection?", *The Review of Metaphysics* 38(4) (1985), 867-880.

Roth, Robert J., "How 'Closed' Is John Dewey's Naturalism", *International Philosophical Quarterly* 3 (1) (1963), 106-120.

Roth, Robert J., *Radical Pragmatism: An Alternative* (New York: Fordham University Press, 1998).

Russell, Bertrand, "Knowledge by Acquaintance and Knowledge by Description", *Proceedings of the Aristotelian Society* 11 (1911), 108-128.

Russell, Bertrand, "William James's Conception of Truth", in *William James: Pragmatism in Focus*, 196-211.

Ryan, Frank X., "Primary Experience as Settled Meaning: Dewey's Conception of Experience", *Philosophy Today* 38(1) (1994), 29-42.

Ryder, John, "Reconciling Pragmatism and Naturalism", in *Pragmatic Naturalism and Realism*, ed. by John R. Shook (Amherst NY: Prometheus Books, 2003), 55-77.

Santarelli, Matteo, *La vita interessata. Una prospettiva a partire da John Dewey* (Macerata: Quodlibet, 2019).

Schultenover, David G. (ed.), *The Reception of Pragmatism in France and the Rise of Roman Catholic Modernism, 1890-1914* (Washington DC: The Catholic University of America Press, 2011).

Searle, John R., *The Mystery of Consciousness* (New York: A New York Review Book, 1997).

Sellars, Wilfrid, *Empiricism and the Philosophy of Mind*, with an Introduction by Richard Rorty and a Study Guide by Robert Brandom (Cambridge and London: Harvard University Press, 1997).

Sfendoni-Mentzou, Demetra, "Toward a Potential-Pragmatic Account of Peirce's Theory of Truth", *Transactions of the Charles S. Peirce Society* 27 (1) (1991), 27-77.

Shapiro, Michael, "History as Theory: One Linguist's View", in *Peirce and Contemporary Thought*, ed. by Kenneth L. Ketner (New York: Fordham University Press, 1995), 304-314.

Sheldon, Wilmon H., *America's Progressive Philosophy* (London and New Haven: Yale University Press, 1942).

Sheldon, Wilmon H., "Can Philosophers Co-Operate?", *The Modern Schoolman* 21 (1944), 71-82.

Sheldon, Wilmon H., "Can Philosophers Co-Operate?", *The Modern Schoolman* 22 (1944), 131-142.

Sheldon, Wilmon H., "Professor Maritain on Philosophical Co-Operation", *The Modern Schoolman* 22 (2) (1944), 88-97.

Sheldon, Wilmon H., *Strife of Systems and Productive Duality: An Essay in Philosophy* (Cambridge: Harvard University Press, 1918).

Shoemaker, Sydney S., "Qualia and Consciousness", *Mind* 100 (4) (1991), 507–524.

Shoemaker, Sidney S., "Self-Reference and Self-Awareness", *The Journal of Philosophy* 65(19) (1968), 555-567.

Shook, John R., "Dewey and Quine on the Logic of What There Is", In *Dewey's Logical Theory. New Studies and Interpretations*, ed. by Tom Burke, Micah D. Hester, and Robert B. Talisse (Nashville: Vanderbilt University Press, 2002), 93-118.

Shook, John R. (ed.), *Pragmatic Naturalism and Realism* (Amherst NY: Prometheus Books, 2003).

Shook, John R., and Richard T. Hull (eds.), *The Dictionary of Modern American Philosophers* (Bristol: Bloomsbury, 2005).

Short, Thomas L., "Hypostatic Abstraction in Self-Consciousness", in *The Rule of Reason: The Philosophy of Charles Sanders Peirce*, ed. by Jacqueline Brunning and Paul Forster (Toronto-Buffalo-London: University of Toronto Press, 1997), 289-308.

Short Thomas L., "Peirce on the Aim of Inquiry: Another Reading of 'Fixation'", *Transactions of the Charles S. Peirce Society* 36(1) (2000), 1-23.

Short, Thomas L., "Peirce's Concept of Final Causation", *Transactions of the Charles S. Peirce Society* 17(4) (1981), 369-382.

Short, Thomas L., *Peirce's Theory of Signs* (New York and Cambridge: Cambridge University Press, 2007).

Shusterman, Richard, "Dewey on Experience: Foundation or Reconstruction?", in *Dewey Reconfigured: Essays on Deweyan Pragmatism*, ed. by Casey Haskins, David I. Seiple (Albany: State University of New York Press, 1999), 193-219.

Skagestad, Peter, "C. S. Peirce on Biological Evolution and Scientific Progress", *Synthese* 41(1) (1979), 85-114.

Sleeper, Ralph W., *The Necessity of Pragmatism: John Dewey's Conception of Philosophy* (New Haven: Yale University Press, 1986).

Smith, Barry D., "John Dewey's Theory of Consciousness", *Educational Theory* 35(3) (1985), 267–272.

Smith, John E., *Purpose and Thought: The Meaning of Pragmatism* (New Haven: Yale University Press, 1978).

Smith, John E., "Religion and Theology in Peirce", in *Studies in the Philosophy of Charles S. Peirce*, ed. by Philip P. Wiener and Frederic H. Young (Cambridge: Harvard University Press, 1952), 251-267.

Smyth, Richard, "The Pragmatic Maxim in 1878", *Transactions of the Charles S. Peirce Society* 13 (2) (1977), 93-111.

Solymosi, Tibor, "Neuropragmatism, Old and New", *Phenomenology and the Cognitive Sciences* 10(3) (2011), 347–368.

Sørensen, Bent, "The Pragmatic Maxim of the Mature Peirce Regarding Its Special Normative Function", *Semiotica* 177-1/4 (2009), 177-188.

Sorrell, Kory S., "Peirce and a Pragmatic Reconception of Substance", *Transactions of the Charles S. Peirce Society* 37(2) (2001), 257-295.

Sorrell, Kory S., *Representative Practices: Peirce, Pragmatism, and Feminist Epistemology* (New York: Fordham University Press, 2004).

Stephens, Lynn G., "Peirce on Psychological Self-Knowledge", *Transactions of the Charles S. Peirce Society* 16(3) (1980), 212-224.

Stoljar, Daniel, "Physicalism." *Stanford Encyclopedia of Philosophy* (2015).

Stoljar, Daniel, "Physicalism and Phenomenal Concepts", *Mind and Language* 20 (2005), 469–494.

Strawson, Galen, "I and *I*: Immunity to Error through Misidentification of the Subject", in *Immunity to Error through Misidentification*, ed. by Simon Prosser and François Recanati (Cambridge: Cambridge University Press, 2012), 202-223.

Strawson, Peter F., *Individuals: An Essay in Descriptive Metaphysics* (London and New York: Routledge, 2003).

Stuhr, John J., "Dewey's Notion of Qualitative Experience", *Transactions of the Charles S. Peirce Society* 15(1) (1979), 68–81.

Stuhr, John J., "Dewey's Reconstruction of Metaphysics", *Transactions of the Charles S. Peirce Society* 28(2) (1992), 161-176.

Stuhr, John J., *Experience as Activity: Dewey's Metaphysics* (Ph.D. Dissertation, Vanderbilt University, 1976).

Sturgeon, Scott, "The Epistemic Basis of Subjectivity", *Mind and Language* 20 (1994), 469–494.

Talisse, Robert B., *A Pragmatist Philosophy of Democracy* (New York: Routledge, 2007).

Taylor, John H., "Physicalism and Phenomenal Concepts: Bringing Ontology and Philosophy of Mind Together", *Philosophia* 41 (2013), 1283-1297.

Thibaud, Pierre, "Peirce on Proper Names and Individuation", *Transactions of the Charles S. Peirce Society* 23(4) (1987), 521-538.

Tiercelin, Claudine, *La pensée-signe: ètudes sur C. S. Peirce* (Nîmes: J. Chambon, 1993).

Tiles, J. E., *Dewey* (London and New York: Routledge, 1988).

Tiles, J. E., "Dewey's Realism: Applying the Term 'Mental' to a World without Withins", *Transactions of the Charles S. Peirce Society* 31 (1) (1995), 137-166.

Tye, Michael, "A Theory of Phenomenal Concepts", in *Minds and Persons*, ed. by Anthony O'Hear (Cambridge University Press, 2003).

Tye, Michael, 2006. "Absent Qualia and the Mind-Body Problem", *The Philosophical Review* 115 (2) (2006), 139–168.

Tye, Michael, *Color, Consciousness, and Content* (Cambridge: MIT Press, 2000).

Tye, Michael, *Ten Problems of Consciousness* (Cambridge: MIT Press, 1995).

Uslucan, Haci-Halil, "Charles Sanders Peirce and the Semiotic Foundation of Self and Reason", *Mind, Culture, and Activity* 11(2) (2012), 96-108.

Veillet, Benedicte, "The Cognitive Significance of Phenomenal Knowledge", *Philosophical Studies* 172 (2015), 2955–2974.

Weber, Eric T., "Proper Names and Persons: Peirce's Semiotic Consideration of Proper Names", *Transactions of the Charles S. Peirce Society* 44(2) (2008), 346-362.

Weiss, Paul, "Charles S. Peirce, Philosopher", in *Perspectives on Peirce: Critical Essays on Charles Sanders Peirce*, ed. by Richard J. Bernstein (New Haven: Yale University Press, 1965), 120-140.

West, Cornel, *The American Evasion of Philosophy: A Genealogy of Pragmatism* (Madison, WI: University of Wisconsin Press, 1989).

Whyte, J.T., "Success Semantics", *Analysis* 50 (3) (1990), 149-157.

Wilson, Aaron B., "The Perception of Generals", *Transactions of the Charles S. Peirce Society* 48(2) (2012), 169-190.

Woodbridge, Frederick J.E., *Aristotle's Vision of Nature* (New York: Columbia University Press, 1965).

Zalamea, Fernando, *Filosofía sintética de las matemáticas contemporáneas* (Bogotá: Editorial Universidad Nacional de Colombia, 2008).

Zalamea, Fernando, *Peirce's Logic of Continuity: A Conceptual and Mathematical Approach* (Boston: Docent Press, 2012).

Zedler, Beatrice, "Dewey's Theory of Knowledge", in *John Dewey: His Thought and Influence*, ed. by John Blewett (New York: Fordham University Press, 1960).

MIMESIS GROUP
www.mimesis-group.com

MIMESIS INTERNATIONAL
www.mimesisinternational.com
info@mimesisinternational.com

MIMESIS EDIZIONI
www.mimesisedizioni.it
mimesis@mimesisedizioni.it

ÉDITIONS MIMÉSIS
www.editionsmimesis.fr
info@editionsmimesis.fr

MIMESIS COMMUNICATION
www.mim-c.net

MIMESIS EU
www.mim-eu.com

Printed by
Puntoweb s.r.l. – Ariccia (RM)
December 2022